INNINGS
OF A LIFETIME

INNINGS
OF A LIFETIME

Ralph Barker

COLLINS
St James's Place, London
1982

William Collins Sons & Co Ltd
London · Glasgow · Sydney · Auckland
Toronto · Johannesburg

First published 1982
© Ralph Barker 1982

ISBN 0 00 211866 1

Photoset in Janson
by Unwin Brothers Limited, Old Woking, Surrey
Made and printed in Great Britain
by William Collins Sons & Co. Ltd, Glasgow

Contents

List of Illustrations		vii
Acknowledgements		ix
Introduction		xi
1	Colin Cowdrey	13
2	Peter Burge	34
3	Graeme Pollock	58
4	Bob Barber	75
5	Gary Sobers and David Holford	97
6	Asif Iqbal	117
7	Glenn Turner	141
8	Doug Walters	172
9	Dennis Amiss	190
10	Derek Randall	223
	Index	251

Illustrations

page

Colin Cowdrey drives Lindwall into the covers   23
Central Press Photos Ltd

Peter Burge pulls Flavell for 4
Sport & General Press Agency Ltd
Burge leaving the field with Hawke
at the end of their partnership   50
Sport & General Press Agency Ltd

Graeme Pollock steps in to drive Titmus
Sport & General Press Agency Ltd
Pollock's controversial dismissal   71
Central Press Photos Ltd

Hawke tries a bouncer   90
The Press Association Ltd

David Holford sweeps Titmus past Milburn
Sport & General Press Agency Ltd
Gary Sobers turns Higgs off his toes   111
Sport & General Press Agency Ltd

Sobers reaches his hundred
Sport & General Press Agency Ltd
Holford's century   113
Sport & General Press Agency Ltd

Milburn's century   114
Sport & General Press Agency Ltd

Brian Close reads the offending note   129
Central Press Photos Ltd

Asif is chaired on reaching his century
Central Press Photos Ltd
Asif with Intikhab — *Central Press Photos Ltd*   134

Glenn Turner — 'Whatever happened to that one?'   155
Ralph Barker

Doug Walters — 'It had to be the bouncer.'
Patrick Eagar
Walters the morning after - caught by Fletcher
off Willis   186
Central Press Photos Ltd

Dennis Amiss moves back and across to play
Holding   217
The Press Association Ltd

Amiss acknowledges the ovation as Holding applauds 218
Sport & General Press Agency Ltd

Derek Randall — 'Well bowled, Mr Lillee!'   237
Central Press Photos Ltd

Two ways of avoiding a bouncer   238
Central Press Photos Ltd

Randall struck by a ball from Lillee   241
Central Press Photos Ltd

Acknowledgements

I should like first and foremost to acknowledge the generous and indeed indispensable help I have received from the men who played these memorable innings; without it I could not possibly have written about their triumphs from the inside, as it were, enabling the reader — as I hope — to identify with the batsman as each innings unfolds.

There is a background to any great innings which contemporary scorebooks and match accounts cannot reveal. It is this background, as well as the innings themselves, that I have endeavoured to re-create.

In addition to the men who played these innings I have received valuable comments and suggestions from players who took part in the matches in which the innings were played. Among these I must mention Ted Dexter and Freddie Trueman on Peter Burge; George Cox and Mike (M.J.K.) Smith on Graeme Pollock; Colin Cowdrey on Sir Gary Sobers and David Holford; Intikhab Alam, Brian Close and Ken Higgs on Asif Iqbal; Mike Denness and Bob Willis on Doug Walters; and Dennis Amiss and Mike Brearley on Derek Randall. To these, and all others who helped, I must record my grateful thanks.

Major sources of information have been the wide range of newspaper accounts, published at home and overseas, made available to me at the British Library Newspaper Library at Colindale; score books and score sheets, kindly lent to me or copied for me by their custodians; numerous reports and articles published in The Cricketer International; and the essential and inexhaustible reservoir of Wisden. Among cricket writers and commentators to whom I owe a special debt I must mention John Arlott, Richie Benaud, Tony Crozier, Michael Melford, Keith Miller, E.W. Swanton, John Woodcock, and the late Denys Rowbotham. I have also referred to and cribbed from all I could find on the selected innings in many volumes of autobiography, biography, and tour records, too numerous to list, to which I have been granted access in the libraries of the MCC and the Cricket Society.

Together these sources have provided a varied and colourful jigsaw on each innings; but the responsibility for fitting the pieces together into the picture presented is entirely my own.

R.B.

Introduction

Ian Botham's astonishing innings at Headingley against Australia in 1981 generated such excitement and enthusiasm, far beyond cricket's mere *aficionados*, that it almost seemed to eclipse Jessop's immortal 102 in 75 minutes at the Oval in 1902, hitherto regarded as the supreme example of how one man's genius can transform a game. Certainly the comparison is both apt and justified: Botham's innings can surely have been not one whit inferior. Yet one does not need to go back to Jessop, or to Hobbs, Hammond, Headley, or Bradman — or even to Hutton, Harvey, Weekes, Worrell or Walcott — to find Test Match innings which for sheer drama and entertainment stand comparison with any other.

Whatever the pessimists may say, cricket's golden age is always with us; or perhaps in our imagination it is just behind us, as even Botham's innings now must be. Thus the greatest difficulty in choosing instances that qualify for the accolade 'Innings of a Lifetime' lies not in a paucity of subjects but in an embarrassment of riches. The reader, I fear, will note some glaring omissions.

Nevertheless, of the ten innings I have chosen — in fact, because I have included a partnership, there is a full team of eleven — it might truly be said that they chose themselves. They are taken from a quarter of a century of great Test centuries, roughly spanning the period 1955 to 1980, and in each case they represent the zenith of achievement of the batsman concerned. Yet they were selected not so much for their quality as for their human interest. Without exception they were played in a dramatic context, against a tense and testing background, and without exception they were the ultimate expression of the character, courage and artistry — and often the patriotism — of the men who played them. It is in this last and often unfashionable quality that the pull of Test cricket lies.

INTRODUCTION

The blossoming of new talent, the maturing of natural gifts, the come-back after failure, the fight-back from adversity — all these are included, while proper tribute is paid to the bowlers; although mastered here, their skills and character, too, form an essential element, without which no truly great innings can be played. Yet for me, and perhaps for the reader, the greatest fascination in these reconstructions has been the confirmation of something all cricketers instinctively know — that more often than not the innings of a lifetime is a triumph not so much of the batsman over the bowler as of the batsman over himself.

R.B.

1

COLIN COWDREY

Sitting in front of the fire at his home on the Kent/Surrey border on an evening in late November, watching television, the 41-year-old former England batsman had a sense of *déjà vu*. What he was seeing threw his mind back to what he still believed was the greatest moment of his life, when two other Australian bowlers were posing the same sort of problems and wreaking the same kind of havoc. That had been twenty years ago, and the bowlers were Lindwall and Miller.

After what he had just witnessed, he was not so sorry as he might have been that the passing years had condemned him to a winter at home. It bordered on the horrific. Dennis Amiss, batting in the first Test of the 1974-75 series at Brisbane, had shaped to play a ball from Jeff Thomson, realised it was shortish and lifting, and ducked. The ball soared over his head, and wicket-keeper Rod Marsh, standing far back, could do no more than deflect it upwards still further as it bent back the tips of his gloved fingers. The ball crashed second bounce into the sight-screen for four byes.

The ex-England cricketer sat back in his armchair. He had been through it all. Nevertheless he was glad he was not up that end. I'm not quite sure, he thought, how I would deal with a ball like that.

When, in the early hours, the insistent ringing of the telephone got him grumbling out of bed, the call was long-distance. Who could possibly want him at this hour? The slight Scottish accent sounded like Mike Denness — but that was ridiculous. Mike

13

was 12,000 miles away, captaining England in Australia. But it *was* Mike Denness.

A lot had happened at Brisbane in the few hours since that explosive delivery of Jeff Thomson's had surprised Dennis Amiss, and, at a distance, horrified many thousands of cricket lovers watching the recorded highlights. Amiss himself, before close of play that night, had had his thumb broken. Early on the third morning another ball of almost undreamt-of velocity had detonated on a length and broken John Edrich's top hand.

There were six specialist batsmen in the touring party, and two of them were out of action. The addition of another batsman to the party was imperative. Who should it be?

What was wanted was somebody who had no fear of fast bowling, preferably someone who could open and who had Test experience. Boycott was not considered as he had already turned down the opportunity to tour. Whoever was selected had to be keen to go, keen to face the physical challenge of Lillee and Thomson, a combination which Ian Chappell, the Australian captain, was already describing as the fastest he had ever played with or against.

'Right from the start the player I had in mind was Colin Cowdrey,' says Mike Denness. The consensus amongst the senior players, too, was that Cowdrey was their man, and Denness booked the call.

Cowdrey could have wished that the call had come sooner, without a gap of three months since the peak fitness of August. This was to be a recurring regret. His enthusiastic response to Denness's call was genuine, but he had hoped for more time to acclimatise. Although he played many staunch innings, it was not until towards the end of the tour that he began to feel capable of asserting himself against Lillee and Thomson as he had once done against Lindwall and Miller, and by then it was too late.

Nevertheless he enjoyed the battle. This was his sixth tour of Australia, and few English cricketers had won such affection and acclaim in that country. Few, too, had warmed to Australia and the Australians quite as Cowdrey had done. It all went back to the way they had taken him to their hearts when he first arrived

14

in Australia with Hutton's team in 1954 as a chubby, cherubic youngster of 21.

*　　　*

The touring party that sailed from Tilbury in September 1954 contained more than the usual surprises. Hutton's appointment as captain, though inevitable, was delayed until mid-July. He was the first professional captain of an MCC touring side. Trueman, Lock and Laker, who had bowled Australia out when the Ashes were recovered at the Oval in 1953 after a gap of 20 years, were all left behind. In addition, said *Wisden*, 'M.C. Cowdrey was given a place although he had not approached his splendid form of the previous year.' Hutton, while supporting his inclusion, thought that this, together with the appointment of Peter May as vice-captain, was the biggest surprise of all.

Cowdrey had been selected largely on the strength of having made two fifties against the Australians for the Gentlemen of England at Lord's a year earlier, while still up at Oxford. How seriously Lindwall and Miller had taken the proceedings was uncertain, but they were both playing, and no one had faced them with more composure. These two bowlers were again expected to form the shock troops of the Australian attack.

Among the crowd on the dockside at Tilbury to wish the players *bon voyage* was Cowdrey's father, the man who had bestowed upon him those magic but daunting initials. The boy had a lot to live up to. Yet with his father's encouragement the young Colin had proved an infant prodigy, and he had been the youngest player ever to appear in a school match at Lord's.

Whether Cowdrey would play any significant part in the defence of the Ashes was doubtful. Selectors sometimes picked the latest 'most promising youngster' to take part in a tour mostly for the experience, to play perhaps in one Test Match if the tour went well and the youngster prospered. A comparatively young side had been chosen, but Cowdrey was very much the baby of it, three years junior to any of the others. In a long chat with Len Hutton at the dockside, Cowdrey senior was deeply impressed by the understanding the England captain showed for the responsibility he was assuming for the youngest of his players. He could hardly get over it, and the son noticed, just before the boat sailed, that the father was moved almost to tears.

A heart condition that had troubled Cowdrey senior had then seemed well under control, and he had been in excellent form that day. Early on the morning of the team's arrival in Perth, however, came news of his sudden death.

The first question to be decided was whether the son ought to go home, and Geoffrey Howard, the tour manager, after making telephone contact with Lord's, brought a message from Cowdrey's mother that without question he was to continue the tour. The last thing his father would have wanted was for him to interrupt it in any way.

By five o'clock that afternoon these matters had been settled, and Geoffrey Howard was advising Cowdrey that all had been done that could conceivably be done and that he should continue to live and behave as normally as possible. He had absented himself from the public rooms of the hotel all day, receiving messages and telegrams in his room. A surprising number of these messages came from unknown but sympathetic Australians. Most remarkable of all was one which said: 'You have the heartfelt sympathy of everyone in Australia.' The signature was that of Prime Minister Robert Menzies.

That evening Cowdrey went down for a drink and a meal. Either beforehand or during dinner, most of the players shook him by the hand and expressed their sympathy. Len Hutton didn't come near him. It was not until they were having coffee in the lounge, and it was getting on for bedtime, that he appeared at Cowdrey's table. Cowdrey immediately realised why he hadn't seen him before. Hutton came up to him shaking his head from side to side, biting his lip and unable to speak. After two agonised expulsions of breath that spoke volumes, he wrung Cowdrey's hand before turning his back. He was too upset to articulate.

Cowdrey's extreme youth, his university background, his amateur status, even those initials, set him apart, and he could easily have found himself isolated in the days that followed. He knew no one intimately, even Godfrey Evans with whom he had played for Kent being of a different generation, and he had never played for England and never toured. He had had only one full county season, players met far less frequently then than they do now, with the proliferation of one-day games, and it took much longer for new players to make friends. So in addition to the shock of his loss he felt very much out of it.

Next morning, on the way to net practice, Cowdrey tagged on to a straggling group of eight or ten players walking across the WACA ground, keeping slightly adrift of the others. He would not, he imagined, be asked to bowl, he didn't want to be one of the early batters, and he made himself as inconspicuous as possible. He was surprised to find that Hutton, although he pretended otherwise, knew exactly where he was. 'Oh . . . er . . . where's . . . where's Colin?'

'Here, skipper.'

'Oh . . . er . . . well . . . I want a spinner in here. You can come and bowl at me. Jim McConnon . . . that's right, I want you in there, Colin in here.' And for the next twenty minutes he had Cowdrey bowling to him. Later he saw to it that Cowdrey got his knock. When it came to fielding practice it was 'Hey, Colin, take some short catches.' Unobtrusively he ensured that Cowdrey kept occupied.

Because of doubts about Denis Compton's knee an extra batsman had been taken, making a party of 18, including eight specialist batsmen. Hutton demanded proved ability at the highest level, and Cowdrey had not even made a championship hundred, so his chances of playing in any of the Tests looked slim. He made a couple of forties impressively enough in the early matches, but it was not until the fifth first-class match, against New South Wales at Sydney, that he forced his way into the reckoning by making a hundred in each innings. MCC were 38 for four when he went in, and then, in partnership with Hutton, he helped to pull the game round under the most searching of scrutinies. Opening the second innings with MCC 130 behind, he scored another hundred to confirm his class and make certain of a place in the first Test.

In that Brisbane Test Australia made 601 for eight declared

after being put in, and England lost by an innings. But Cowdrey batted reasonably well and did his cause no harm. 23 and 54 in the second Test at Sydney, which England won after being put in, were valuable innings in a low-scoring game in which Tyson and Statham tipped the scales. Thus the sides went to Melbourne all square, guaranteeing 60,000-plus crowds and an exciting atmosphere.

Whoever batted first at Melbourne, it was predicted, would face a tough first session until the moisture dried out of the wicket, and the dilemma of what to do on winning the toss exercised both captains. Hutton had put Australia in at Brisbane and lost. Arthur Morris, deputising for an injured Ian Johnson (Keith Miller was also absent with a knee injury), had put England in at Sydney and lost. But was this relevant? There was a great deal of coming and going to and from the middle, and Hutton even put on spiked boots to test the amount of moisture in the wicket. The light was bright but the sky was overcast, promising good conditions for swing bowling. But the ghost of W.G., or at least an echo of his philosophy — thinking about putting the other side in and then batting — haunted the England camp, and when Hutton won the toss he decided to bat.

Hutton himself, if not exactly a sick man, was far below peak form. It had been doubtful if he would play. A heavy cold and a stiff neck caused by fibrositis had contributed to a general malaise. In addition Denis Compton, having missed the previous Test through damaging a hand in a collision with a boundary fence at Brisbane, had played no cricket since then and was still feeling some soreness and discomfort. Against this, Keith Miller, his knee heavily bandaged, was thought unlikely to bowl. Doctors had stated emphatically that if he bowled at all it must be in the briefest of spells, so this was a balancing factor.

At precisely twelve o'clock Lindwall opened the 90-minute morning session from the pavilion end to Hutton (Tests in Australia then comprised six five-hour days). With his first ball he surprised Hutton with an in-swinger, but the ball veered so much that it eluded the wicket-keeper too and raced away for four byes. The next ball lifted disconcertingly from only just

18

short of a length and Hutton had to take avoiding action. The third ball was pitched up and Hutton pushed it through the empty covers for 3. A lightning glance for 4 by Hutton's opening partner, Bill Edrich, meant that eleven runs came off the first over, but any complacency was shattered by the fact that Edrich, too, had twice to avoid the lifting ball.

Ian Johnson was talking to Keith Miller. The wicket was distinctly lively, that much was clear. But the moisture might not last. Miller didn't need much persuasion to have a go under conditions like this. Ron Archer was in the side to cover for Miller, but he was going to have to wait for his chance. Miller was going to bowl after all.

Miller began as though bent on bowling England out before lunch. Even in a brief spell he aimed to deal a blow from which England might not recover. He hadn't bowled since Brisbane five weeks earlier, but now the pent-up energy was released in a torrent. The pitch had an arid look, but a dark brown tinge confirmed that some dampness remained. Miller bowled spitefully fast from the start, disdaining a gradual acceleration. Pitching the ball well up, he forced a gasp of astonishment from the crowd in his first over when a ball of almost reachable length reared up and struck Edrich a painful blow on the bicep.

Lindwall at the other end was scarcely less fierce. He too got a ball barely short of a length to rear nastily to Hutton, and only the deadest of bats kept the resultant catch short of gully. A second lifter in the same over dropped perilously close to short leg.

The ball was moving in the air, too, though not so alarmingly as off the pitch, the way it kept climbing off a length being especially perturbing. From Miller no two balls were alike, and when Edrich tried to glance the third ball of his second over as he had already glanced Lindwall, the bounce betrayed him and he steered it straight to Lindwall himself at leg slip.

This brought in the 24-year-old Peter May, whose 104 (and a stand of 116 with Cowdrey) had helped to win the previous Test. What mattered here was survival until the wicket dried out, and May was content to defend.

19

When Lindwall bowled a half-volley Hutton drove it straight for 4, and then, off the seventh ball of the over, he turned him square for 3. This gave Lindwall one ball at Peter May.

No one respected Peter May more than Ray Lindwall, and the respect was mutual. On first acquaintance eighteen months earlier, at the Oval against Surrey in 1953, Lindwall had bowled the over of his life at May, quite deliberately, suspecting May's potential. May, out of his depth, had played and missed at every ball. Next over Lindwall had had him caught behind for nought, effectively shutting him out of the England side for the first four Tests of that series. May had got the better of Lindwall in the Sydney Test, which was all the more reason for sending him back promptly now.

Over by over, Lindwall was not as quick as he had been, but he could still bowl a very fast ball. This one rose wickedly off a length and hurried May into a stroke of body protection. The result was a half-cock shot, head not quite behind the ball. It spooned via glove and handle in a gentle arc to Richie Benaud in the gully.

The batsman replacing May would normally have been Compton, but he had asked to bat No. 5, and Hutton had agreed. There were two reasons, of which the first was pure superstition. Compton had batted No. 4 all his life, yet the only innings he had played of any substance in Tests in Australia had been at No. 5. Both his hundreds in 1946-47, and a 76, had come from that place in the order. In his disastrous tour of 1950-51 he had reverted to second wicket down, and he had been scheduled to bat there when he broke his finger at Brisbane. So why not try No. 5? A more practical reason was that by the time he got there it was hoped that the devil would have gone from the wicket, reducing the chances of further damage to his hand. Thus with England 21 for two and Lindwall and Miller on the rampage, the man who came in to face the barrage was Cowdrey.

Cowdrey's only thought was to cling on if he could, and he set his sights, so far as he thought about runs at all, on reaching double figures. Here he was, batting with the master for the first time in a Test Match, with a new ball buzzing around his ears

20

— very much, had he but known it, as another famous pair were to buzz it twenty years later. But bouncers were the least of his worries. He was watching Hutton goggle-eyed, not so much to admire his technique as to decide whether or not the great man wanted to run. Hutton had a way of playing the ball to one side or the other and trotting off, with no discernible call. It was a question of watching his face, and this was where Cowdrey's gaze was fixed as he backed up for each ball. He would not dare to send Hutton back, but he was absolutely petrified that he might run him out.

As though to make all the clichés about his bowling come true in one over, Miller proceeded to toss back his mane and project a pot-pourri of in-swingers and out-swingers, of bouncers that flew and round-arm deliveries that squatted, the mixture delivered without loss of rhythm off a varied and unmeasured run. Hutton somehow survived, and then Cowdrey took guard.

Lindwall's first ball was an out-swinger, which he wisely left alone. His second ball, too, was the out-swinger, but it was too straight this time to ignore, and it drew Cowdrey forward. He got a thick edge and it raced away along the ground, eluding third slip. There was no third man and it went through for 4.

Perhaps he should have avoided that one, too, but there had been no time to withdraw the bat. He thrust his head down all the more firmly, resolving not to be drawn again.

Next ball was the in-swinger, and he was well over the top of it, or so he thought; but again the best he could do was a very late middle-and-edge. The ball squirted through the leg trap, again there was no deep fielder, and that was his second lucky 4. A minute ago ten runs had seemed a scarcely attainable target. Now he was 8 not out.

Miller had bowled three overs, but despite his heavily-bandaged knee he showed no sign of wanting a rest. The advice of doctors was easily ignored when there was juice in the wicket. The first ball of his fourth over was of fairly full length and Hutton, pushing rather gingerly forward, without much adjustment of the feet, was lured into playing at it. He found himself reaching it without quite covering the swing, and the resultant

21

edge was greedily devoured by first slip. England were 29 for three, and Miller had taken two for nought.

The Australians always showed a special elation at the dismissal of Len Hutton. But the euphoria was expressed less demonstratively than in later years.

Compton came in at 12.39 and was beaten at once by Miller, who appealed not to the umpire but to the heavens. 'All these years, Denis,' he said, 'and you don't seem to get any better. You'd think with all this experience I keep reading about you'd at least get a touch.' This sort of badinage, greatly enjoyed by both Miller and Compton, provided a fascinating eye-opener to the inexperienced Cowdrey. He had no idea this sort of exchange was possible in a Test Match. Neither of the protagonists wished each other evil, but Cowdrey knew he was watching the unforgiving clash of two great competitors. 'Give me the ball,' grumbled Miller. 'I'd better bowl him something he might get a touch to.' As soon as he pitched one up, Compton cover drove it for 3.

Two balls later Cowdrey steered Miller backward of point to reach double figures. In two overs he had reached a landmark that he had expected to take him an hour. These five runs were the first off Miller that morning, and perhaps he would now ask to come off. But after a single to Compton off Lindwall and a crisp drive through the covers by Cowdrey, Miller stood ready to bowl.

The fifth delivery of this his fifth over moved off the seam and lifted so steeply that it may well have been unplayable. It was certainly, as someone called it, 'a fearful ball'. Compton, wringing his hand in agony, sustained a badly bruised thumb; not until it was x-rayed could he be sure nothing was broken. Long before that, though, Harvey at wide gully had taken the catch.

Fifty minutes gone, the juice in the wicket still lethally active, and England 41 for four. Situations like this called for a Trevor Bailey, and in the 1950s he was generally on hand. It was the Barnacle himself, relishing the crisis, who emerged to take

Cowdrey drives Lindwall into the covers early in his innings as Hutton backs up. Keith Miller at slip.

Compton's place, and he blocked the rest of Miller's over. To him, Lindwall and Miller were familiar adversaries.

Of this great pair of bowlers the fiery and less predictable Miller was the more volatile; but he was incomparably more skilful than the average tearaway fast bowler. Both were masters of the art of intimidation, showing no mercy to the faint-hearted. Indeed Miller's whole approach exuded physical challenge. With the wicket encouraging a full length, however, Cowdrey had scarcely been tested with the bouncer, but when it came it was on target. Miller's bouncer looked the more alarming, but Lindwall's was the more dangerous, and he rarely wasted it. It didn't fly over the batsman's head, it sprang at him shoulder-high, and it had an uncanny habit of 'homing' onto his person. Cowdrey grinned as a Lindwall special squeezed past his chest, brushing his shirt, and the crowd shivered with excitement.

Lindwall's greatest strength, though, lay in his classic away swing. He would aim the ball at middle and leg and suddenly it would go late. It was one of these that Cowdrey had edged for 4. Now, following the bouncer, he showed Cowdrey that he was also master of the yorker. It pitched at Cowdrey's toes, and he only just managed to dig it out, while the crowd roared again at his discomfiture.

Lindwall also bowled a well-disguised slower ball, and he tried it now. Cowdrey, picking it, turned it with what seemed a mischievous grin to mid-wicket for 3, a riposte which the crowd much enjoyed. They were now on his side. Bailey got off the mark with a 4 down the leg side next ball, and Lindwall, having run through the gamut, came off.

Thinking that his knee might stiffen up later, and in any case enjoying himself, Miller bowled right through to lunch, nine eight-ball overs in 90 minutes, every over a maiden except the fourth. Keeping the ball up, pitching straight, and combining speed and surprise with remarkable control, he was almost unplayable for an hour. Cowdrey, however, continued to divine his every change of pace, length and swing, almost as if by intuition. His method was strictly correct; even when the ball climbed he was always right over it. This had not always been true of his seniors, and that such great players could be criticised — as they were — for being forced into protective strokes and failing to get behind and over the ball, might offer some comfort to a later generation.

By the time Archer replaced Lindwall the overcast had lifted and the wicket had blenched, its moisture evaporating under the emerging sun. The ball, too, was softer and losing its shine. The odd ball still climbed; but although Archer began with two maidens, batsman and bowler alike were aware that it was becoming a different game. If Cowdrey and Bailey could get through to lunch, some sort of recovery might still be possible. In this resolve they succeeded, and after an over of leg-breaks from Benaud had brought a swept 4 to Cowdrey, lunch intervened. England were 59 for four, Cowdrey 22, Bailey 8.

Miller's figures at this point were 9 overs, 8 maidens, five runs, 3 wickets. As an example of new-ball bowling in helpful conditions it was compared with the famous morning spell on the same ground by S.F. Barnes 43 years earlier, in 1911-12 — 9 overs, 6 maidens, 3 runs, 4 wickets. On that occasion Australia, 32 for four at lunch, had recovered to make 184. Could England manage something similar?

Archer came on to bowl the first over after lunch and the twentieth of the match from the end opposite the pavilion — the end from which Miller had bowled all morning — and he began with a maiden to an apprehensive Bailey, but the bounce was true. Cowdrey took a single off Lindwall's second ball, and Bailey played out the over. Archer's first ball was steered a little uppishly through a vacant gully by Cowdrey for another single, and again Bailey presented a barn-door bat.

The cricket came to life in the fourth over of the afternoon as Cowdrey drove Lindwall regally past mid-off to the boundary and then on-drove him off his toes for an all-run 4, taking him into the 30s. A vivid square cut off Archer streaked to the fence, and when Lindwall was replaced by Benaud, Cowdrey jumped in to drive him past extra for 3. Another 3 to Cowdrey off the first ball of Archer's fifth over since lunch gave Bailey seven balls on which to gorge himself, but then, tiring perhaps of his role, he pushed Archer towards mid-off and had the temerity to suggest a run. Archer swooped to intercept, Cowdrey sent Bailey back, and if Archer's throw had hit the stumps Bailey would have been out.

When Benaud pitched one of his leg-breaks a trifle short Cowdrey late cut him for 4, and another cheeky deflection past slip, executed with an almost audible chuckle, took him to his fifty in 103 minutes, made out of only 69 scored while he was at the wicket. (England were now 90 for four.) The achievement came 40 minutes into the afternoon, and the warmth of the reception it got was astonishing. The innings, a combination of 'high seriousness with a schoolboy sense of fun', as one writer felicitously put it,[1] had charmed the assembled 63,000.

Cowdrey's transparent enjoyment of his success infected Bailey, who celebrated by sweeping Benaud for 4. Bill Johnston replaced Archer, and his mixture of left-arm in-swing and floating out-swing restored order. Benaud's variations of flight presented problems too, but by their very nature they generally offered a chance of one firm stroke per over, and Cowdrey took his score to 56 with a straight drive that put up the hundred. Total disaster had been averted, but there was still a long way to go.

Bailey's forward defensive prod was well in the groove, but he was ever alert for the loose ball, and he blossomed out with a 2 and a 3 off Johnston, then stepped back twice to pull Benaud, taking six runs off him in the over. But curiously the emergence from the chrysalis of stroke-maker Bailey found Cowdrey withdrawing into his shell. Johnston's floating half-volleys, bowled to a packed cover field — five men from just behind square to mid-off — were designed to tempt Cowdrey into indiscretion, and after playing two maidens he was barracked, by a section of the crowd for whom, a few minutes earlier, he could do no wrong.

With two batsmen established, the Australian captain had gone on to the defensive, and with Johnston concentrating on length and line the action stultified. For Cowdrey the whole fun

[1] The late Denys Rowbotham in the *Guardian*.

of batting lay in playing his shots, and when these were cramped or cut off he lacked the experience to change his tactics and pick up the singles. Thus he remained bogged down.

Sensing that Cowdrey had been seized by some kind of atrophy, Ian Johnson removed wrist-spinner Benaud as more likely to afford Cowdrey relief and came on himself from the pavilion end. Bailey took a single off his second ball to take him to 30, and Cowdrey, as Johnson had hoped, played the ballooning, flighted off-breaks which were Johnson's speciality from the crease, suddenly mistrusting his footwork. A close leg-side catcher also restricted him, and he eschewed the leg glance, letting the ball hit his pads.

The first ball of Johnston's next over looked like a long hop, and Bailey, trying to swing it away down the leg side, snicked it on to his pads. From there it rose in a brief parabola, to be eagerly grabbed by wicket-keeper Maddocks. Bailey had helped to add 74 precious runs, making 30 himself, and England were 115 for five.

Godfrey Evans came in to play out the over, and Johnson, turning the ball hardly at all but teasing with flight, bowled another maiden to Cowdrey. It was not that Cowdrey attempted no shots. As the run-getting dried up, the field looked impenetrable, and two lovely cover drives with the typical Cowdrey follow-through were cut off in goalkeeper fashion by a diving Neil Harvey.

Even at this early stage of his career it was being said of Cowdrey that he was a batsman of moods. He had suffered a similar palsy in the previous Test at the same stage of his innings — on 54 — and been caught off Benaud attempting to hit his way out. This, for all its risks, remained the only avenue of escape he could think of.

What kind of player was it who made 56 runs in the course of 28 of the most testing overs imaginable — two runs an over — and then went through the next eleven overs without scoring at all? The noisy perplexity of the crowd was understandable. Now Johnson was preparing to bowl an over which, if Cowdrey failed to score off it, would make the twelfth.

Evans got a single off the second ball, and Cowdrey, facing, knew that he had to try something. The first two balls, driven strongly into the thickly populated covers, yielded him nothing. He had played 45 balls without scoring, and there was nothing for it but to take his life in his hands.

The next ball was flighted as all the others had been, but this time Cowdrey moved down the pitch. To some it seemed that he lashed out wildly; to others the shot looked controlled. The fact was that Cowdrey had simply made up his mind to hit through the line. He felt the ball on the bat, and the contact was good, but there was a lot of right hand in the shot. The ball flew fast and low straight at mid-on, where Archer, focusing against the crowd background, shaped for the catch.

As Archer peered to pick up the line, Cowdrey thought it would hit him smack in the temple, he had struck it so well. As though possessed of some dynamic force of its own the ball was gaining both speed and height. Archer, spotting the trajectory, raised his hands and jumped, but the ball scorched the tips of his fingers before sailing past him and crashing into the pavilion rails.

The spell was broken, and in Johnson's next over Cowdrey pierced the covers at last for his ninth 4. In the last over before tea a quick reaction saved him from playing on to Johnston, but reassurance followed as he hooked him superbly for another 4. England's tea score was 130 for five, Cowdrey 68, Evans 3. For Australia, Johnston had bowled ten overs that afternoon for 13 runs, Johnson five overs for 10.

Lindwall came back at the pavilion end after tea, and singles to both batsmen left Cowdrey to face Johnston. The tall, good-natured Victorian was still tempting Cowdrey outside the off stump, and Cowdrey, accepting the challenge, drove him majestically past extra cover for 4, drawing a 'Good shot, Col,' from Johnston. Cowdrey acknowledged this pleasantry by sweeping Johnston's in-swinger for 4.

Two more overs and Cowdrey moved into the 80s, and the total to 147. Then a Lindwall bouncer caught him flat-footed and despite his well-covered figure he was palpably hurt. The rubbing of the bruise, however, was accompanied by the broadest of grins. Next ball was outside the off stump and he came down right on top of it, thumping it for 4. Evans had previously put up the 150.

Miller came on for two bustling, erratic overs, and when he pitched one up Evans hit him for 4 over mid-on. A triumphant Evans walked down the wicket towards Miller and the two men ceremonially shook hands. If not exactly burnt out Miller was far removed from the bowler of the morning, and after Evans had hit him for another 4 he came off. 35 runs had been added in 40 minutes since tea.

Archer replaced Miller, and in his first over he got Evans lbw with a ball that kept low. That was 169 for six. Evans had made 20, Cowdrey was on 90.

Thinking perhaps that Cowdrey might be eminently teasable in the 90s, Johnson came back at the pavilion end for Lindwall. For seven balls he tantalised Cowdrey, but then another delicious late cut, making room against the spin, produced three runs, took Cowdrey to 93, and gave him the strike. Cowdrey quite clearly had looked for the shot.

Archer, having just got a wicket, was full of running, and he aimed at the stumps. Cowdrey responded with a crashing straight drive, so tremendous that Archer skipped out of its way. This was Cowdrey's fifteenth 4, making 60 out of 97 in boundaries, and although a fast outfield had helped, it confirmed Cowdrey's predilection for hitting the ball rather than looking for singles. He had scored only 14 singles so far — fewer singles than 4's.

Furious with himself for overpitching, Archer stumped off back to his mark. As Cowdrey, having followed through down the pitch after the shot, wandered back to his crease, the thought occurred to him that Archer would be intent on not over-pitching again. There were three balls left of the over, and they would be short of a length.

A glance round the field disclosed that third man was rather finer than he would have expected. Harvey had moved round in the covers to narrow the gap, but if Archer pitched short there were four certain runs to be had fine of square cover.

Sure enough the ball was short of a length. But it was straight — too straight to cut. He would have to play a forcing shot to leg off the back foot. He came down on it nicely, getting his right hand into the shot, and he connected in exactly the right spot on the bat. As soon as he hit it he knew it would beat mid-on, and he called for a run. He thought there would probably be two in it, and if they ran quickly there might just possibly be three.

As the crowd saw the run being attempted they roared their encouragement. It was one nearer the target. Then, absorbed in their own calculations of distance and time as mid-on chased the ball, they lapsed into a sudden, staccato silence, like a choir under the baton, finding their voices again with renewed gusto as the batsmen turned to run two.

There had been no flourish with the shot, no extravagant follow through, and two runs had been the limit of expectation. Only Cowdrey himself knew how sweetly he had timed it. As the batsmen completed the second run, and the fielder stooped to pick up the ball, a second and even more pregnant hush fell over the arena. Might the batsmen, after all, look for a third?

They were going! With the last of the three-tiered crescendos of sound the crowd orchestration swelled into pandemonium, and Cowdrey, half-way to the bowler's end, knew he was safe.

The applause for Cowdrey's hundred rivalled anything heard on a cricket ground in Australia in living memory. The only comparable ovation anyone could think of was that accorded the Don himself when he reached his hundredth 100 at Sydney. Cowdrey's youth had a lot to do with it, as did the merit of his performance: coming in at 21 for two, he had made his hundred out of 158, and five wickets had fallen while he was in. But this was not all. There was a profound and compassionate empathy for the boy who had lost his father at the beginning of his first tour abroad. Sentimental it might be, but when sentiment takes hold of a crowd the impact can be devastating, as it was now. The emotions had been touched, and the cheering went on and on.

Les Favell, whose fielding and throwing in the deep had been a feature in this his first Test series, felt a tingling in his spine at the thunderous intensity of the applause. He thought it would never stop. It surged again to a new fortissimo as Ian Johnson shook Cowdrey's hand.

The Barnes match on this same ground was recalled again as statisticians confirmed that Cowdrey was the youngest Englishman to make a Test hundred in Australia since Jack Hearne on this same ground 43 years earlier.

When the game eventually resumed Cowdrey, facing Johnson, could not get going again until the last ball of the over, when a stroke through the covers that looked like producing three was cut down to two by a quick chase and return. This gave Archer the chance of bowling at the new batsman, Wardle, and a well-directed off-cutter — a leg-cutter to the left-hander — bowled Wardle behind his legs. That was 181 for seven.

Only Benaud had turned the ball more than an inch all day, and when Johnson, in the next over, pitched two feet outside Cowdrey's off stump, Cowdrey moved across automatically to cover any possible movement with his pads. He did not attempt a stroke. But the ball pitched in the rough made by Bill Johnston's boots (bowling left-arm over). It spun viciously, flicked the buckles of Cowdrey's pads, and hit the unguarded leg stump. Maddocks, covering the turn, finished up yards across on the leg side. Thus a freak ball ended Cowdrey's innings. After patting the offending spot incredulously, he departed.

This time the commotion swept round the ground like a whirlwind, gusting to gale force whenever it seemed like abating. The boy who had gone on the tour as a learner had established himself under exceptional pressure, lifting the innings from abject failure towards something almost respectable. He had gone in to bat at the moment of crisis, when Lindwall and Miller were sending England's premier batsmen staggering with their supercharged speed. The only other batsmen to reach double figures were Bailey 30, Evans 20, and Hutton 12. Entering the fire when the furnace was fiercest, he had dowsed and all-but extinguished the flames.

England were all out soon afterwards for 191, but in a low-scoring match it was enough to keep England on terms. 91 from Peter May provided the core of England's second innings, and then, as Australia set out to make 240 to win, Tyson and Statham proved supreme; England went one up in the series, and despite further shock-bowling from Miller they went on to a five-wicket victory at Adelaide (Hutton 80, Cowdrey 79) to retain the Ashes.

*   *

Cowdrey's total of 7,624 runs in Tests was recently beaten by Geoffrey Boycott, but his record of six tours to Australia, spanning 20 years, may last longer. Runner-up to Cowdrey is the late Sir Jack Hobbs, who made five such tours over a period of 21 years and would in all probability have made a sixth but for the First World War.

AUSTRALIA v ENGLAND 1954-55 (3rd Test)
at Melbourne, December 31, January 1, 3, 4, 5
England won by 128 runs

ENGLAND: First Innings

*L. Hutton, c Hole b Miller	12
W. J. Edrich, c Lindwall b Miller	4
P. B. H. May, c Benaud b Lindwall	0
M. C. Cowdrey, b Johnson	102
D. C. S. Compton, c Harvey b Miller	4
T. E. Bailey, c Maddocks b Johnston	30
†T. G. Evans, lbw b Archer	20
J. H. Wardle, b Archer	0
F. H. Tyson, b Archer	6
J. B. Statham, b Archer	3
R. Appleyard, not out	1
Extras (B 9)	9
Total	191

Fall of wickets: 1-14, 2-21, 3-29, 4-41, 5-115, 6-169, 7-181, 8-181, 9-190, 10-191.

Bowling: Lindwall, 13-0-59-1; Miller, 11-8-14-3; Archer, 13.6-4-33-4; Benaud, 7-0-30-0; Johnston, 12-6-26-1; Johnson, 11-3-20-1.

AUSTRALIA: First Innings

L. Favell, lbw b Statham	25
A. R. Morris, lbw b Tyson	3
K. R. Miller, c Evans b Statham	7
R. N. Harvey, b Appleyard	31
G. B. Hole, b Tyson	11
R. Benaud, c sub b Appleyard	15
R. G. Archer, b Wardle	23
†L. Maddocks, c Evans b Statham	47
R. R. Lindwall, b Statham	13
*I. W. Johnson, not out	33
W. A. Johnston, b Statham	11
Extras (B 7, LB 3, NB 2)	12
Total	231

Fall of wickets: 1-15, 2-38, 3-43, 4-65, 5-92, 6-115, 7-134, 8-151, 9-205, 10-231.

Bowling: Tyson, 21-2-68-2; Statham, 16.3-0-60-5; Bailey, 9-1-33-0; Appleyard, 11-3-38-2; Wardle, 6-0-20-1.

ENGLAND: Second Innings

L. Hutton, lbw b Archer	42
W. J. Edrich, b Johnston	13
P. B. H. May, b Johnston	91
M. C. Cowdrey, b Benaud	7
D. C. S. Compton, c Maddocks b Archer	23
T. E. Bailey, not out	24
T. G. Evans, c Maddocks b Miller	22
J. H. Wardle, b Johnson	38
F. H. Tyson, c Harvey b Johnston	6
J. B. Statham, c Favell b Johnston	0
R. Appleyard, b Johnston	6
Extras (B 2, LB 4, W 1)	7
Total	279

Fall of wickets: 1-40, 2-96, 3-128, 4-173, 5-185, 6-211, 7-257, 8-273, 9-273, 10-279.

Bowling: Lindwall, 18-3-52-0; Miller, 18-6-35-1; Archer, 24-7-50-2; Benaud, 8-2-25-1; Johnston, 24.5-2-25-5; Johnson, 8-2-25-1.

AUSTRALIA: Second Innings

L. Favell, b Appleyard	30
A. R. Morris, c Cowdrey b Tyson	4
R. Benaud, b Tyson	22
R. N. Harvey, c Evans b Tyson	11
K. R. Miller, c Edrich b Tyson	6
G. B. Hole, c Evans b Statham	5
R. G. Archer, b Statham	15
L. Maddocks, b Tyson	0
R. R. Lindwall, lbw b Tyson	0
I. W. Johnson, not out	4
W. A. Johnston, c Evans b Tyson	0
Extras (B 1, LB 13)	14
Total	111

Fall of wickets: 1-23, 2-57, 3-77, 4-86, 5-87, 6-97, 7-98, 8-98, 9-110, 10-111.

Bowling: Tyson, 12.3-1-27-7; Statham, 11-1-38-2; Bailey, 3-0-14-0; Appleyard, 4-1-17-1; Wardle, 1-0-1-0.

Umpires—M. J. McInnes and C. Hoy

2

PETER BURGE

'As for Burge, he was *Australia.'*
— *Denzil Batchelor*

The burly, balding six-footer who had been summoned to face a partners' meeting of his employers could see the sense of what they were saying. An accountant by profession, not yet fully qualified, he had been in and out of the Australian Test side for four years without ever quite making the grade. Now he had been selected for what would be his fifth overseas tour. His firm had given him a pretty fair crack, keeping his job open for him while he was away, and releasing him for the eight Sheffield Shield matches of the Australian season, but another overseas tour, it seemed, was out of the question. The firm had internal problems and he simply couldn't be spared. There was also the question of the examinations he still had to take.

'We think your future lies in accountancy,' one of the partners was saying. 'We think you should pull out of this Indian tour.'

At the back of his mind was the feeling that the partners were right. He had recently married, and Joan, his wife, was expecting their first child. He had them to think of too.

'If you decide to go on this tour,' he was told, 'we shall have to engage a replacement. That means that when you get back you'll be out of a job.'

There was no money to be made out of State cricket, and precious little to be saved out of an overseas tour. All top cricketers in Australia had to have the security of a regular job. With no savings to fall back on, he couldn't argue. He wasn't really sure that with Joan pregnant he wanted to go anyway. 'Yes,' he said, 'I think you're right. I think I'll withdraw.'

'We think that's for the best.'

One of the partners, who had not spoken before, intervened. 'Quite frankly, Peter,' he said, 'we don't think you're good enough to consolidate your position in the Test side.'

Didn't they indeed? The 27-year-old Peter Burge, normally the most phlegmatic of men, felt his gorge rise. Job security was one thing. Being told he wasn't good enough was another. He wasn't going to give up so easily. They had said they could replace him, so he wouldn't be letting them down.

'I'm going to see if I can find a job in another office, so that I can stay in the accountancy game and still go on the tour.'

'Someone who'll give you a job and then release you for the next three and a half months? We don't think you'll find one.'

'Just give me two weeks. Then I'll let you know what I'm going to do.'

'Very well.'

But as the partners had forecast, finding a new employer on such terms looked well-nigh impossible. When the time approached for acceptance or rejection of the invitation to tour India, he sat down and wrote out his withdrawal. Then at the last moment, through a friend of his father's, he got an appointment with a man called Harry Bolton, and he put his cards, such as they were, on the table. Bolton took a liking to this uncomplicated, open-faced Queenslander, but it was some time before he made up his mind. At length he said: 'I'm prepared to give you a go.' He offered Burge a substantial rise and unfettered freedom to pursue his cricket career.

Hurriedly arranging a street-corner meeting with his wife, Burge gave her the news. 'It means I can go to India,' he said, 'but it also means that you would be by yourself again.' 'We can't afford not to take it,' said Joan. 'We're going to be better off whatever happens.'

Burge accepted the job, starting a relationship that was to become more like father and son than employer and employee, and he got a special satisfaction out of going back to tell his old employers of his decision. This, for the good-natured Burge, was an uncharacteristically abrasive gesture, but he had to get back at them for that tag of 'not good enough'. Somehow, in the years to come, he would show them.

*   *

Peter Burge was born to play cricket. Like Colin Cowdrey, he was doing what his father wanted him to do. Although never a great cricketer himself, Burge senior lived for cricket, and the young Peter Burge made his first hundred for his State school at the age of nine. But he earned his father's wrath on another occasion when, after making 200, he retired 'tired'. 'Don't ever do that again,' warned his father. A schoolboy prodigy, he also took up wicket-keeping, and he hardly knew what it was to field out when he played his first game for Queensland in 1953 at the age of 21. But with Don Tallon still playing and Wally Grout about to take over, Burge had to make his way as a batsman, and learn how to field.

By this time his father was a Queensland selector, but when the possibility of Burge's selection arose he resigned to avoid any suggestion of nepotism. This did not altogether silence innuendoes of favouritism, either then or when the son was chosen for his first overseas tour, to the West Indies in 1955, with the father as manager.

For Burge it proved a disappointing tour. There was a batting place available, in support of four established players — Morris, McDonald, Harvey and Miller — and Burge was given it for the first Test. But he failed, and his subsequent form did not warrant further opportunities. He came to England for the first time with Ian Johnson's 1956 side, but when he lost his place to Ian Craig after failing twice to Laker in the third Test at Leeds — and thus avoiding being 'Lakered' at Old Trafford — he was averaging only 16.

On the way home from that tour the Australians played three Tests in India, and Burge played in them all and averaged 49. But he could not maintain this form when he toured South Africa a year later, losing his place after a disastrous first Test. Thus he was psychologically vulnerable when the invitation came to tour India.

36

The way that tour began he almost regretted his decision to go. Australia were scheduled to play three Tests against Pakistan and five against India. Against Pakistan he got a duck in the first Test, was dropped from the second, and made 14 in the third. He was left out of the first three Tests against India, and scores of 35 and 60 in his only innings in the last two Tests amounted to no more than modest reparation. It did not greatly surprise him when he was left out of the side against Worrell's West Indians in the home series of 1960-61. With McDonald, Simpson, Harvey, O'Neill and Favell filling the first five places, and his Queensland colleague Ken 'Slasher' Mackay at No. 6, there was no place for him. Then one of his closest mates, Neil Harvey, pulled a muscle, and he was recalled for the fourth Test at Adelaide.

His selection aroused such controversy, and brought such a fierce denunciation from Phil Tresidder in the *Sydney Morning Herald*, that he accepted the popular view that this was the make-or-break moment. Before the game he told Harry Bolton that if he didn't make runs in this match he would give up the game.

The contest proved almost as exciting as the tied first Test, and with the West Indies in control all the way, every run had to be earned. Burge's 45 and 49, made under pressure, were such valuable contributions towards saving the game that they drew a handsome apology from Tresidder, while *Wisden* noted that Burge had 'justified his return to Test cricket'. Two half-centuries in the final Test helped towards a narrow Australian victory, and Australia had become, esteemed *Wisden*, 'thankful for the aggressiveness of the broad-shouldered Burge'.

On the 1961 tour of England under Richie Benaud, Burge was an automatic choice for all five Tests, and he finished by making 181 at the Oval. Then, for England's tour of Australia under Dexter in 1962-63, it was another case of *déjà vu*, Burge being replaced by Barry Shepherd after the first two Tests. Brought back for the decider, he made 103 in the first innings, pulling the game round with O'Neill in what was described as 'the best batting of the match', and 52 not out in the second.

These two innings took him to the top of the Australian averages for the series and fully vindicated his decision four years earlier to stay in the game.

At the age of 32, however, he was by no means certain of a third trip to England in 1964. A veteran by Australian standards, he was also unfit. Throughout that Australian season he was suffering from what he took to be a pinched nerve in his left foot, causing him agonies of pain and slowing him down noticeably in the field, where he had never been the most athletic of performers. The doctors diagnosed a neuroma — a growth on the nerve about the size of a grape, like a tumour but non-malignant. 'There's eight weeks to go before the team goes to England,' Burge told the doctors. 'Can you fix it in that time?' 'If you have the operation straight away,' they said, 'we reckon she'll be right.' The team were going by sea to India and flying from there, and that would give him another week or so to recover.

When he went for his medical for the tour he was still on crutches. 'What are we supposed to do?' asked the members of the board. 'Pass you fit for a cricket tour?' Fortunately they accepted the report of the orthopaedic surgeon who had operated, but he was unable to play in any of the preliminary tour matches — two in Tasmania, one in Perth and one in Ceylon — and he could only join to a limited extent in the exercises and work-outs on the boat.

By the time he got to England his foot was more comfortable, but he still found running difficult, and after the long lay-off he was over-weight and out of touch. A wet start to the season denied him the net practice he needed, and after a fair start in the first match his batting fell away. To make matters worse he was consistently getting out to blinding catches. One match where he expected to play himself back into form was against Oxford University in late May, but a perfect square cut, as good as any he had ever made, was clutched in two fingers by a young undergraduate after an acrobatic swoop. With the first Test only a week away, and his likely replacement, the 24-year-old Bob

Cowper, on his first tour, averaging 70, only an act of faith by the selectors could save him.

That night in his hotel room he could not shake off his depression. Already he was fond of saying that he had made more come-backs than Dame Nellie Melba. He would soon be facing the need to make another. For some people this would be the time to break out and have a few pots, but Burge, though not teetotal, rarely drank. What he needed was company, preferably someone outside the team, not too closely involved, and at the nadir of his depression it was forthcoming.

The knock on the door was sounded by the knuckles of an old friend and champion of Burge's, Alan McGilvray, and knowing Burge's abstemious habits he had brought his own bottle. They sat on the floor of the hotel room and talked it out until three in the morning, and while Burge poured out his woes, McGilvray poured out his Scotch. He didn't bother taking the bottle back with him when he left.

Burge, as it happened, was not the only established Australian Test batsman struggling to find his touch. Bill Lawry was in similar travail. But when the selectors — Simpson, Booth and Lawry — came to choose the side for the first Test they plumped for experience. The younger players would get their chance later. The game — at Trent Bridge — was rain-ruined, and no changes were made for the second Test at Lord's.

A failure in the first innings, lbw to Dexter for 1, held ominous implications for Burge, especially as the bowler, until getting O'Neill caught at long leg just beforehand with a long hop, had taken only two wickets that season. Australia were 70 behind on first innings, and despite breaks for rain they were in real danger on the last day before Burge joined Redpath. While Redpath defended, Burge played his natural game, and according to *Wisden* he 'hit forcefully for 59 in an hour and forty minutes'. But he didn't really feel things were coming right until Coldwell bowled him one just about on a length and he lifted it between Father Time and the Nursery-end clock for 6.

There was only one first-class game for the Australians between the second and third Tests and that was against Northants. Burge made 5 and Cowper 87, and again there was newspaper speculation that Burge might be on the way out. Burge himself was far from confident of playing. But Simpson, particularly, believed that Burge had the big-match temperament, and he was duly chosen for the Leeds Test, Cowper being left out.

Roughly half the scheduled time had been lost through rain in the first two Tests, and this served to sharpen the appetite for Leeds, where the forecast was for a firm pitch, a fast outfield, and fine weather. Good judges also predicted that the ball would turn, slowly at first but more sharply later on, and they assessed the advantage of winning the toss at 75 and perhaps a hundred runs. No side required to make 250 in the last innings, it was thought, was likely to do so.

Winning the toss and avoiding that fourth innings on a wearing wicket seemed doubly desirable when arguably the best batsman on each side, Colin Cowdrey and Norman O'Neill, dropped out at the last minute through injuries. England substituted the 29-year-old Yorkshireman Ken Taylor. For Australia, Bob Cowper got his chance after all.

Dexter had won the toss at Trent Bridge and again at Lord's, and when Simpson called wrongly for the third time he threw up his hands in chagrin. The previous two encounters at Leeds had ended in victory for England. Like the toss, it looked like being three in a row.

Headingley, with its perimeter of red-brick houses and town-bred trees, had never looked in better shape when Boycott and Edrich, both playing in their first Test series against Australia, began to the bowling of McKenzie and Hawke. A strong cross-wind helped the bowlers to swing the ball disconcertingly, but their direction was erratic, and the first wicket fell through a misjudgement by Edrich. Hooking too late at McKenzie, whose speed and lift surprised him, he was caught at backward short leg off his glove.

Dexter set the example with a succession of irresistible strokes, including four 4's in one over off Hawke, mostly thumping square cuts. Boycott responded with one great back-foot force past cover, and after an hour's play England were 56 for one. Corling was tried, and at 74 he had Boycott caught by Simpson at slip for 38, which included eight 4's. *The Times* opined that Boycott had come to stay. . . .

At lunch England were 112 for 2 off 38 overs, Dexter's new partner being Barrington. It was eight years since England had made a first innings 400 against Australia, but that was the aim. Perhaps they were too eager to reach their goal. McKenzie, strong and persevering, and banging the ball in just as hard and rather more accurately than in the morning, achieved the break-through, getting first Dexter and then Barrington. Hawke, too, bowling round the wicket, found the right line and was moving the ball just enough to be dangerous. At tea England were struggling at 199 for five, and despite a partnership of 69 between Parks and Parfitt they were all out by ten past six for 268. Hawke, in his final spell, took four for 30, and the advantage of the toss was gone.

With a maximum of three overs in which to strike back before stumps, Trueman, after a dummy run-up, pawed the turf with frustration as Simpson and Lawry appealed against the light. Their appeal was granted and England were denied any chance of a consolation wicket.

Bad starts by Australia in the first two Tests had finally convinced Simpson that he must open, and he had relegated Redpath to No 3. It was the task of England's opening bowlers to confound this strategy. But if Burge was a veteran, how much more so were Trueman and his new-ball partner Flavell. At 32 a batsman might be adjudged to be in his prime, but this could hardly be said of a fast bowler at that age. Flavell, much respected on the county circuit for his aggression and fire, had never been truly fast, and he was 35. The role of third seamer was filled by Ted Dexter, with the spin entrusted to Titmus and Gifford.

On the second morning Trueman opened from the Kirkstall Lane end, down hill and with the advantage of a slight breeze. Simpson looked rusty and was twice hit by Trueman, the ball lifting nastily, but each time it pitched too short for real danger. Flavell was as accurate and aggressive as usual, but the bat was seldom beaten. Trueman was having trouble with the front-foot law, an experimental change introduced for the first time in Test cricket that season, in which the front foot had to land behind the popping crease. When Trueman erred in length Lawry, more sure than Simpson, drove him through the covers or square cut.

Fifty runs came in less than an hour, and the England score began to look puny. Then Gifford, who had replaced Flavell, induced Simpson to drag a ball into his stumps. 50 for one. But Lawry went on leaning into his off drives, often beating the field, and Titmus, who had worried Redpath at Lord's, was not introduced until just before lunch, when Australia were 95 for one.

A flurry of runs after lunch off Flavell, off whom Lawry took 22 in six overs, was counterbalanced by frugality at the pavilion end, where Titmus provided the contrast. When Gifford replaced Flavell, both batsmen were confined. Using a slight cross-wind to float the ball almost imperceptibly, the spinners tightened their grip. Only 29 runs came in 20 overs after lunch, despite Flavell's largesse.

When the crowd became fractious, Lawry laid his bat on the ground. But it was Redpath, who had been similarly barracked at Lord's for inaction, who became restive. Backing up when Lawry moved out of his crease after edging Titmus to Boycott at shortish third man, Redpath called for a run and set off. Lawry, watching the ball, looked up to see Redpath almost upon him. Judging that it was too late to say no, he ran, knowing his case was hopeless unless Boycott misfielded. But Boycott's throw to Titmus was unerring, and even before Titmus broke the wicket Lawry turned for the pavilion. Lawry's comment, although unreported, is vouched for as unprintable. Redpath, for his part, held his head in his hands. Lawry was on 78 and was not likely to miss a hundred, perhaps a lot more, so it was a lucky dismissal for England. But the tourniquet applied by Titmus and Gifford had been the cause.

Redpath, constrained and remorseful, was not the most relaxing company for a new batsman. Australia at 124 for two still held the advantage, but they looked nervous and tentative against spin, and Peter Burge, the new batsman, was fighting for his Test future, with little behind him but a string of low scores.

Burge shrugged his broad shoulders and pulled his cap forward as he emerged into the afternoon glare. Simpson knew what he wanted to say to him but he could only mutter it under his breath. 'Peter, this is going to be the most important innings you'll ever play, for me, for your country, or for yourself. Go out there and belt the daylights out of them.'

Burge's horizon at this point was much more limited. The landscape was empty, with not a belt in sight. He had often been told that he was one of the worst players of all time on nought, and he was more than ready to believe it. He suffered agonies in the dressing-room beforehand and became progressively neurotic until he got off the mark. All he was looking for was his first single. Beyond that his mind was a blank.

Several times he tried to tickle one round the corner, but Dexter was alert to his need. Titmus's first ten overs yielded three runs, and Gifford was equally stingy. Then Redpath, trying to cut, dragged a widish ball from Gifford that drifted in late on to his stumps. He had spent 2¼ hours over 20.

The tempo of the game had atrophied, and although only the odd ball was turning, Burge and his new partner, Brian Booth, suffered torments as they struggled to get off the mark. For twenty jittery minutes Burge fretted, not seeing half a chance of a run. The crowd, no longer peevish, relished the Australians' discomfiture.

Facing Titmus, Burge struck the ball a shade too firmly to Edrich at mid-off — but nevertheless called for a run. If Edrich picked the ball up cleanly and hit the stumps in one movement, Burge was a goner. But the Australian had learned to pick his marks. He respected Edrich as a gritty batsman, but he had noted that he was not the quickest mover in the field. Edrich did what he could to abort the run but Burge galloped home.

The ground was full, the gates were closed, the fielding had suddenly become menacing, and the crowd were enthralled. Booth, going like Burge for a risky first run, would have been out had Taylor's under-arm throw to the bowler's end hit the stumps.

Defending resolutely but always looking to score, Burge brought a protracted round of applause by straight-driving Gifford for 4 to put up the 150. But for a long time this was his only belligerent stroke. Titmus was playing on the batsmen's anxieties with subtle changes of pace and flight. Once Burge made room to square cut him to the boundary with surprising elegance for such a big man, but Booth, normally quick on his feet, chafed at being pinned down. When he left his crease to get to the pitch of the ball, Titmus saw him coming, and a faster ball, tossed a bit wider, had him stumped.

At 154 for four, with only one recognised batsman to come, the Australian position was precarious. The over before Booth's dismissal, Dexter had recalled Trueman, and Cowper, playing in his first Test, now had to face him. The Yorkshireman's method for Cowper's baptism was classic but simple. A confident stroke off Cowper's legs for 2 drew a well-directed answering bumper. Then came the in-swinging yorker. Cowper, trapped on the back foot when he should have gone forward, tried too late to smother it, and to the unrestrained delight of Trueman's many thousands of fans his leg stump went down. It was the first time he had failed on the tour. Australia were 157 for five and England were unquestionably on top.

Burge, still struggling himself, was not able to do much about it. He rated Titmus, with his curving flight and occasional turn, the best off-spinner in the world on good wickets. This was the testing time, and although irked at being tied down, he went on pushing out doggedly. A miscued hook off Trueman trickled into the gully, but when Trueman produced a yorker he stunned it incisively. To the onlooker, at least, he didn't look like getting out. Tom Veivers, who had saved the Australian first innings at Lord's, held fast with Burge until tea, when Australia were 172 for five, Burge 30 not out. For Australia, as for England the previous day, it had been a disastrous afternoon.

With the game so far advanced by tea-time on the second day, an outright win for one side or the other looked certain. It might be more difficult to force a result at Old Trafford or the Oval, and in a series where the sides seemed closely matched, the Leeds game looked likely to decide the destiny of the Ashes.

Australia were still 96 behind and in the toils against spin. But nothing very dramatic was said in the dressing room during the break. 'Put your heads down,' said Simpson, 'See what you can do.'

Soon after tea, Veivers tried to cut Titmus and edged the ball to Parks. 178 for six. McKenzie, presumably on instructions to knock Titmus off, lunged across the line, missed, and was bowled. 178 for seven. That left Burge with three tail-enders — Hawke, Grout, and Corling — to come. Australia were still 90 behind.

Despite McKenzie's failure, Simpson did not change his tactics. 'Tell Peter to try to take charge, to try to hit the bowlers off their length,' he told Hawke. 'Now's your chance, Hawkeye. Let's see if you're as good with the bat as you say.' Hawke had long been bemoaning his lack of opportunities with the bat, and Simpson, weakening, had promoted him above Grout, to the latter's disgust.

All too often Hawke didn't get to the wicket at all, and at Northampton he had finally sunk to No. 11. An Australian Rules footballer, of splendid physique and fitness, he had been primarily a batsman before switching to seam bowling, and he had once made 89 in a State match. More important, he was endowed with his full share of Aussie competitiveness. Now he passed on Simpson's message. 'Simmo says we're not doing any good this way. See if you can have a bit of a go.'

Simpson was right: only if Burge took charge could Australia recover. But there was no point in getting himself out. Titmus remained tantalisingly accurate: of his first 18 overs 14 had been maidens, he had bowled 21 overs between lunch and tea, and Burge was still wary of chancing his arm. Gifford had bowled eleven overs for 16. Burge did respond to Simpson's instructions to the extent of advancing once to drive Titmus for 4, but otherwise the spinners held sway.

Of the two captains, it was Simpson whose brow was the

45

more furrowed. But Dexter had his worries too. The new ball was due and Titmus and Gifford must surely be tiring. It was always better to rest the spinners before they got collared. Then they could reweave their spell when brought back. At the moment, ringed by close catchers, the batsmen were strokeless, but McKenzie's heave had suggested that soon they would try to break out. No one, in Dexter's experience, played off-spin better than Burge. Meanwhile Trueman and Flavell were itching to clean up nine-ten-jack with the new ball.

It was an unenviable and perhaps a crucial decision, and Dexter delayed it until the 89th over. Two factors settled it. He must test Hawke with pace before he got in. And he had in Trueman potentially one of the most destructive bowlers in the world, most of all so against tailenders. Trueman, indeed, had already castled Hawke cheaply once that season.

Burge saw Dexter signal that he was about to take the new ball. For Burge it looked like a reprieve, a release from the straitjacket imposed by the spinners. He walked down the wicket to Hawke. 'Ted's taking the new ball. Let's make the most of it. The spinners will be back soon enough. We've just got to take it out of this new ball.'

Burge reasoned that he had a lot of things in his favour. He was 38 not out, and if he wasn't seeing the ball now he never would. The new cherry would look like a football. The wicket was slow, the bounce was even, and there had been no indication that the ball would swing over-much. He and Trueman were old adversaries, and over the years Trueman had hurt him many times and often got him out. Generally speaking, indeed, Trueman had got the better of him; he had to admit that. But Fred wasn't the bowler he had been. When the conditions were right he could still find that extra yard of pace and bowl as well as ever, but the conditions weren't right for him today. Burge believed that Dexter was throwing the life-line, and he was determined to grab it.

On the other hand, Trueman, having got Burge out before, believed he could do it again. And he thought he knew how. He was prepared to give Burge a single to get at Hawke if that

proved necessary, but for a start he would try to find the edge
of Burge's bat. If that didn't work he would bowl a few bouncers.
Burge would answer the challenge and go for the hook, as he
always did. Fresh from his extended rest, and with the extra
bounce of the new ball, Trueman was confident he would get
Burge caught. Meanwhile the crowd perked up. What had
Dexter been waiting for? Fred was taking the new ball. About
time!

Burge told Hawke: 'I'll take as much of Freddie as I can. Give
me the strike and I'll get stuck in.'

Dexter gave Trueman an umbrella field, but Trueman failed
to keep the ball up, and twice in his first over Burge hit him hard
and square on the off side. An answering bouncer, pitched nearer
the bowler's end than the batsman's, flew out of reach over
Burge's head.

Flavell likewise bowled too short, and Burge had time to pull
him to mid-wicket. The umbrella field backed off. It hadn't
worried Burge anyway. Even if he made a mistake he felt it gave
him a chance, so long as he went for his shots. A thick edge
could go anywhere.

As Trueman and Flavell continued to pitch short, Burge
hooked and cut gratefully. Determined to prove his point, and
with his home crowd roaring him on, Trueman overdid the
bouncers, and on this slow wicket Burge stood his ground and
pulled them safely in front of square.

Burge was now hammering both bowlers at will. Three overs
from Trueman cost 25 runs, including five 4's to Burge, and
three overs from Flavell cost 15. A ferocious pull off Flavell put
up the 200, and Burge reached his fifty, made out of 87 in just
under two hours, with a thunderous on-drive off Trueman. Two
balls later he straight-drove him for his ninth 4 with the best
shot of the lot. Dexter came on for Flavell, and Flavell, switching
to Trueman's end, and urged not to pitch short, was twice
cover-driven for 4. So devastating was Burge's assault that
Hawke's susceptibility to fast bowling and the new ball was
barely tested.

Dexter's first ball, though, might have had Hawke caught if

he could have afforded a third slip. Had the catch gone to hand, Dexter would have been a hero. But for persisting with pace for 15 overs while 63 runs were added, taking the score from 187 to 250, he was severely criticised. He could hardly be blamed for taking the new ball, and it was not his fault that Trueman and Flavell bowled badly. While the ball was new, too, he was surely entitled to have a go himself: he nearly broke the partnership. But all this was forgotten, and for not cutting his losses after eight or nine overs and reverting to spin he was roundly condemned.

To the home supporters it seemed that a hard-won advantage had been squandered. To the impartial it was clear that the Australians had played some magnificent cricket. But Burge himself had expected the spinners back sooner. 'I don't know how long this is going to last,' he told Hawke between overs, 'but I'm going to make the most of it.'

Burge had not wrought the miracle alone. Hawke, less gainly but with sound commonsense, played many firm strokes. But Burge, solid in defence, unshakeable in application, massive in composure, was majestic. When Titmus and Gifford were cheered back to the bowling crease at six o'clock — a rare rebuff for Trueman at Leeds — the batsmen were going so well that the old authority exercised by the spinners was lacking. A leg glance from Burge took him to 80, and Australia were only 18 behind.

After four uneventful overs from Titmus, Dexter brought Trueman back for a final fling before stumps, this time from the pavilion end. Australia were now in the lead, and Burge was on 89. He pulled Trueman's first ball to the mid-wicket boundary, then off-drove him for 2, putting up the 100 partnership and taking his score to 95. One by one the Australians crowded on to their dressing-room balcony, their grim expressions of an hour or so earlier transformed into grins. Once assembled, none of them dare move, for fear of changing the luck.

Trueman's next over would be the last of the day, but the light had deteriorated. As Trueman walked back to his mark, Burge appealed. With maddeningly measured tread the umpires strolled towards each other to confer, and the crowd booed. But they cheered when the umpires resumed their vigil.

Trueman, perhaps, was trying too hard, and Burge square cut his second ball for 4 to take him to 99. Then the game was interrupted yet again as Dexter, plotting to save the one, rearranged his field.

There were four balls to go. It didn't occur to Burge that he ought to play them out. He could see those magic three figures on the board, and for the first time that day he thought of himself. The pressure building up on him, from the Australian balcony and from all over the ground, to get that single tonight became palpable. The chance did not come until the fifth ball of the over, and it was little more than half a chance even then. But the temptation was irresistible. It would be a scrambled single, stolen from the packed covers, but he could see that Hawke was ready to come, and he set off.

The fielder was throwing to the wicket-keeper — Hawke's end! He felt a stab of fear for Hawke. What a ghastly finish! How could he have been so foolish? He would never forgive himself. Then came the uproar, the clapping and cheering, and immense relief at the knowledge that Hawke had scraped in. He lifted his cap briefly, undemonstrative but aglow. He had demolished the crowd's idol, and they had forgiven him.

Then he remembered there was still one ball to go, and another fear gripped him. That single had been irresponsible. He should never had exposed Hawke to Trueman at this stage. Trueman had a lot to prove, and he would go all out to get Hawke with the last ball of the day.

Trueman did not fluff his chance. He found just the right ball, leaving the bat, one which only a top player might shun, Hawke flirted briefly, and Parfitt at slip took a comfortable catch.

Overcome with penitence and remorse, Burge felt all the joy of getting a hundred evaporate. He had committed a monstrous tactical blunder. Worse than that, he had put himself first. It was unforgiveable, and in this his greatest moment of triumph he hung his head in shame. Everyone was congratulating him,

Burge pulls Flavell for 4 during his match-winning innings as Parfitt, Barrington and Parks look on.

Hawke and a self-accusing Burge leave the field at the end of their great partnership.

and all he could do was lament his selfishness and stupidity in getting Hawke out.

He and Hawke had put on 105, and they might have put on another 105 tomorrow. At 283 for eight Australia were only 15 in front, and everyone had said they needed at least 75.

He sat in the dressing room with his pads on, cap and gloves laid at his side, head forward, too tired to move. Batting for three hours in a packed arena, before a knowledgeable but partisan crowd, with everything depending on him, had exhausted him, mentally as much as physically. Someone brought him a cold drink, and the twelfth man started undoing his pads for him. Simpson came and talked to him, so did all the boys one by one, so did the manager, but they couldn't relieve his guilt. 'It's a bloody sight better than it was three hours ago, anyway,' they said, and they patted him on the back. 'Well played.'

It took him twenty minutes to relax and collect his thoughts. By the time he'd had a shower, the euphoria came flooding back. Things weren't so bad. They could have been all out for under 200. He shouldn't have exposed Neil in that last over, but it wasn't as though Neil had just come in. He'd been batting for 95 minutes and had made 37. It was natural to have looked for his hundred that night. Anyone else would have done the same. And he wouldn't have cared to be 99 not out overnight. For a cricketer, 99 and 100 were oceans apart. Cricket history was littered with innings which had blossomed one day only to wither the next. He had got a hundred, just when it was wanted. And it was still all to play for.

That, too, was the majority view. 'What now?' asked 'Jim' Swanton in the *Daily Telegraph*. The wicket was still plumb, though the spinners might get some help later, and Australia would have to bat last. Burge was still there, though, and there was nothing in the game as it stood. 'What a fascinating situation!' concluded Swanton.

The Australian team were driven back to their hotel at Harrogate, where they had a quiet meal, then sat in the lounge, talking the day through, discussing the morrow. They still needed a lot more runs. They wouldn't want to have to make much more than 150 in the last innings. 200, they thought, might be beyond them as the wicket wore.

After a couple of soft drinks, Burge went to bed. He could always sleep before a big match, but that night he was restless, playing his innings over again. It had been his longest innings by far since his operation, and he felt stiff next morning. Back at Headingley, he went into the nets for a loosener, sweating out the stiffness, sharpening his reactions against McKenzie and Hawke. Then he went for a shower.

Grout, too, was in the nets early, but he couldn't middle the ball at all. He batted so atrociously that there seemed no chance of extending that slender lead of 15.

Burge didn't strap his pads on again until Charlie Elliott and Fred Price, the umpires, put their heads round the dressing-room door. 'Ten minutes, boys.' He hated sitting around. He hadn't quite exorcised the ghost of last night's blunder, but it was consoling to have his fellow Queenslander Wally Grout, the veteran of the side at 37, to accompany him to the wicket. The old Grout, a seasoned campaigner, was not the batsman he had been, but he had gone in ahead of Hawke in the first two Tests and would be doubly keen to surpass Hawke now. Having played with him for years, Burge knew of his intense will to win.

Simpson called encouragingly to them as they left. 'We need another 150.'

'That's no trouble, Bob,' said Grout.

Having watched Grout in the nets, Simpson was not so confident. 'Wally — let Peter take it as much as you can.'

Grout nodded, and the two batsmen walked out. Burge, letting Grout go first, heard Simpson say, when Grout was out of earshot, 'The old fellow will do it'.

Grout had already endeared himself to English crowds by not removing the bails after Titmus had collided with Hawke in mid-pitch at Trent Bridge, allowing Titmus to regain his feet and complete the run. But he was about to draw heavily on his balance of good will. When Trueman resumed at the pavilion end after an over to Burge from Titmus, Grout hit his first three balls for 4, 4, 1, the boundaries coming from a square cut and a hook. Grout was a fierce and notorious hooker, and Dexter, dismayed at this ragged start, asked Trueman a question that amounted to a rebuke. 'Why are you dropping them short to this fellow?'

Burge, too, had a question to put. Grout was supposed to be leaving it to him. After playing out the over he asked Grout: 'What's going on out here?'

'We'll have to change the instructions,' said Grout. 'You hold your end up and I'll get the runs!' Despite his woeful exhibition in the nets he had middled his first three balls beautifully and was relishing the paradox.

Titmus continued from the Kirkstall Lane end, and Burge glanced him for 4. Another pull by Grout off a Trueman long hop brought up the 300. That was enough for Dexter, and Flavell came on for Trueman, only to be thumped off the back foot through the covers by Burge.

Grout, mischievously hogging the strike, dominated the scoring, making 16 of the first 23. When Burge hurried Grout into a quick single to pinch the bowling, Grout glared down the wicket at him in mock fury. He defended dourly when confronted by spin but flailed at anything short from the quick men. Between overs he talked and laughed. The previous day had been a grim, humourless war of attrition. Today was almost light-hearted.

If Trueman couldn't bowl them out he could at least try and talk them out, and he sauntered up to Grout between overs, prodding the pitch. 'I wouldn't like to be you fellows,' he said, 'batting on this in the second innings.' 'The way you've been bowling, Freddie,' countered Grout, 'we won't have to.'

England did not find it so funny. Flavell, limping from a strained Achilles tendon, left the field, and a young Glamorgan player named Allan Rees with a reputation as a fielder came on as substitute. Dexter tried Gifford at the pavilion end, and in his first over Burge hit one almost straight back, slightly to the on, hard and low to Gifford's right. He barely got his fingers to it, and it was his wrong hand anyway, so it was scarcely a chance.

Burge was then 117. In Gifford's next over Burge unleashed two tremendous drives, straight and to the on, which no one could touch.

First came the 50 partnership, and then, at 12.45, after Dexter had replaced Titmus, a leg-bye brought up the 350. Australia led by 82, and it seemed impossible that they had once been 178 for seven. Titmus changed to the pavilion end, and Burge twice made room to hammer him square for 4.

Old hands were talking about McCabe's match-saving 232 at Trent Bridge in 1938, when Bradman had called his team out on to the balcony, telling them they'd never see anything like it again. Burge's total command was reminiscent of that innings.

Sooner or later, Burge knew, Grout would have a woof at the spinners. But when he did, he swept Titmus to the fence. Perhaps this scared Grout as much as it did Burge, as next ball, which looked suspiciously straight, he failed to offer a stroke. Titmus appealed, and Grout looked ostentatiously at his leg and then checked the line by running his gaze down the wicket. His dumb show did not impress umpire Elliott, and Grout departed, the picture of outraged innocence. But he'd made 37, the same number as Hawke, and Australia at 372 for nine were 104 ahead.

'I'll just give it a go now,' Burge told Corling, the last man in. 'If we can get another 20 or so that'll do.' (Corling had no great pretensions as a batsman.) Burge reached 150 by sweeping Titmus for 4 — a stroke he used sparingly in this innings because of its danger — and he and Corling were still together at lunch, after which Dexter took the third new ball. Surely Trueman could not bowl so badly this time.

Stubbornly convinced that sooner or later Burge must mishook, Trueman tempted him with yet another long hop, and Burge smote it high towards the square leg boundary, either for 4 or 6, he didn't know which. He was surprised to see — for a fast bowler with the new ball — a fielder stationed at deep mid-wicket, but he eyed him complacently, knowing there was no one in the England side capable of getting anywhere near the ball. He had forgotten about substitute Allan Rees. Sprinting round the boundary, Rees hurled himself through space and brought off a miraculous catch.

It was a fitting end to an innings which turned defeat into victory. Australia led by 121, and nothing went right for England from then on. Boycott, for the third time running, was caught at first slip by Simpson off Corling, and Parfitt, batting No. 3 this time, had a knuckle broken first ball. Taylor had chipped a bone in his right hand in the first innings, and with Flavell still limping England were a team of crocks. Only a patchy 85 from Ken Barrington raised Australia's second innings target to three figures, but Titmus then pressed them so hard that they took 57 overs to score the 109 they needed, losing three wickets in the process. They might not have won had not Redpath, by making 58 not out, finally established himself as a batsman of Test class.

All Simpson now had to do to retain the Ashes was to avoid defeat at Old Trafford, and for this he took out his own personal insurance policy by batting for 12¾ hours, the longest innings ever played against England, and scoring 311. (On a placid pitch, Trueman had the good fortune to be left out.) For England, Barrington countered with 256 and Dexter with 174, and the match was drawn; but the best England could do now at the Oval was to square the rubber. The faint hope they had of doing so was frustrated when the last day was rained off.

Thus the game that will always be referred to as 'Burge's Match' decided both the destination of the rubber and the Ashes. 'Considering the circumstances in which it was played,' wrote Denis Compton, 'it was possibly the greatest innings I had seen.' Simpson called it 'one of the great innings of all time'.

Ted Dexter likened it recently to Ian Botham's innings at Headingley in 1981. Australia in the 1964 match, he believed, were also 500-1 against. 'It didn't *matter* at the time,' he added, 'whether England took the new ball, kept on with the old one, or swapped it for a grape-fruit. Just as Kim Hughes might just as well have bowled himself against Botham.

'The greatness of these very similar innings was that they changed the course of the match well before anyone — including Burge and Botham — realised what was happening.'

The last word, perhaps, may be allowed to Freddie Trueman, who in that truncated game at the Oval reached 300 wickets in Tests. He could rightly claim that he had known all along how to get Burge out; but he had to admit that the execution was a trifle tardy. He called it, with wry humour, 'proving a point'.

ENGLAND v AUSTRALIA 1964 (3rd Test)
at Leeds, July 2, 3, 4, 6
Australia won by 7 wickets

ENGLAND: First Innings

G. Boycott, c Simpson b Corling	38
J. H. Edrich, c Veivers b McKenzie	3
*E. R. Dexter, c Grout b McKenzie	66
K. F. Barrington, b McKenzie	29
P. H. Parfitt, b Hawke	32
K. Taylor, c Grout b Hawke	9
†J. M. Parks, c Redpath b Hawke	68
F. J. Titmus, c Burge b McKenzie	3
F. S. Trueman, c Cowper b Hawke	4
N. Gifford, not out	1
J. A. Flavell, c Redpath b Hawke	5
Extras (LB 9, NB 1)	10
Total	268

Fall of wickets: 1-17, 2-74, 3-129, 4-138, 5-163, 6-215, 7-232, 8-260, 9-263, 10-268.

Bowling: McKenzie, 26-7-74-4; Hawke, 31.3-11-75-5; Corling, 24-7-50-1; Veivers, 17-3-35-0; Simpson, 5-0-24-0.

AUSTRALIA: First Innings

*R. B. Simpson, b Gifford	24
W. M. Lawry, run out	78
I. R. Redpath, b Gifford	20
P. J. Burge, c sub (A. Rees) b Trueman	160
B. C. Booth, st Parks b Titmus	4
R. M. Cowper, b Trueman	2
T. R. Veivers, c Parks b Titmus	8
G. D. McKenzie, b Titmus	0
N. J. N. Hawke, c Parfitt b Trueman	37
†A. W. T. Grout, lbw b Titmus	37
G. E. Corling, not out	2
Extras (B 1, LB 8, W 2, NB 6)	17
Total	389

Fall of wickets: 1-50, 2-124, 3-129, 4-154, 5-157, 6-178, 7-178, 8-283, 9-372, 10-389.

Bowling: Trueman, 24.3-2-98-3; Flavell, 29-5-97-0; Gifford, 34-15-62-2; Dexter, 19-5-40-0; Titmus, 50-24-69-4; Taylor, 2-0-16-0.

ENGLAND: Second Innings

G. Boycott, c Simpson b Corling	4
J. H. Edrich, c Grout b McKenzie	32
P. H. Parfitt, c Redpath b Hawke	6
K. F. Barrington, lbw b Veivers	85
E. R. Dexter, c Redpath b Veivers	17
J. M. Parks, c Booth b McKenzie	23
N. Gifford, b McKenzie	1
K. Taylor, b Veivers	15
F. J. Titmus, c Cowper b Corling	14
F. S. Trueman, not out	12
J. A. Flavell, c Simpson b Corling	5
Extras (B 6, LB 6, W 1, NB 2)	15
Total	229

Fall of wickets: 1-13, 2-88, 3-145, 4-156, 5-169, 6-184, 7-192, 8-199, 9-212, 10-229.

Bowling: McKenzie, 28-8-53-3; Corling, 17.5-6-52-3; Hawke, 13-1-28-1; Veivers, 30-12-70-3; Simpson, 1-0-11-0.

AUSTRALIA: Second Innings

R. B. Simpson, c Barrington b Titmus	30
W. M. Lawry, c Gifford b Trueman	1
I. R. Redpath, not out	58
P. J. Burge, b Titmus	8
B. C. Booth, not out	12
Extras (B 1, LB 1)	2
Total (3 wkts)	111

Fall of wickets: 1-3, 2-45, 3-64.

Bowling: Trueman, 7-0-2-1; Titmus 27-19-25-2; Gifford, 20-5-47-0; Dexter, 3-0-9-0.

Umpires—W. F. Price and C. S. Elliott

3

GRAEME POLLOCK

'If you ever score a century like that
again I hope I'm there to see it'
— Sir Donald Bradman

In a corner of the playing field under the pine-trees, against a background of stolid, Dutch-style school buildings, the old Sussex professional mopped his receding brow. Only a light, cooling breeze and the shade of the pine-trees made the day tolerable. 'Take the boys into the nets this morning,' the headmaster had said. 'You can have them four at a time. They can manage without their lessons for an hour or so, but they can't do without their cricket.'

For 46-year-old George Cox these coaching engagements at Grey High School, in South Africa, were both pleasurable and rewarding, never more so than when some young player of promise emerged. Such was the case today. Indeed the lad in the nets was an artist in miniature.

Cox had never seen anything like it. He knew something about the boy — he was a left-hander — and his background, but the progress he had made since Cox's last visit was astonishing.

On a concrete wicket, fast and bouncy, the boy was cutting and pulling the rising ball with precocious certainty. He was hitting through the line of anything on a length, and moving unerringly to the pitch of the ball when anyone tossed it up — not merely to kill the spin and the bounce but to drive, never lifting the ball. Most amazing for a boy was his quick and accurate judgement of length, always seeming to be balanced and in position without any elaborate footwork.

Cox recognised the boy from his rather low forehead and prominent ears; but these things were superficial and he would grow out of them. What struck Cox most forcibly was his *compactness*. Most boys of his age — he could not have been more than 13 — were hampered by the awkwardness of growing. They were angular, or leggy, or unco-ordinated. Coaching helped them to go through the motions, to adopt the right postures and play a straight bat, but it did not teach them timing or elegance. This boy not only did everything right: he middled the ball.

Cox knew the boy as a nice little chap with a round, rather florid, cherubic face who had always shown exceptional ability. His father, Andrew Pollock, editor of the *Eastern Province Herald*, was a native of Scotland who had played as a wicket-keeper for the Orange Free State. The boy was Graeme Pollock, and he had a brother at the same school, nearly three years his senior, who had already grown tall, filled out, and developed into a youthful but rampaging fast bowler.

Cox himself came from a cricketing family; that was traditional in his home county of Sussex. Of a genial, relaxed disposition, he was a man of discernment and charm. His one fear, where this boy was concerned, was that someone might presume to coach him, at the risk of disturbing his natural talent. His technique was already immaculate; on no account should it be tampered with.

Someone far closer to the family than Cox had once tried to do so — and failed. This was the boy's mother. Seeing him, as a three-year-old, take up his stance at the wicket left-handed, Edith Pollock had sought to correct him; he had done everything else right-handed up to that time. A wilful child, he had resisted; but soon Mrs. Pollock accepted that it was a question of heredity, not naughtiness. The boy's father, right-handed in everything else, batted left-handed. A games player herself, she bowled to her younger son from then on without comment, as she had bowled to the older boy Peter.

For George Cox, musing under the pine-trees, the boy had a glittering future. He imagined him playing on all the great cricket grounds of the world, scoring many thousands of runs and giving pleasure to millions. His future looked as unclouded as the South African sky. Yet out there on the playing fields, where no shade existed, the sun, near its zenith, threw one tiny shadow. It was the foreshortened image of someone whose prospects were not quite so glittering, the shadow of a Cape Coloured ground-boy, whose chances of entertaining millions, at cricket or anything else, were millions to one.

*   *

Rumours of 'the best schoolboy cricketer ever seen' were brought back to England a year or so later by the Warwickshire batsman Fred Gardner, Cox's successor at Grey High School. The information was not forgotten by Warwickshire captain M.J.K. 'Mike' Smith when he was appointed to lead the MCC tour of South Africa in 1964-65. But as it happened he had fresher intelligence available. The South Africans had toured Australia in 1963-64, halving the rubber, and of several individual stars that of the 19-year-old Graeme Pollock had twinkled the brightest. His hundred in 88 minutes against a strong Combined XI at Perth at the start of the tour drew the remark from Sir Donald Bradman already recorded. He made 122 out of 186 scored while he was at the wicket in the third Test and an exhilarating 175 in the fourth, when his stand of 341 with Eddie Barlow set a new South African record for any wicket. These Test centuries of Pollock's were hailed as 'two of the finest innings ever seen in Australia'.

Thus Mike Smith knew what to expect. During the 1964-65 tour he felt that the England bowlers made Pollock struggle and restricted him pretty well, and it wasn't until the final Test that he really took them apart. He averaged 57 in the series; but England enjoyed an unexpected success by gaining the only positive result of the series in the first Test at Durban, through getting first knock on a pitch that took spin. Subsequently they hung on somewhat ingloriously to their lead.

Following that series, the South Africans arrived in England in mid-June to play three Test Matches in the last two months of the season. Strange as they nearly all were to English conditions, they were not thought likely to extend England at home. Yet they proved one of the most popular of all touring teams.

Previous post-war South African sides had been lacking in enterprise, always excepting the great Roy McLean. But under an untried skipper in Peter van der Merwe, with only one fast bowler in Peter Pollock, and with no experienced spinner apart from the 33-year-old Athol McKinnon, they played such exciting cricket that the crowds flocked to see them, not just for their batting and bowling but also for their fielding — or anyway the wonderful fielding of Colin Bland. On a blank day at Canterbury the crowds actually turned up to see Bland give a fielding exhibition.

Luckier with the weather than New Zealand, who played three Tests in the first half of the summer, they worked up slowly to their opening Test at Lord's in July. In a fluctuating game they finished on top, which gave them confidence for the second Test early in August at Trent Bridge.

England were forced to make two changes from the Lord's side through injuries, Peter Parfitt coming in for John Edrich, who had been hit on the side of the head by Peter Pollock at Lord's, and John Snow replacing David Brown. Another change brought in Tom Cartwright instead of a third fast bowler. South Africa made one change only, McKinnon replacing off-spinner Bromfield.

The Trent Bridge pitch had been flooded a week earlier, and the prophecies on how it would play were exceedingly gloomy. It would be soft and slow and easy-paced, too slow for stroke-play, though it would allow the bowlers some movement off the seam. This was what encouraged the England selectors to sacrifice a fast bowler for Cartwright. But both seam and spin were expected to be too slow to trouble top-class batsmen, and the best hope of a result, it was thought, lay in the uncertain weather forecast. This added to the importance of winning the toss.

Thursday morning August 5th began cool and blustery, but by the time the two captains went out to toss a warm but rather watery sun was pushing its way through the overcast. To the delight of the South Africans van der Merwe won the toss, and no one was more pleased than Graeme Pollock, for whom getting first knock was always a relief. Batting second meant a ready-made area of rough outside the left-hander's off stump, churned up by the bowlers' footmarks.

Mike Smith, too, would have batted, but for him the loss of the toss was no great disappointment. Strong sun on the previous day had drawn most of the moisture out of the wicket, but the overcast sky and damp atmosphere, allied to a lively cross-breeze, promised the sort of conditions which his bowlers were far more skilled in exploiting than their opponents. The morning's play, he hoped, would provide a severe examination for the South African batsmen.

England opened the attack from the pavilion end with the giant fast bowler David Larter; John Snow started from the Radcliffe Road end. Larter's length and direction, although better than they had been at Lord's, were erratic, and he could get no bounce out of the wicket, while Snow bowled too much down the leg side. However, neither Barlow nor Lance, the opening batsmen, found the pace of the wicket to their liking. Both played too soon and missed, and both made misjudgements which resulted in vociferous lbw appeals. The two batsmen survived uneasily, the only belligerent stroke in the first eight overs being a pull to the square-leg boundary off Larter by the sturdy, bespectacled Barlow.

Speed through the air, on this wicket, was clearly less important than accuracy and movement, and Smith soon introduced Tom Cartwright at the Radcliffe Road end, switching Snow to the pavilion end to relieve Larter. Cartwright, feeling his way, pitched somewhat negatively at first, and he began with two maidens. But in his third over he pitched one further up and Lance, trying to drive, was beaten by an in-swinger and hit on the back leg. On appeal he was given out.

The new batsman, Derek Lindsay, played and missed at his first ball, let the second alone, and drove rather desperately at the next. This time it moved away and found the edge of the bat for Parks to take the catch.

After 50 minutes' play and fourteen overs, South Africa were 16 for two. Perhaps it had not been such a good thing to win the toss after all. So far as the new batsman was concerned, however, his preference remained firm; it was the 21-year-old left-hander Graeme Pollock.

Since leaving school Pollock had grown several inches, and he was now 6' 2½", the same height as his brother. But he had filled out proportionately, and although still comparatively slim and lissom he exuded the same aura of compactness that had so impressed George Cox eight years earlier. The rather low forehead was hidden under a cap, but the ears still slightly protruded.

Forecasts that Pollock would not be able to repeat his overseas successes on English wickets had been widespread, and he had made a modest start to both the tour and the Test series, scoring 56 and 5 at Lord's. But in his most recent innings, at Canterbury, he had reminded the spectators of their old idol Frank Woolley in a wonderful double century — 203 not out, out of 365 for three. The bowling may not have been the most penetrative, but on the same wicket Kent were bowled out cheaply twice — producing the spare day on which Colin Bland gave his exhibition.

Fresh from that triumph, Pollock had approached this match with confidence. He had listened to all the talk about the wicket, but he had no preconceived ideas about how he would play. As for the bad start, he would not allow that to inhibit him. As always, he would treat each ball on its merits.

A natural sideways player, studiously correct, Pollock maintained a perfect balance for every shot. He appeared to have no weakness, and Mike Smith, having had plenty of time to study his methods in South Africa, gave no special instructions to his bowlers. It was sufficient that the ball was moving in the air and off the seam and that Cartwright had only just begun an inspired spell.

Lindsay had been out to the last ball of Cartwright's third over, so Barlow faced Snow. He got a single off the first ball, and Pollock took guard. A single off the fourth ball took him down to face Cartwright.

Cartwright had caused the batsmen few worries in South Africa, but they had all been assured that he was a vastly different proposition in England. Nevertheless Pollock felt that his experience of Cartwright in South Africa gave him a psychological advantage. This belief was somewhat dented when he went to cut Cartwright's second ball and snicked it uppishly between wicket-keeper and first slip. The ball didn't go to hand, so technically it wasn't a chance, but it was the narrowest of escapes.

These runs, off the edge, were the first conceded by Cartwright. Three balls later Pollock re-asserted himself by driving him through the covers for 4.

He was seeing and middling the ball, but he knew the bowlers were after him. Snow got one to cut into him off the wicket and he was lucky to edge it down to fine leg for 4.

There was certainly movement in the wicket, as everyone had promised, but to Pollock it seemed little different from the wickets he'd played on so far on the tour. It wasn't going to stop him going for his shots.

For a time Barlow got most of the strike — an unusual experience for Pollock, who was an adept at farming the bowling. After taking 65 minutes to reach double figures Barlow suddenly got in two pugnacious blows off Cartwright, a square cut of terrific force and a straight drive, both of which reached the fence. This brought a double change, Cartwright moving down to the pavilion end to replace Snow and Titmus coming on for Cartwright.

The introduction of Titmus at this early stage — after 80 minutes' play, at 41 for two — might seem incompatible with the conditions, which remained favourable to seam and swing. But Smith had his reasons. In South Africa, against Eastern Province before the Tests, Titmus had bowled Pollock first ball. In the first Test, at Durban, Titmus had bowled him for 5 in the first innings and Smith had caught him close in off Titmus for a duck in the second. Much the same thing had happened in the first innings of the second Test at Johannesburg, when Pollock had made 12. That had been the extent of Titmus's successes, but the memory of them lingered. More recently, Titmus had dismissed Pollock in the first innings at Lord's.

For Pollock, batting against Titmus was always a contest; but it was a contest he enjoyed. After that string of failures, Titmus had always been brought on early against him. Pollock had eventually got after him, but he rated Titmus the best off-spinner he'd met and responded to the challenge of batting against him.

The double change brought three successive maidens, two from Titmus and one from Cartwright. Then Barlow, trying to break out of the strait-jacket, drove at Cartwright, only to snick the ball to first slip. It was falling short of Cowdrey, but Parks dived and knocked it up. Cowdrey completed the catch, and that was 42 for three.

Confirmation of the difficulty of run-getting that morning lay in Barlow's figures: an aggressive player, he had batted 90 minutes for 19.

Bland got a single off the last ball of Cartwright's over, then faced Titmus. With 39 and 70, Bland had been the most successful of the South African batsmen at Lord's. Now Titmus floated one up to him and Bland pushed forward to smother the spin. But he didn't quite succeed in stunning it, and the ball spun back towards Parks. Parks grabbed it and swept it into the stumps in one movement, Bland couldn't get his foot down in time, and that was 43 for four.

It was an unlucky dismissal no doubt, but it was a disaster for South Africa. All advantage of winning the toss was gone. Indeed the match looked as good as lost.

Next man in was the 23-year-old Ali Bacher. Although new to Test cricket this series, he had batted staunchly in the second innings at Lord's. Now he dealt safely with the remainder of Titmus's over.

With the South African innings on the brink of collapse, what would be Pollock's reaction? Pollock himself supposed that he ought to be thinking about survival, of concentrating, at least for a time, on defence. But he just couldn't play that way. With a mind untrammelled by notions of what was and was not possible on this type of wicket, he decided his job must be to see that Cartwright and Titmus didn't get completely on top. Cartwright, about to bowl to him from the pavilion end, was the immediate consideration. Pollock had always been partial to medium-pacers, and he decided to go after Cartwright. Not that he proposed to take risks. He was playing well within himself, and there was no need to panic as yet. But if shots were there he would go for them. Somehow he must take command.

Mike Smith anticipated something like this, and he strengthened the off-side field. Pollock's response was two tremendous boundaries, a square cut and a cover drive, the latter a lovely flowing stroke that left the fielders standing. These two shots put up the 50 after 95 minutes' play and brought appreciative applause from the crowd.

Cartwright's face was a study. His look, first at the umpire and then at the heavens, was comically expressive. What did one bowl to this chap? The ball he had cover-driven for 4 had not been a half-volley; it had been right on a length. How had he done it? It was a new experience for Cartwright. On the county circuit he was never driven like this.

At the other end, Bacher was happy to allow Titmus to bowl his fourth maiden in succession, and then Pollock resumed his assault on Cartwright. Again the packed covers were somehow sent the wrong way. With a firm stroke that brought 2 and another scorching drive for 4 Pollock became, at 21 years five months, the youngest player to reach 1,000 runs in Tests. While his colleagues had been in all kinds of traumas against some very good bowling, Pollock had made it look easy.

Bacher got going with a 3 off Titmus, and when in the next over he turned Cartwright neatly off his toes for 4, Cartwright was rested. His figures read 12 overs, 4 maidens, 36 runs, 3 wickets.

Titmus tied Pollock down until the last ball of the next over, when Pollock, swift-footed and poised, moved to the pitch of the ball, leaned into and over it with exquisite balance, and pierced the field yet again.

Larter came back at the pavilion end, to be cross-batted by Bacher straight back past his ankles for the morning's eleventh 4. Lunch came after 37 overs with South Africa 76 for four, Pollock 34, Bacher 12. They had put on 33 for the fifth wicket, staging a partial recovery, but England were very much in the ascendancy.

Nothing much was said by the South Africans at lunch. Only Graeme Pollock seemed unworried. The others looked deflated and glum. The side that lost this match could still draw the series, but it couldn't win it, and the tourists were dead keen to avenge their defeat in South Africa. Everything depended on Pollock.

It was not only among the South Africans, however, that a discreet silence was maintained. Those who had pontificated on the impracticability of stroke-play on this wicket kept quiet as well.

They were inclined to excuse themselves by concluding that only a very great player could have done it. But they couldn't blame the wicket when Snow returned at the pavilion end after lunch and Bacher, playing a half-defensive shot with a fatally angled bat, dragged the ball into his stumps.

Van der Merwe, who came next, had already earned golden opinions by his handling of the side, both on and off the field. He had batted soundly in the two Tests he had played in at home, but in thirteen innings on this tour his top score had been 33, and his average was under 15. Three times he had been dismissed without scoring. Yet somehow he had to put this behind him and play a captain's part.

Pollock saw him glance at the score board as he walked to the wicket; he knew exactly what was in his skipper's mind. 80 for five. They had started the day with such high hopes, and now they would do well to get 150. Then, with all movement drained from the wicket, England would pile on the runs.

No words passed between the two men; there was no need for them. It was axiomatic that van der Merwe would get his head down and Pollock would go for the runs.

Van der Merwe looked desperately unsure of himself, but he managed to stick. Pollock moved into the 40s with a 4 off Snow. Then, for half a dozen overs, even Pollock went warily as Titmus closed one end and Snow flung himself into the task of destroying all chance of a recovery. At length a series of wristy deflections off Snow took Pollock to his fifty. He had batted 95 minutes.

Standing his full height, Pollock began hitting through the line with such devastating effect that Snow, struck for two 2's and a 4 in one over, had to come off. Cartwright came back at the Radcliffe Road end, where he had started that morning, and

Titmus changed ends. Manipulating the strike, Pollock bided his time before hitting Titmus for nine runs in four balls, including a hook and another glorious swift-footed drive through the covers. The Titmus ploy had failed, and van der Merwe rubbed it in by sweeping the last ball for 4.

The 15,000 spectators were now treated to some of the fiercest hitting they had ever seen. Yet not a ball left the turf. Pollock drove Cartwright to the onside and square to the off to take his score to 77, and when Smith tried Bob Barber with his leg-breaks and googlies Pollock late-cut him adroitly, the ball gathering speed as it raced to the ring. When Barber over-pitched or dropped marginally short, Pollock swung or hammered him to leg, the shot off the back foot between mid-wicket and mid-on being peculiarly his own.

With all this array of strokes — only the hook was never attempted — there was not a trace of a mis-hit, the batsman seeming immune from error. Changes of pace and flight failed to deceive him, and his choice of stroke, as he moved through the 80s, remained unerring. The top hand was invariably in control, the shoulder pointing the stroke. Yet his greatest asset, as George Cox had once noted, was his instant and infallible judgement of length. He was never hasty, never hesitant, he never needed to improvise, and for all his power of shot his swing was easy and languorous.

How was it done? Much of it is unaccountable except by the use of an overworked word: genius. But Pollock did have natural advantages. He believed that to have his right hand — his dominant hand — at the top of the bat-handle exerted a decisive influence on his play. He was leading all the time with his stronger hand, helping to keep the bat straight. Players who placed the dominant hand at the top, he believed, were always good drivers.[1] This was the secret of his ability to control the ball and keep it down when hitting on the up.

Batting left-handed was an advantage in itself, he believed, despite the problem of the bowlers' footmarks. Frank Woolley,

[1] See Chapters 4 and 9.

with whom Pollock was so often compared, had held that it was a disadvantage, because the left-hander had to cope so much more often with the ball that moved away — in theory the most dangerous ball. But Pollock found that being left-handed gave him more room to play his shots. Earlier in his career, before he developed his leg-side play, he had countered a deliberate attack on his leg stump by making room to drive the leg-side ball to the off. For right-handers, in-slant bowling, or off-spin, cramped their off-side strokes.

Pollock compounded these natural advantages by using a heavy bat, much heavier than average. He was one of the first top players to do so in the modern era; the habit has been much copied since. Pollock used a bat 3lbs in weight (he still does): he had the strength of wrist and forearm to wield it. It did much to account for his effortless power.

A 4 and a single off Cartwright took Pollock to 90, and by treating Barber's next over similarly he reached 95. The first ball of Cartwright's next over was driven to the boundary, and a pull off the next gave him his fifteenth 4 and his hundred. A third 4 in the same over took him to 107.

Pollock's first fifty had taken 95 minutes, and it contained seven 4's, two of them off the edge. His second fifty, with nine 4's, came in 33 minutes. In the Press Box, Richie Benaud, anxious to get to a telephone, dared not move from his seat for fear of missing a stroke.

Barber brought crowd and critics down to earth by bowling a maiden to van der Merwe. But Pollock was irresistible, Cartwright's first and fourth balls were despatched to the boundary, and after taking a single off the fifth ball he again showed his impartiality by hitting Barber, too, for 4, 4 and 1 to take his score to 125. In 70 minutes since lunch he had made 91 out of 102, and his last 25 runs had come in eleven minutes.

The first ball of Cartwright's next over was directed outside the off stump, and Pollock shaped to stroke it smoothly into the covers. The ball was of full length, too far up for a half-volley, not quite a yorker. What happened next is conjecture.

In attempting to cover the ball Pollock scraped the ground

with his bat. The ball flew to Cowdrey at slip, either off the edge of the bat or out of the rough. It must have been one or the other. Pollock felt no contact with the ball and was convinced it had turned so much that he wasn't anywhere near it; he had stopped his shot. Cowdrey made the catch, and when Pollock remained statuesque at the crease, head down, showing no interest, Cowdrey and others appealed. It could well be that Pollock made contact with ball and ground simultaneously, in which case he might be unaware that he had played the ball. Anyway, umpire Jack Crapp gave him out.

The crowd, spellbound by the pace of the cricket, were bemused for a moment, unable to take it all in. But when they saw Pollock turn slowly and head for the pavilion, they rose to their feet and applauded him all the way in. 'Not since Bradman's day could anyone recall having seen an England attack treated in such cavalier style,' wrote John Woodcock in the *Cricketer*. 'I think it was the *ease* with which Pollock batted which was more astounding than anything.' The way Pollock stood alone, he wrote, was a sure sign of greatness.

This, in the minutes after dismissal, was little help to the disconsolate Pollock, and he sat miserably in the dressing room, scarcely able to credit that his innings was over. As he was often to show, he could fix his eye on a mammoth score, and he had done so today. At that temporary trough in his fortunes, someone came into the dressing room and asked for him, and Pollock, naturally enough, was in no mood to see anyone. 'I'd like to congratulate you on a very fine innings,' said the intruder. Pollock had recovered his normal friendly manner even before he recognised that the visitor was Sir Leonard Hutton.

Bradman at Perth, Hutton at Trent Bridge. Nowhere in the world of cricket could he have found more distinguished and knowledgeable champions.

He remembered something else, too, that cheered him up even more. It was his mother's birthday, and she would want no better birthday present than to hear of his hundred. He hoped she might have heard it on the radio — but he knew that when things went wrong for South Africa she could not bear to listen and

Pollock, beautifully balanced, steps in to drive Titmus.

Pollock's controversial dismissal — c Cowdrey b Cartwright as Parks looks on.

switched off, and he rightly guessed that at 43 for four she would have been too upset to listen. Charles Fortune, the South African radio commentator, came to the rescue, including a message for her in his broadcast, to be passed on by a neighbour in case she wasn't listening. 'Can someone please tell her,' he said, 'about Graeme's hundred, and wish her a happy birthday from her two boys.'

As it happened it was a great day for Peter Pollock as well. The last four South African wickets added 91, Peter making a useful 12 not out, and the total was advanced to 269. Van der Merwe made 38. Then in 35 minutes before the close Peter Pollock got Boycott for nought and Barrington for one, and despite a grand fighting century from Cowdrey England finished 29 behind. on first innings, and failed, at a second attempt, to make up the ground. They eventually lost by 94 runs. The third Test was drawn, so South Africa had their revenge by winning the series.

The match was a triumph for the Pollock brothers, Graeme making another 59 at a second go and Peter taking five wickets in each innings and 10 for 87 in the match. 'Their fraternal effort,' said *Wisden,* 'is without parallel in Test cricket.'

As has been hinted, Graeme Pollock's international career, for political reasons, was sadly truncated. He came to England again to play for the International Cavaliers — to the incalculable profit of one Asif Iqbal, as will be related[2]— and he played for the Rest of the World against England in 1970, after the South African tour was cancelled, scoring a memorable hundred in partnership with Gary Sobers at the Oval. But all attempts to lure him into the English county game, one as recently as 1981, failed. Although loving his cricket, he never wanted to make it a career.

He played in two more Test series in South Africa, his final Test appearance being at Port Elizabeth in March 1970. He was then 26, just approaching the height of his powers. Twelve years later, at the age of 38, he remained an automatic choice for his

[2] See Chapter 6.

ENGLAND v SOUTH AFRICA 1965 (2nd Test)

at Nottingham, August 5, 6, 7, 9

South Africa won by 94 runs

SOUTH AFRICA: First Innings

E. J. Barlow, c Cowdrey b Cartwright	19
H. R. Lance, lbw b Cartwright	7
†J. D. Lindsay, c Parks b Cartwright	0
R. G. Pollock, c Cowdrey b Cartwright	125
K. C. Bland, st Parks b Titmus	1
A. Bacher, b Snow	12
*P. L. van der Merwe, run out	38
R. Dumbrill, c Parfitt b Cartwright	30
J. T. Botten, c Parks b Larter	10
P. M. Pollock, c Larter b Cartwright	15
A. H. McKinnon, not out	8
Extras (LB 4)	4
Total	269

Fall of wickets: 1-16, 2-16, 3-42, 4-43, 5-80, 6-178, 7-221, 8-242, 9-252, 10-269.

Bowling: Larter, 7-6-25-1; Snow, 22-6-63-1; Cartwright, 31.3-9-94-6; Titmus, 22-8-44-1; Barber, 9-3-39-0.

SOUTH AFRICA: Second Innings

J. D. Lindsay, c Cowdrey b Larter	9
H. R. Lance, c Barber b Snow	0
A. Bacher, lbw b Larter	67
E. J. Barlow, b Titmus	76
R. G. Pollock, c Titmus b Larter	59
K. C. Bland, b Snow	10
P. L. van der Merwe, c Parfitt b Larter	4
R. Dumbrill, b Snow	13
J. T. Botten, b Larter	18
P. M. Pollock, not out	12
A. H. McKinnon, b Titmus	9
Extras (B 4, LB 5, NB 3)	12
Total	289

Fall of wickets: 1-2, 2-35, 3-134, 4-193, 5-228, 6-232, 7-243, 8-265, 9-269, 10-289.

Bowling: Larter, 29-7-68-5; Snow, 33-6-83-3; Titmus, 19.4-5-46-2; Boycott, 26-10-60-0; Barber, 3-0-20-0.

ENGLAND: First Innings

G. Boycott, c Lance b P. M. Pollock	0
R. W. Barber, c Bacher b Dumbrill	41
K. F. Barrington, b P. M. Pollock	1
F. J. Titmus, c R. G. Pollock b McKinnon ..	20
M. C. Cowdrey, c Lindsay b Botten	105
P. H. Parfitt, c Dumbrill b P. M. Pollock	18
*M. J. K. Smith, b P. M. Pollock	32
†J. M. Parks, c and b Botten	6
J. A. Snow, run out	3
J. D. F. Larter, b P. M. Pollock	2
T. W. Cartwright, not out	1
Extras (B 1, LB 3, W 1, NB 6)	11
Total	240

Fall of wickets: 1-0, 2-8, 3-63, 4-67, 5-133, 6-225, 7-229, 8-236, 9-238, 10-240.

Bowling: P. M. Pollock, 23.5-8-53-5; Botten, 23-5-60-2; McKinnon, 28-11-54-1; Dumbrill, 18-3-60-1; R. G. Pollock, 1-0-2-0.

ENGLAND: Second Innings

G. Boycott, b McKinnon	16
R. W. Barber, c Lindsay b P. M. Pollock	1
F. J. Titmus, c Lindsay b McKinnon	4
J. A. Snow, b Botten	0
K. F. Barrington, c Lindsay b P. M. Pollock	1
M. C. Cowdrey, st Lindsay b McKinnon	20
P. H. Parfitt, b P. M. Pollock	86
M. J. K. Smith, lbw b R. G. Pollock	24
J. M. Parks, not out	44
T. W. Cartwright, lbw b P. M. Pollock	0
J. D. F. Larter, c van der Merwe b P. M. Pollock	10
Extras (LB 5, W 2, NB 11)	18
Total	224

Fall of wickets: 1-1, 2-10, 3-10, 4-13, 5-41, 6-59, 7-114, 8-207, 9-207, 10-224.

Bowling: P. M. Pollock, 24-15-34-5; Botten, 19-5-58-1; McKinnon, 27-12-50-3; Dumbrill, 16-4-40-0; Barlow, 11-1-20-0; R. G. Pollock, 5-2-4-1.

Umpires—C. S. Elliott and J. F. Crapp

country in the unofficial Test and one-day series against Graham Gooch's English XI. But never again, from the age of 21 on, did he play for his country on an English cricket ground.

Those who were fortunate enough to see his 125 at Trent Bridge in 1965, or one of his big innings in Australia the previous year, recognised at the time that they were the privileged few. But it was some years before they realised just how lucky they were.

4

BOB BARBER

*'Barber is the most dynamic England
opener I have seen'*
— Bobby Simpson

'Your Yorkshire friends tell me that you like to run on the sixth
ball of the over,' said the tall, lissom Lancastrian to his younger
but less athletic Yorkshire partner. 'Please understand that I'm
not prepared to run on the last ball of the over unless you're
equally prepared to run on the first ball of the next.'

This uncompromising broadside provided the abrasive introduction to an association of opposites which was to prove one
of the most exciting opening partnerships in Test cricket. The
Yorkshireman thus addressed was Geoffrey Boycott. The Lancastrian — born in Manchester, though his father was a Yorkshireman — was Bob Barber.

After opening together for the first time in the final Test at
the Oval against the Australians in 1964 and putting on 44 and
80, Boycott and Barber went to South Africa in 1964-65 as
England's opening pair. Boycott at 24 had already proved himself
a player of international class, Barber at 29 had yet to do so.
Thus Boycott hardly took the threat seriously. But when, early
in that South African tour, Boycott blocked the first five balls
of an over before turning the sixth down to long leg and setting
off for a run, Barber responded with an emphatic 'No!' Boycott
protested, as well he might, but Barber simply restated his case.
'I'm sorry, but I've explained the position. Either accept it or do
the other thing. There's two of us out here and that's all there
is to it.'

Boycott ran promptly and was a good judge of a run, so he
was an excellent partner provided he could be persuaded to run

for others as well as for himself. When Boycott realised that Barber meant what he said, the two men struck up a good working relationship.

The predilection for dominating the strike was typical of Geoff Boycott. But the confrontation was even more revealing of the character of Bob Barber. An individualist who conformed to no pattern, he was seen by some as unorthodox, even capricious, with a mind and temperament all his own.

Typical of how quixotic Bob Barber could be was the manner of his dismissal in the second Test of that South African tour. When he had made 97 of the first 146 — and for all but ten of those runs his partner had been Ted Dexter — he went up to Dexter and said 'Right — six or out.' 'Don't be so bloody stupid,' said Dexter. But Barber said 'I mean it.' Off-spinner M.A. Seymour was bowling at the time, and Barber, advancing to hit him straight, allowed for the spin that wasn't there and deflected the ball into his wicket.

Barber departed with a shrug. With Dexter established and a strong batting line-up to come, he was satisfied that he had done his job. More remarkable was the fact that he was not in the least disappointed at not getting a hundred. He had gambled and lost.

This sort of eccentricity could sometimes be disconcerting to others. In the 1965 home season, in the first Test against New Zealand, England were set 95 to win, and Boycott and Barber had scored 92 of them when, according to *Wisden*, Barber 'tried to finish the match with a 6, only to be caught in the deep.' The truth was more whimsical. Barber had conceived the notion of getting Ted Dexter to the wicket before the game was over, for the amusement of the crowd, and had given his wicket away. Dexter, on a hiding to nothing, did not particularly savour the joke.

'You're crazy,' Barber was told afterwards. 'Why throw your wicket away?' 'Why not?' said Barber. 'Why is it important, when there's nothing in the game?' For Barber there had to be a purpose, and the purpose of winning by ten wickets instead of nine, or of improving his average, was an empty one. He needed a challenge, and when that was absent he got bored.

Like many gifted cricketers Barber could be a reluctant per-
former; to be at his best he had to really *want* to play. But he
had always wanted to express himself through his cricket. It was
not until he was close on 30 that he succeeded in doing so, but
when that happened he immediately established himself in the
England side.

*   *

Bob Barber had been a schoolboy prodigy, scaling the heights
at an early age, very much the golden boy. At Ruthin School he
did the 'double' — 1,000 runs and 100 wickets — in his penultimate year, and he played in three matches for Lancashire
while still at school. He batted left and bowled right, and under
the tutelage of the Australian all-rounder George Tribe — a
friend of his father's — he really spun the ball. At Cambridge
he gained a double blue — cricket and athletics — and great
things were expected of him in the first-class game, perhaps too
much. In 1960 at the age of 24 he was appointed captain of
Lancashire, and in the same year he won his first England cap.
His natural ability was undoubted, and his background — he
was a genuine amateur, working in the winter for a small public
company — made him a strong contender to captain England
one day. Yet ten years after his first appearance for Lancashire
he seemed about to become yet another schoolboy wonder who,
although successful up to a point, had not quite fulfilled his early
promise.

Barber was ambitious and competitive, but cricket wasn't the
be-all and end-all for him, and this reinforced his independent
outlook. There were other things in life that he wanted to
achieve. On the MCC tour of India and Pakistan in 1961-62 he
played in all eight Test Matches and performed creditably, but
he was too outspoken for some, and he guessed he had been
labelled 'unco-operative' by the management. He was not a
'hungry' cricketer, dependent for his career and livelihood on
success in the middle, and there were times when he found it
difficult to motivate himself on the county circuit. He took little

77

account of figures, and if runs weren't wanted he might not bother to get them.

Barber was an unselfish cricketer. For all his individualism he always put the team first. First-class cricket, as he fully realised, was a spectator sport, and he genuinely wanted the public to enjoy their day out. But this did not turn him overnight into the joyous, carefree cricketer one might expect. One reason for this was the tendency of the Lancashire batting to collapse. He had to provide a steadying influence. He thus acquired the reputation of being stodgy and inhibited — 'tediously introspective' was one description.

As a captain he was criticised for not bowling himself enough — but this again was largely unselfishness, since he had in Tommy Greenhough a rival leg-spinner who was bidding for international honours. His outspokenness, too, was not always supported by the Lancashire committee, and after two years they relieved him of the captaincy, on the grounds — specious, as he saw it — that the responsibility was handicapping his development as an England player.

Unco-operative or not, he was still in contention for a place on the 1962-63 tour of Australia under Ted Dexter when in mid-July 1962 he was selected to play for the Gentlemen against the Players (amateurs v professionals) at Lord's, a game that by tradition formed something of a Test Trial. It proved a disaster for Barber. Yet the first glimpse of the metamorphosis that was to follow may be traced to it.

After being run out for nought, Barber was asked to bowl when Trueman and Titmus were shoring up the Players' innings after a poor start. Lord's with its slope is a good ground for a leg-spinner, but Barber, fearful of muffing his chance, tightened up with nervous tension. The spring-heeled step by which he was instantly recognisable seemed incompatible with muscular tension, but this was what Barber was suffering from. His first ball, a long hop, was promptly pulled first bounce to the grandstand boundary, and the second was shorter still and landed over the fence. A third long hop was so short that Trueman lifted it gratefully on to the grandstand balcony. 'I've blown it,'

thought Barber. 'I've had my chance and I've blown it.' But as
the crowd hugged themselves with delight he caught something
of their mood, and suddenly he was laughing with everyone else.
The worst had happened, there was nothing more to fear, and
from then on he bowled well. It was this relaxation that was the
essential ingredient of the sort of cricket Barber wanted to play.
It had been missing for too long.

The diagnosis was the first step towards a cure. But there
wasn't much time. He was nearly 27, he was married, and he
had business responsibilities. He had always intended to retire
from big cricket at 30.

Crucial perhaps, was a change of scene, and at the end of that
season he sought and obtained a special registration with Warwickshire. The new relationship proved a happy one, and in his
first season at Edgbaston he emerged as one of the country's
leading all-rounders. Outstanding was an innings of 113 against
the West Indian tourists with Hall and Griffith at their fastest.
(Warwickshire were all out for 210.) He had not completely
shaken off the inhibitions he had developed at Old Trafford as
yet, and it was the 'touch of Northern dourness' that he brought
to Warwickshire's middle batting that was chiefly remarked on,
but the innings against Hall and Griffith was a milestone. The
better the opposition the better he played; that had always been
a characteristic. He relished the challenge of pace, was stimulated
rather than unsettled by the element of risk. He had always
preferred to open the innings, and his fearless approach to fast
bowling convinced Mike Smith, the Warwickshire captain, that
this was his proper place in the order. Another factor was the
coaching of E.J. 'Tiger' Smith, the old England wicket-keeper.
'Why do you have to think about playing forward or back'? he
demanded. 'Stand up and hit through the ball.'

There was no parallel with the conversion of Saul on the road
to Damascus, as has been suggested. The process was slower and
more subtle. But the result, in 1964, was an exhilarating hundred
in the third round of the newly established Gillette Cup, and an
innings of 76 which took Warwickshire into the final. Then
came the knock which 'dwarfed everything else' — a hundred

before lunch against the Australians at Edgbaston in August (he made 138 out of 209 in 2¼ hours), just in time to win him a place in the final Test of the series at the Oval, when he opened for the first time with Geoff Boycott.

It was on the South African tour that followed that Barber really found himself as an international cricketer. One of the things he liked best about touring was that with 16 or 17 players and not too crowded an itinerary he had time to prepare himself mentally for each game. The longer preparation helped him to relax. He still required the stimulus of *wanting* to play, but the rest between games suited his need.

There were other important factors. Barber's sight was imperfect — he suffered from blurred vision in the left eye. This may well be why he learned to bat left-handed, although he was right-handed in everything else — an involuntary adjustment to bring his leading eye into line. In the brighter light of South Africa he found it easier to pick up the flight of the ball, and there were better backgrounds, too, with good sight-screens. Finally there were the wickets themselves, wickets on which he could safely hit through the line of the ball. This had become his greatest strength, but it was ill-suited on English wickets against bowlers who moved the ball off the seam. Swing he found little different abroad from at home, but on most grounds the bounce was consistent, and provided he picked up the line he could commit himself early to an aggressive shot, rather than curb his strokes as he often had to do in England.

It was in South Africa that he proved to everyone that he had the big match temperament. There was an element of the showman in him, and he reacted positively to the atmosphere of a packed house. In the first four Tests he played only four innings, and he missed the fifth through a broken finger, but with scores of 74, 97, 58 and 61 he left an indelible mark on the series.

He had wanted to go on the South African tour for its own sake, although his father had questioned whether he ought to spare the time. But he had also had his eye on a more distant target. If he turned down South Africa he was unlikely to get

80

the chance to go to Australia the following year. Now that he had established himself as a batsman ideally suited to overseas conditions he was certain to be picked to go to Australia.

*   *

From the moment when the England party first assembled at Lord's for a pre-tour get-together, the idea that they were going to play attacking cricket was fostered by the manager, S.C. Griffith. 'Win or lose,' said Griffith, 'we're going to have a go.' The previous tour of Australia had ended in anti-climax, and the appointment of 'Billy' Griffith, then secretary of the MCC, was made in response to the intense criticism that cricket at all levels, and especially English cricket, faced at that time.

The selection of Mike Smith as captain was similarly welcomed, not so much because he was a noticeably aggressive skipper as because he was known as a captain who respected his players and encouraged them to play their game. But overseas tours were notorious for pious promises of belligerent intent which were never fulfilled, and scepticism was widespread. How was it possible to change the approach of the average English cricketer when his livelihood depended on personal success?

Bob Barber, in this context, was unique. He had reached a stage in his career when he was determined to play in his own individual style and in a manner of which he could be proud. He had already advised Warwickshire that, through giving up the winter to the Australian tour, he would be available for only a handful of matches in the following summer, for business reasons. This meant his virtual retirement from Test cricket. The England selectors were aware of the position, but they asked Barber to keep it to himself for the moment. The policy of picking a man with no future in international cricket might be questioned, and in any case they hoped to persuade Barber to change his mind. But so far as Barber was concerned, the tour of Australia was to be his swan-song.

Griffith's attitudes and enthusiasms soon permeated the party, and to Barber especially they were a call to the colours. Independently of the management, he had his own sense of mission.

He would be opening the innings, and it was up to him to set the tempo, to translate words into deeds. The chat was meaningless unless the right action followed. Yet such was the paradox of his nature that he did not approach the task without a certain off-handed cynicism. 'Are we slogging or fielding today?' he would ask, when the coin had been tossed — to the amusement of some and the irritation of others.

It did not take Barber long to create the desired image. 'The touring team's most aggressive batsman,' said *Wisden*, 'hit the first two centuries.' These were in the opening matches at Perth, 126 out of 197 in 44 overs against Western Australia, and 113 out of 145 in only 26 overs against a strong Combined XI. Each time Barber opened with John Edrich, and with Eric Russell at No 3 also in the runs, Boycott arrived at Adelaide for the third match, having been delayed in Ceylon with stomach trouble, to find his place in jeopardy. When Barber and Russell visited his room to see how he was, he reacted testily. He would soon be back, he warned them, to claim his rightful place. Barber had no reason to be dismayed, but he too reacted typically. 'Look Geoff,' he said, 'when you get out of bed you can go on the park and play in every game if you want, and if I spend the rest of the tour on the beach that'll suit me fine.'

Boycott played against South Australia and got 94, and he batted, according to *Wisden*, with 'refreshing enterprise'. Griffith was asking for an overall rate of a run a minute, others were doing their best to comply, and Boycott had got the message.

After standing down at Adelaide, Barber made 28 out of 39 off 29 balls against Victoria, then ran himself out for 90 against New South Wales looking for a hundred before lunch. He and Russell made 151 off 22 overs. New South Wales just escaped defeat by an innings, and when Barber went in with Russell to make the two runs needed to win he was caught first ball off a 'joke' bowler for nought. Why chuck his wicket away so pointlessly? Barber's reaction would have been an unanswerable 'Why not?'

The first Test at Brisbane was ruined by rain, but it settled the problem of who was to open with Barber. Had it not been for

Cowdrey's absence through injury Boycott might not have played, but as it was he was scheduled to bat No. 6, Russell being chosen to open. But Russell split his right hand while fielding, and Boycott moved up to open. He made 45 in the first innings and 63 not out in the second, and from then on it was not Barber and Boycott but Boycott and Barber. Barber got out in Hawke's first over in the first innings, but the contrast with Boycott was particularly marked in the second. With England in no danger, Barber hit 34 out of 46 in 45 minutes, and his innings ended in knockabout farce. All the England bowlers had suffered at the hands of newcomer Doug Walters (155 in his first Test against England), and Barber's five overs of leg-breaks, googlies and flippers had cost 42 runs, so when Walters came on to bowl Barber went after him. He didn't always connect, and the astonishment and incredulity of the close fielders as he survived being bowled or getting a touch provided a sibilant accompaniment. Next over he hit Walters' first two balls for 6 and 3. Boycott, disdaining such frivolities, was content to take his usual single off the seventh, and Barber prepared to hit the last ball of the over out of sight. 'You boys save your "Oohs" and "Aahs",' he advised the Australians, 'until you've seen this one.' Coiling himself up like a spring as Walters bowled, he reduced the fielders to near hysterics by spooning a dolly catch. Boycott's 63 not out, out of 186 for four, took 3¾ hours — but Boycott was playing for his place, and indeed for his career.

Restored to No. 1 for the second Test at Melbourne, Boycott was so galvanised by his partner that he actually outscored him as they put on a brisk 98 for the first wicket, after Australia had been dismissed for 358. With Edrich, Barrington, Cowdrey, Smith and Parks to come — the run-accumulators, as Barber called them, somewhat slanderously in some cases — Barber believed that a score of 70 or 80 for the first wicket, with a personal forty or fifty made in quick time, was what was needed to set the innings in motion. Edrich and Cowdrey duly obliged with centuries, and Barber would have been the match-winner as a bowler had a stumping chance not gone begging off his bowling. Burge, who went on to make 120, was yards out of his ground at the time. As it was, Australia saved the game.

Barber as a bowler caused almost as much controversy as Barber as a batsman. 'All Australians recognised the potential of Barber's spin,' wrote E.M. Wellings, who thought that Barber should have been kept hard at work as an attacking bowler, instead of being held in reserve for occasional use. Without him the side was short of penetrative bowling. But Barber the bowler was a difficult man to skipper. As with his batting, he had to *want* to bowl, and although he never refused, he could make his reluctance plain.

England were left with ten minutes' batting on the last day of this Test match (two overs), but Boycott prevented any further Barber antics by keeping the strike.

The third Test, at Sydney, followed directly after the second, with a two-day break in between. Right round Australia Barber had given the crowds a sparkling aperitif, creating a hunger that sooner or later he would have to appease, and this was especially true of Sydney, where his 90 before lunch had left the crowd titillated but unsatisfied. He liked the Sydney ground, and he had felt a rapport with the crowd. He very much wanted to play one Test Match innings, in the course of the tour, that would stamp his attitude to the game on the series, and he knew that 80s and 90s were not enough. Where better for the big one than Sydney, taking on the Australians on their own patch, as he judged it to be?

He felt in his bones the imminence of a big innings. He was going to give the Australian bowlers some stick before the series was out. If it didn't come here at Sydney then it would come somewhere else. But he hoped very much it would come here.

Two days before the start he learned that his father was flying out to watch the game. His wife and small daughter were already in Australia. It had to be Sydney.

He thought about the bowlers he would be facing. The one who concerned him most was not Graham McKenzie, splendid bowler though he acknowledged him to be; it was Neil Hawke. Despite a slightly awkward action Hawke could swing the ball both ways, and he varied his angle of attack, sometimes over, sometimes round the wicket. He wasn't as accurate as McKenzie, but he was less predictable, adding an involuntary element of surprise. McKenzie would bang the ball in, Hawke would slant it across or bring it back. He wasn't worried about the Australian spinners. Indeed, by using his feet he had already put one or two of them out of the reckoning.

In the clash between bat and ball someone had to dominate. Failure to do that, for Barber, meant letting the fast bowlers whistle them around his ears and letting the slow bowlers pin him down. He liked nothing better himself, when bowling, than being treated with respect.

He set out to take on the opposition early. It spread the field and lowered the pressure. It was good, he felt, both for him and his partner, reducing the chances of a mistake bringing retribution. It wasn't easy, he reflected, to get caught in the slips in the Gillette Cup.

Early on Friday morning, January 7th 1966, Barber drove in a borrowed car to Sydney Airport to meet his father. From there he drove to the ground. He had not reserved a seat, and he deposited his father in the middle of the animated and colourful crowd that was assembling on the Hill.

Barber was not a great believer in pre-match net practice, but he liked to have the ball thrown at him from fifteen yards or so to get the feel of it on the bat. He even demanded a few bouncers, hurled with venom, just to wake him up.

Bobby Simpson, the Australian captain for the series, was absent with chickenpox, and it was Brian Booth who went out with Mike Smith to toss the coin, on the result of which much was expected to depend. The Sydney curator had left the pitch well grassed to prevent it from crumbling, and although he had forecast that it would 'roll out a beauty on Friday morning', the impression was that a perfect batting track on Friday and Saturday might take spin on the Monday. Thus both sides fielded two spinners — the finger spin of Titmus and Allen for England, and the wrist spin of Philpott and Sincock for Australia. It was not a game where defensive tactics were expected to pay; both sides were going all out for a win. Mike Smith called correctly, and at eleven o'clock that morning Boycott and Barber began the England innings to the bowling of McKenzie (pavilion end) and Hawke.

The importance of capitalising on the luck of the toss was obvious, and even Barber began in decorous mood. Both bowlers extracted a degree of lift, and Boycott especially had a torrid time, being hit on the forearm by McKenzie and then edging him for 4. Barber meanwhile was weighing up the bowling and the wicket, attempting nothing flamboyant. But the omens were good. Twice in the opening overs, with no conscious thought of belligerence, he struck square drives, one off each bowler, so sweetly that they pierced the field and went for 4.

After McKenzie and Hawke had bowled three overs each, Walters came on for one over to allow them to change ends. Barber took eight runs off the over, but four of them came from an edge through the slips that didn't carry. Next over, Boycott turned a McKenzie in-swinger chest-high to Sincock at backward short leg but the chance went down.

Barber's driving of the good length ball perplexed both bowlers, who often pitched short in consequence. In fielding one of Barber's drives McKenzie fell heavily, and after he had bowled two overs from the Hill end Booth took him off. Thus, by the time morning drinks were served, Walters had had a turn at both ends. Walters bowled tidily while Hawke attacked, and for a time they kept both batsmen quiet. Nevertheless, the first 19 overs yielded 64 runs.

At this point Booth introduced Philpott with his leg breaks, and in his third over Boycott, influenced perhaps by Barber, so far forgot himself as to loft him straight for 4. McKenzie returned for Hawke at the pavilion end and aimed his attack outside Barber's off stump; going for his shots in this area as Barber did, he was always giving the slips a chance. But Barber himself welcomed this form of attack (as Graeme Pollock did), feeling that it gave him a free hit. He believed bowlers reduced their chances of getting him out when they failed to bowl straight.

McKenzie discovered a fleeting fallibility in both batsmen as first Barber and then Boycott edged him for 4. But between these two streaky strokes Barber reached his 50, made out of 75 in 105 minutes. The challenging element of animosity he had now come to expect from the Hill was matched by the generosity of their applause. Barber relished taking on the more volatile section of the crowd, winning them over by displaying his skill.

Shouts of 'Put Sincock on' for the last over before lunch found favour with Booth, but the ginger-haired Sincock was unable to pitch his left-arm googlies and Barber, eschewing the tennis shots that the high full tosses invited, waited for the short one and despatched it for 4. At lunch England were 93 for 0 off 26 overs, Barber 59, Boycott 34.

After lunch Philpott tried his luck from the pavilion end, with McKenzie opposite, but with Barber taking charge the hundred was hoisted in McKenzie's first over. Boycott responded by doing his share; it was their second hundred partnership in Tests.

Opinion on their compatibility as partners was divided, some thinking the contrast — right- and left-handed, dour and free-scoring, even amateur and professional (in the cerebral sense) — ideal, others greatly regretting the misfortune which had put Eric Russell out of the reckoning for the series. It was difficult to guess to what extent Barber stimulated Boycott into playing his strokes or conversely Boycott tempered Barber's wilder extravagances. Both in their way were of an obdurate nature, not easily led. Jim Parks thought the pressure on Boycott during this tour affected his performance, but inevitably it was Boycott who came in for criticism. Wellings thought him 'not really the right partner for Barber, the brilliant go-getter who should have been given as much of the bowling as possible', and this was fair comment: Boycott certainly tended to hog the strike. But Barber felt he understood Boycott, understood the background from which he had emerged by his own efforts and why it was so terribly important to him not to fail. He asked for no more dependable and dedicated partner than Boycott.

The two men had made their England débuts in the same series, against the Australians in 1964, after which came their association in South Africa, and their record as an opening pair provided a sufficient answer to criticism. This was their 19th opening stand for England, and although they had only once before put on a hundred they had exceeded fifty nine times and averaged — before this match — 48 in partnership. With no marathon stand to boost their figures, this showed their consistency. Amongst post-war English openers they were only surpassed by Hutton and Washbrook, whose average together was 55.

Barber's swift footwork against Philpott, his impeccable timing of the ball when hitting on the up, and his sheer weight of shot, opened the way for Boycott's short-arm forcing and cutting, confirming their value to each other. In the first hour of what developed into a gloriously sunny afternoon they added 76 runs. Barber moved into the 80s and Boycott reached his fifty, and indeed in the fourth over of McKenzie's post-lunch spell he moved from 49 to 58. This brought Hawke on at the Hill end for McKenzie.

Hawke tried a few bouncers, which Barber enjoyed. Three 2's off Hawke's first over took Barber to 89, and although Boycott allowed him only two balls in the next three overs he despatched them for 4 and 2 respectively to take him to 95. At this half-way stage in the afternoon session, with England 168 for 0, Barber 95, Boycott 58, Barber's progress to his hundred was interrupted by a break for drinks.

Hawke continued on the resumption to Boycott, and a single off the first ball gave Barber the rest of the over to reach the target. A sizzling drive through the covers took him to 99, but the single eluded him.

Looking for something different, something that might be unfamiliar, Booth brought Cowper on at the pavilion end; the slightest turn of one of his off-breaks might find the edge of the left-hander's bat. But Boycott was facing, and with 2 off the fifth ball and a single off the last he severely tested the crowd's patience.

So far Sincock had been given two overs only, the last before lunch and the last before mid-afternoon drinks. But he was the type of bowler who could spin the ball on any wicket, and in two outings for South Australia against the MCC tourists he had taken eleven wickets, all of recognised batsmen. He was in the side to be given a long bowl, and now was the time. He struck a length at once, and the best Boycott could do was to take two runs off the sixth ball. That left Barber to face Cowper.

Cowper was a genuine all-rounder, with a fine record in Test cricket. But he was not the sort of bowler likely to achieve much turn on the first day of a Test Match. Although differing in type, he resembled Doug Walters in that he was the sort of bowler more likely to induce error through relaxation or over-confidence on the part of the batsman than through any particular cunning or skill. Therein lay the danger. But Barber was on his guard against this; and he had the added advantage of having batted against Cowper during his hundred before lunch for Warwickshire against the Australians at Edgbaston in 1964. Advancing to Cowper's second ball, he off-drove it firmly for one to reach his first Test century, out of 175. He had batted 198 minutes, faced 147 balls, and hit ten 4's.

The applause for Barber's hundred was more than mere recognition of a milestone reached. It was a fulsome expression of gratitude for pleasure enjoyed. Nowhere was it more protracted than on the Hill, where the secret of the presence in their midst of the centurion's father had inevitably got out.

Barber had already shown his ability to master and even demolish an attack. But this innings, begun with due caution before timely acceleration, stood out for its maturity as well as for its entertainment value. A sense of inevitability had accompanied the brilliance. Such aggression, in that period, was rarely seen in Test cricket except from West Indians, and Bobby Simpson was one of the first to recognise that it was Barber, more than any off-the-field influence, who was the inspiration of the England team. He was, in Simpson's opinion, 'the most dynamic England opener I have seen', totally transforming the usual war of attrition in the fight for the Ashes.

Simpson correctly diagnosed Barber's greatest strength. 'He is an unusual player in that he does not seem to be greatly worried by the length of the bowling. No matter where the ball

'Hawke tried a few bouncers,
which Barber enjoyed.'

is pitched he seems able to hit it on the rise off the front foot. This is a most difficult thing to do.' The secret almost certainly lay in Barber's exceptionally high grip on the bat, giving him the maximum swing through the line, and the control he derived from his left-handed stance, placing the stronger hand (as Pollock did) at the top.

The applause had scarcely subsided when Boycott took a single off Cowper's next ball and Barber again faced the bowling. The glow of achievement was still on him, and after playing two balls sedately he swept the next off his stumps for 4 and drove the seventh for another. At this Boycott waved him down like a traffic cop. 'Stick around,' he muttered. 'Take it easy.' They needed a lot more runs yet.

Barber saw his role as giving the side a boost at the beginning, something on which his designated 'run accumulators' could build. They were the heavy scorers, the people equipped to cash in on a good start. But he had wanted to play one really big innings, and he took Boycott's caution to heart. Yet he had long since decided that once he had begun to strike the ball it was best to keep going, that a change of tempo was almost always a mistake. Thus he continued his exhibition of controlled stroke-play almost without pause.

At this stage in his career Barber would sometimes make up his mind where he was going to hit the bowler before he actually bowled — a course of action not recommended by the coaching manuals. He found this especially easy with a bowler like Sincock, who gave the ball so much air that Barber could get to him on the full at least twice an over and steer the ball anywhere from the covers right round to square leg. Only through failing to play a bowler like Sincock positively could one get into trouble. Placing a field for such bowling, whose strength lay in its variety, was difficult enough anyway, and Barber simply advanced and picked out the gaps.

Standing out above all else was the exceptional vigour of his driving, mostly through the covers and wide of mid-off, and the wristy cuts for which he continually made room. In three overs after reaching his hundred he took his score to 123, at the same time putting up the 200; he and Boycott were only the fourth England pair to achieve this against Australia. He was then halted by an over from Cowper in which two off-breaks turned enough to beat his forward defensive stroke. While a slightly pensive Barber was contemplating the best means of counter-attack, Titmus and Allen were moistening their fingers.

Barber's answer was to hit Cowper out of the firing line, and this he encompassed with two ferocious straight hits, the second, for added emphasis, dropping not far short of the sight-screen. Both these strokes were premeditated. The second took the partnership past the 219 put on by Hutton and Barnett at Trent Bridge in 1938 and left only Hobbs and Rhodes (323) and Hobbs and Sutcliffe (283) to beat.

Philpott duly relieved Cowper, and with tea approaching the run-rate slowed, Boycott scoring only two singles in six overs. Then, with one more ball to come before the break, Boycott pushed forward to Philpott without quite killing the spin and the ball cocked up, carrying far enough for a surprised Philpott, tumbling forward, to take the catch on his knees. The consummation thus came simultaneously with the prayer.

Thus by teatime on the first day England at 234 for one were in a virtually impregnable position, with time on their side, while the wicket was already showing signs that the susceptibility to spin forecast for the Monday might materialise. The England opening pair had scored at a rate of more than four runs an over, and Boycott, although overshadowed, had played an innings of almost equal merit, his homespun dedication being the perfect foil to the dashing elegance of Barber. Their only weakness as a pair had been an occasional difference of opinion in the calling.

Barber himself had a healthy suspicion of the relevance of figures as a yardstick, believing that they distorted as much as they revealed, but in this instance the score book amply confirms his dominance. Boycott received 254 balls and made 84, Barber up to this point had received 49 fewer balls and made 63 more runs.

After tea Barber continued as though there had been no interruption, leaving Edrich, his new partner — another left-hander — to work out his problems against the spin combination of Philpott and Sincock. Barber reached 150 in the first over after tea, and with Edrich, despite a typically hesitant start, unerring in his treatment of anything loose, the 50 stand came in 38 minutes. That was 284 for one after 65 eight-ball overs, Barber 172, Edrich 20. At once the new ball was taken.

Finally deciding that he preferred to bowl towards the pavilion, McKenzie began from the Hill end, with Hawke opposite. Barber was undoubtedly tiring, but he was scarcely aware of it, and he had conceived an ambition, uncharacteristically, to get 200. True to his philosophy, however, he went on playing his shots. Two in particular off McKenzie, square on either side of the wicket, were as good as any seen all day. Between these two strokes McKenzie put up the 300 with a no-ball. Edrich had already taken three runs off the first two balls, and with a single off the seventh Barber made it eleven off the over and at the same time kept the bowling.

Perhaps the pace had become too hectic. The first ball of Hawke's second over with the new ball was a widish long hop, bowled from round the wicket, and Barber, seeing the chance of another four-pennyworth, rose on his toes to flail it to the off. It did not swing — it was too short for that — but it came on to him slightly and he got a bottom edge. He turned round to confirm what he already knew — that he had chopped it on to his wicket.

Even that day at Johannesburg when he had got out for 97 through his own prodigality he had felt no chagrin. Now he was deeply disappointed. This would be his last overseas tour, that much was certain, and very probably it would be his last Test series. There were still two Tests to come, and he would be looking for another big score yet, but he was realist enough to accept that he might not get quite so near 200 again. He would dearly have loved to emboss his name on the series by making 200.

In fact he had no cause for dejection. His innings of 185, out of 303 for two, stood out above all others in the series. He had batted four minutes short of five hours without giving a chance and hit nineteen 4's, and his personal scoring rate had fallen not far short of three runs per over, despite the fact that for long periods he had got less than his share of the strike. He had scored his last 85 out of 129 in 108 minutes.

When Barber got out there were 64 minutes left for play, and in that time England lost the wickets of Barrington, Cowdrey and Smith for the addition of only 25 runs, the damage being done by Neil Hawke. So, far from Barber's 'run accumulators' building on the foundations he and Boycott had laid they collapsed, causing a panic that turned the England dressing-room, complacent all-day, into a confused mêlée reminiscent of a club side. Mike Smith, the No. 6, was bowling to Jeff Jones behind the M.A. Noble stand when Barber got out, and within a quarter of an hour he was taking guard in the middle.

After passing the 300 mark with one wicket down, England thus ended the day at 328 for five. But the platform had been erected, and next day Edrich, 40 not out overnight, battled on to a century, completed by a straight drive for 6 off the last ball before lunch. Parks, Titmus and Allen all helped in useful stands, and Mike Smith's coaching of Jeff Jones, inopportune though it seemed at the time, finally paid off in a last-wicket stand of 55.

Having totalled 488 in quick time, England were left with 3½ days to bowl Australia out twice, a task they duly achieved. It was Jones and Brown who got on top in the first innings and made the vital break-through and then, with the ball turning as promised and the Australians demoralised, Titmus and Allen took four second innings wickets a piece.

That McKenzie and Hawke in harness were a great opening pair was better appreciated by the England batsmen than by the Australian selectors, and they omitted McKenzie from their side for the fourth Test. Unfortunately for England, injury to the chosen alternative resulted in McKenzie's recall in chastened mood, and with Simpson returning as captain England were as decisively outplayed at Adelaide as Australia had been at Sydney. To underline the comparison, Lawry and Simpson went ten better than Boycott and Barber by putting on 244. With the final Test, on which the rubber depended, spoiled by a combination

AUSTRALIA v ENGLAND 1965-66 (3rd Test)
at Sydney, January 7, 8, 10, 11

England won by an innings and 93 runs

ENGLAND: First Innings

G. Boycott, c and b Philpott	84
R. W. Barber, b Hawke	185
J. H. Edrich, c and b Philpott	103
K. F. Barrington, c McKenzie b Hawke	1
M. C. Cowdrey, c Grout b Hawke	0
*M. J. K. Smith, c Grout b Hawke	6
D. J. Brown, c Grout b Hawke	1
†J. M. Parks, c Grout b Hawke	13
F. J. Titmus, c Grout b Walters	14
D. A. Allen, not out	50
I. J. Jones, b Hawke	16
Extras (B 3, LB 8, W 2, NB 2)	15
Total	488

Fall of wickets: 1-234, 2-303, 3-309, 4-309, 5-317, 6-328, 7-358, 8-395, 9-433, 10-488.

Bowling: McKenzie, 25-2-113-0; Hawke, 33.7-6-105-7; Walters, 10-1-38-1; Philpott, 28-3-86-2; Sincock, 20-1-98-0; Cowper, 6-1-33-0.

AUSTRALIA: First Innings

W. M. Lawry, c Parks b Jones	0
G. Thomas, c Titmus b Brown	51
R. M. Cowper, st Parks b Allen	60
P. J. P. Burge, c Parks b Brown	6
*B. C. Booth, c Cowdrey b Jones	8
D. J. Sincock, c Parks b Brown	29
K. D. Walters, st Parks b Allen	23
N. J. N. Hawke, c Barber b Brown	0
†A. T. W. Grout, b Brown	0
G. D. McKenzie, c Cowdrey b Barber	24
P. I. Philpott, not out	5
Extras (B 7, LB 8)	15
Total	221

Fall of wickets: 1-0, 2-81, 3-91, 4-105, 5-155, 6-174, 7-174, 8-174, 9-203, 10-221.

Bowling: Jones, 20-6-51-2; Brown, 17-1-63-5; Boycott, 3-1-8-0; Titmus, 23-8-40-0; Barber, 2.1-1-2-1; Allen, 19-5-42-2.

AUSTRALIA: Second Innings

W. M. Lawry, c Cowdrey b Brown	33
G. Thomas, c Cowdrey b Titmus	25
R. M. Cowper, c Boycott b Titmus	0
P. J. P. Burge, run out	1
B. C. Booth, b Allen	27
K. D. Walters, not out	35
D. J. Sincock, c Smith b Allen	27
P. I. Philpott, lbw b Allen	5
N. J. N. Hawke, c Smith b Titmus	2
A. T. W. Grout, c Smith b Allen	3
G. D. McKenzie, c Barber b Titmus	12
Extras (B 3, LB 1)	4
Total	174

Fall of wickets: 1-46, 2-50, 3-51, 4-86, 5-86, 6-119, 7-131, 8-135, 9-140, 10-174.

Bowling: Jones, 7-0-35-0; Brown, 11-2-32-1; Titmus, 17.3-4-40-4; Barber, 5-0-16-0; Allen, 20-8-47-4.

Umpires—C. J. Egar and L. P. Rowan

of caution and rain (Barber in the first innings was badly run out by Boycott), England were left to regret their failure to ram home their advantage in the second Test at Melbourne, and Australia, by halving the rubber, retained the Ashes. On the whole they did so deservedly, but England, ignited by the unorthodox Bob Barber, fulfilled their secondary objective (some would say their major one) of blazing a trail of enterprise and aggression across Australia, correcting the unflattering impression of English cricket gained rightly or wrongly on previous tours.

Barber never toured again, and although he was picked several more times for England at home he did not play enough cricket to give himself a fair chance. His 185 at Sydney, however, will always be remembered: Walter Robins spoke of it as 'the best I have ever seen by an Englishman in Australia'. For that caustic critic E.M. Wellings, Barber was 'emphatically the Number One, playing attacking cricket from start to finish', and he rated his innings at Sydney 'the superlative achievement of the whole tour'.

5

GARY SOBERS AND DAVID HOLFORD

*'No cricketer can truly be designated
"great" unless he can save games as
well as win them.'*
— Peter Roebuck,
Cricketer International

They came as world champions, and richly they deserved the label. In 1963 under Frank Worrell they had beaten England 3-1. In 1965 under Gary Sobers they had won the rubber in the West Indies 2-1 against Australia. All their great players, apart from Worrell, were available again. Since England had halved the rubber in Australia in 1965-66, it was fair to bill the 1966 series as for the world championship.

If bowlers win matches, then Wes Hall, Charlie Griffith, Lance Gibbs, and Sobers himself, were there to do it. And where could stronger batting be found than from such artists as Conrad Hunte, Rohan Kanhai, Seymour Nurse, Basil Butcher, and — again — Garfield Sobers? It had been, and remained, one of the great international sides.

To call it an ageing side might be accurate, but it would also be misleading. The players, as a simple matter of arithmetic, were three years older than on their last visit. But of the bowlers only Gibbs was over 30. Hall was 28, Griffith 26, Sobers 29. The other batsmen, although mostly over 30, were at their peak. Of the established players only Joe Solomon, 35, and Conrad Hunte, 34, could be classed as veterans.

Nevertheless, the side had its weaknesses, which England hoped to expose. There was no proven Test-class opening batsman to partner Hunte. And the presence of so many established stars had left little room for the blooding of youngsters.

Even amongst the remaining members of the party, only three were new to the international scene, and two of these, Rawle Brancker, 28, and David Holford, 26, were hardly youngsters. Holford, perhaps, was the most interesting of the newcomers. A university graduate, he had spent four years studying agricultural science at the University of the West Indies in Trinidad and a further year in Canada. He was also a cousin of Gary Sobers. But as a cricketer — unlike his cousin — he was a late developer. Whereas Sobers had played in his first Test Match before he was 18, Holford at 26 had played no Test cricket at all.

Indeed one had to comb the records to find out anything about him. He had played for Barbados Colts against the MCC on the 1959-60 tour. While at university he had played once for Trinidad — and caught the eye of Jeffrey Stollmeyer, himself a Trinidadian, with his leg-break bowling. But his only other Shell Shield appearances had been for Barbados earlier in 1966, when he had turned in some useful analyses. He had done nothing of note with the bat. Had it not been for the coincidence of Jeffrey Stollmeyer's appointment as manager of the tour and that game for Trinidad, the lack of a competing leg-spinner, and perhaps the accident of birth that linked him to the world's greatest cricketer, he would scarcely have made the tour.

When the tourists went to Lord's for the match against MCC they chose what by general consent was their strongest side, and Holford was not in it. The No. 7 spot, for which Holford was competing, went to left-hander Rawle Brancker. Although a bowler of a different type, Brancker turned the ball away from the bat as did Holford, and as a batsman he had several centuries to his credit in Shell Shield cricket. Holford had never made a hundred in a first-class match.

In that MCC game at Lord's Brancker picked up a couple of wickets and made a few runs. But in the course of the match he came in for a murderous and calculated assault from Mike Smith.

Writing that week in the *Cricketer*, Smith had forecast what might be called 'sweeping' changes for the slow left-hander. 'I don't think ever again we are going to see the really packed off-side field for the slow left-hander,' he wrote. Like the off-spinner he was likely to be swept from outside the off stump. 'This may sound a dangerous shot,' continued Smith, 'but it is worth it in that almost every shot is 4.' With Brancker bowling from the pavilion end, Mike Smith made his point by sweeping ball after ball from outside the off stump to the Tavern boundary in an innings of 140, thereby putting Brancker out of the reckoning.

The way was open for Holford, and in the next match, against Lancashire at Old Trafford, he went in at 132 for five and made his first century in first-class cricket, enabling acting captain Hunte to declare at 295 for eight. And as if this were not enough, he proceeded to take twelve wickets for 115 against Cambridge University. Weak though they were, the feat made him a certainty for the first Test. (It went unnoticed at the time that he clean bowled Mike Brearley for single figures twice.)

The first Test, at Old Trafford, was a disaster for England — and, as it happened, for Mike Smith. England dropped many catches and batted badly, compounding their failure to win the toss on a newly-laid pitch that responded to spin. West Indies made 484 (Hunte 135, Sobers 161), and then Gibbs (10 for 96), with useful help from Holford (4 for 83) and Sobers (3 for 87), bowled England out twice, so that West Indies won by an innings with two days to spare. As Holford also helped his cousin to add 137 for the sixth wicket (his own contribution was 32), he had what John Woodcock called 'a notable first Test'. 'Holford,' said Woodcock, 'is becoming worth his place at No. 7.' If that seems a trifle patronising it was consistent with Holford's rating at the time.

England's performance at Old Trafford had been too bad to be true. But they had always been bad starters at home, and few games were awaited more keenly than the second Test at Lord's — the Command Performance of the season, it was called, as the Queen and the Duke of Edinburgh were expected to attend. The sacking of Mike Smith after one Test may or may not have been premature, but by obliterating Brancker and letting in Holford he had unwittingly left his mark on the series.

Certainly the changes that were made strengthened the side overall. Cowdrey was appointed captain — for the 13th time in Tests — and Boycott returned, but the most significant changes were the selection for the first time of Basil D'Oliveira and the recall after three years and 38 Tests of Tom Graveney in his 40th year. This, and the inclusion of Barry Knight, so lengthened the batting that Titmus, who had gone in No. 7 at the Old Trafford, was now placed more realistically at No. 9.

West Indies made two changes. Easton McMorris, who had failed at Old Trafford, was replaced by left-hander Joey Carew, and David Allan replaced an injured Jackie Hendriks behind the stumps.

One down already, England could not afford to lose this game. And on paper they looked worthy challengers for world supremacy. If the West Indies had the edge at all it was only through the incomparable Sobers. Against this the West Indians as cricketers, feared and respected though they were, were suspected of having an Achilles heel. Whereas England sides had the reputation of being defiant in adversity, and Australians never knew when they were beaten, West Indian cricketers were still thought of as lacking in resilience — spectacular but brittle, easily demoralised when things went wrong. Under Frank Worrell the defect had been remedied and the image lived down, but the tendency was thought to be dormant, the inevitable obverse of a glittering but mercurial coinage. Under Gary Sobers, a man of convivial personality, and a somewhat reluctant captain, a relapse seemed possible.

The suspicion seemed amply confirmed on the Monday before the Lord's Test when the West Indies, 62 behind on first innings against Sussex, collapsed for 67 on a green Hove pitch, the second lowest total ever recorded by a West Indian side in England. Losing by nine wickets in less than two days, they showed a lack of resolution of which John Snow (11 for 47 in the match) took full advantage. The England side, however, had already been chosen without him.

Sobers again won the toss, but the first day went well for England, and especially for Ken Higgs. Bowling from the Nursery end, keeping the ball up and moving it a little either way, he took the wickets of Carew, Kanhai and Hunte in his first nine overs for 14 runs. Despite these shocks the batsmen went for their strokes, and at the end of a rain-shortened day West Indies were 155 for four, Nurse and Sobers being together. They put on another 50 runs next morning before both made fatal misjudgements, offering no stroke to balls that in both cases moved up the hill, Nurse being bowled and Sobers lbw. Holford made a useful 26 before falling to the second new ball, and another three-wicket spell by Higgs (6 for 91) finished off the innings for 269.

Colin Milburn, opening for England with Boycott, failed, but Graveney, whose entrance came at a critical moment, found plenty of time to play Hall and Griffith, making everyone wonder why he had ever been left out. Boycott made 60, and at the close of the second day England were well placed at 145 for two, Graveney 65 not out.

On the third morning the West Indies bowlers hit back, Sobers being superb and Hall at his fastest. They dismissed Barrington and Cowdrey cheaply, and Graveney was caught behind off Hall looking for the 4 that would have completed his hundred. Nevertheless it was a triumphant return to Test cricket. Parks and D'Oliveira took England past 250, but then Parks drove a Hall half-volley hard back and it hit D'Oliveira, backing up, on the boot before rebounding on to the bowler's wicket. D'Oliveira thought he was out and made no attempt to get back, but Hall knew better. Grabbing the ball with one hand, he pulled up a stump with the other, and that was 251 for six. It was a tragedy for D'Oliveira in his first Test, but he had put on 48 with Parks and done enough to show his worth. Higgs helped Parks (91) in a ninth-wicket stand of 59, and England gained a lead of 86.

In nine overs on that Saturday evening West Indies reduced

101

the deficit by 18, but they lost Carew in doing so, brilliantly caught by Knight at leg slip off Higgs.

With England having to bat last on a wicket that might by then be taking spin, critics were undecided on who had the advantage. But England's position looked rather better on Monday when, after weekend rain and the threat of more that morning, the covers were not removed until shortly before play was due to resume, to reveal that the wicket had sweated. Evaporation was far from complete when, promptly at 11.30, Higgs opened the attack to Kanhai and Hunte from the Nursery end. With two days to go and very little separating the two sides much depended on what England could achieve while the moisture lasted — and on what West Indies could deny them.

Both batsmen got going with singles off Higgs. At the pavilion end Cowdrey chose Knight as the most likely to take advantage of the conditions, and this proved a good choice as Knight, in his second over, got a ball to lift and move down the hill for Hunte to give a sharp catch to Milburn at backward short leg.

Butcher replaced Hunte and got off the mark with a single. But in Higgs's next over he was trapped lbw by a ball that came back, and West Indies were 25 for three.

Kanhai and Nurse answered the challenge by counter-attacking in the traditional West Indian manner, oiling the hitherto parched vocal chords of a group of calypso singers. Nurse especially played some glorious shots, and both batsmen were intent on winning back the initiative rather than merely concentrating on survival until the moisture dried out. Not that the wicket was doing anything extravagant by English standards. It wasn't the sort of wicket, in Cowdrey's view, on which one posted four slips and two gullies. Nevertheless both batsmen lived somewhat dangerously, and Cowdrey himself just failed to hang on to a difficult chance at first slip offered by Nurse off Higgs. But the wicket appeared to be easing, Higgs and Knight had expended themselves, and the arrears were cleared to another cadenza of calypso enthusiasm.

Replacing Higgs at the Nursery end was D'Oliveira, and the change produced a wicket. Kanhai and Nurse had put on 66 in

GARY SOBERS AND DAVID HOLFORD

48 rather hectic minutes when Nurse was deceived by a slower ball which found the edge of his bat and Parks, diving forward, took the catch.

That brought in Sobers at 12.40, bare-headed as always, carriage inimitable, top section of outsize pads flapping loosely but not untidily against the thigh. If his reception was more muted than usual, that was in recognition of the load that he carried: West Indies were 91 for four.

Cowdrey had substituted Jones for Knight at the pavilion end, but he was not bowling well, and before Sobers could get established he restored Knight. The move paid off, though the victim was not Sobers but Kanhai. Again Knight got a good-length ball to lift and move, this time away from the bat, and Kanhai was good enough to get the touch that mattered, Parks taking the catch.

Cowdrey could hardly believe his luck. The score, he believed, flattered his bowlers. But at 95 for five, only nine runs in front, and with all but Sobers gone, West Indies were a beaten side.

England had ridden their luck and played the better cricket, and they thoroughly deserved to square the series. The West Indies had batted far too freely, as they were wont to do in a crisis. The wicket had never been so spiteful that resolute defence would not have preserved the bulk of the batting, and all the old clichés about the Caribbean character were trotted out. The most charitable conclusion was that they had not yet recovered from their experience at Hove. But whatever the cause, in their impatience to get on top they had thrown the game away.

By 12.50, when David Holford emerged from the pavilion to join his cousin, it was the home supporters who were buzzing with excitement. The gait of the new batsman, unlike that of Sobers, was totally unfamiliar to them, and most people had to consult their score-cards to see who it was. Holford? Don't know him. A tall enough fellow, over six feet by the look of him, but as befitted a minor actor he was making his entrance with diffidence. To follow Holford were Allan, the wicket-keeper, and then Hall, Griffith and Gibbs. There was virtually nothing to come.

103

One end was open. Sobers could hardly work the miracle now. All England had to do was deny Sobers the strike and concentrate on the weaker vessel. Put the champagne on ice!

Another school of thought held that Sobers, with his high back-lift, was an uncertain starter, and that there was always a fifty-fifty chance of getting him early. Cowdrey accepted this, but he did not believe, as a captain, in flamboyant gestures of aggression. All too often they proved futile and expensive. He preferred the subtle approach. He had played many times against Sobers and thought he knew his likely reaction better than most. So far Sobers had sought to play freely, as his team-mates had done, looking to hit his way out of trouble. The departure of Kanhai meant that crisis point had been reached, perhaps even passed, and Sobers was trying to work out how best to react. Even the approach of his cousin, in whom he had considerable faith, did not raise his spirits. He thought all was lost. Puzzled and despairing at the way wickets had fallen, he could think of only one remedy, and that was attack.

This was what Cowdrey wanted. Sobers was in a punishing mood: if he could be encouraged to feel that the situation was irretrievable by dogged methods, and that he must make what runs he could before he ran out of partners, there was all the better chance of getting him out. As for worrying him with close fielders, that, Cowdrey knew, was a vain hope. You could surround Sobers with close catchers and he wouldn't bat an eyelid; he was too self-assured. Such an obvious attempt at pressurising him, indeed, would only stiffen his resolve.

Cowdrey didn't want to see Sobers of all people steeling himself to play a long innings. When Sobers was in that sort of mood he gave bowlers no chance.

Holford had left a dressing room sepulchral with gloom. He was always nervous and tense when he went in to bat, and he knew he was a poor starter, but he tried to relax. Although chosen primarily for his bowling, he was filling the place of a middle-order batsman. Yet No. 7, he had always felt, was a tough place to bat. You rarely had a chance to plan an innings. Either you were chasing runs against the clock or a declaration was imminent, or, as today, you were expected to hang on grimly where far better players had failed.

That thought, paradoxically, helped to calm him down as he walked to the wicket. Hunte, Kanhai, Nurse and Butcher — all, in the context of the match situation, had failed. So, on Saturday evening, had Joey Carew. He couldn't really do any worse than them. He was looking at it from the negative side, perhaps, but it worked. With the realisation that he had nothing to lose, he felt better already.

His only other thought was survival. While Gary was at the other end there was always hope.

It was characteristic of Sobers that he never sought to tell his partners what to do or how to play. He showed them by example. But on this occasion he did proffer four words of advice as Holford joined him. He knew that his cousin liked to hit the ball, but he knew too, that he had developed qualities of application and self-discipline in his academic life which he was capable of applying to his cricket. At 26 he was unusually inexperienced for a West Indian cricketer, but he had a maturity that marked him as a potential leader. What Sobers needed now was a partner, and if Holford could bat with discretion, something might yet be done. He had shown a stubborn streak at Old Trafford. 'You just stay here,' Sobers told him. Coming from the senior cousin to the junior, it was enough.

Cowdrey, too, was assessing Holford's potential. Like many non-specialist batsmen he might be capable of making 30 or 40, but he would lack the mental stamina to play a long innings. He had put on over a hundred with Sobers at Old Trafford, but Sobers had been so much the dominant partner, and Holford so self-effacing, that his innings had attracted little notice. In any case the circumstances had been vastly different. Holford had come in at 284 for five with Sobers established, and the pressure had not been comparable.

Holford got the first two balls he received from Knight away for 2, but the strokes were as much nervous reaction as anything. D'Oliveira then gave him a terrible time, so much so that he found his inability to lay bat on ball embarrassing. D'Oliveira was moving the ball off the wicket both ways at medium pace, and Holford, continually playing and missing, could not hide his confusion.

Cowdrey felt that in Knight and D'Oliveira he had the right combination. They bowled accurately and gave nothing away, other than the singles to Sobers that Cowdrey intended. This was the professional approach — to contain Sobers by spreading the field, giving him one at the beginning of an over if he would take it. Mid-off and mid-on, especially, were sufficiently deep to invite the single, and mid-wicket, too, was pushed back. Sobers took the bait without hesitation, leaving Holford exposed.

Certainly Holford looked very much like getting out. But the drawback with this approach was that the batsman whose dismissal, if it could be effected, would be decisive was allowed to find his rhythm and play himself in. While the bowlers were attacking Sobers he had flashed unwisely more than once. Now he was steadying down. He went on trying to pierce the field, but he took all the runs that were offered.

This was a conscious decision on Sobers' part. He believed in letting his partners stand on their own feet. He would work to keep the strike when seven or eight wickets were down, but if a worthwhile target was to be set for the fourth innings, Holford would have to take care of himself.

Psychologically this was good for Holford. Instead of being humiliated as though he were a tail-ender, he was being treated, by his cousin at least, with respect. He resolved to deserve it. And the more he got of the bowling, the less tense he became.

The interplay between the two men went further than this. When Sobers saw his cousin defending grimly, as though his life depended on it, yet keeping amazingly cool, his own mood changed. There might be a chance to play a long innings yet.

The pattern of the game, with a single to Sobers on the first or second ball of the over, followed by four or five blocked deliveries to Holford, became monotonous as the wicket eased, the atmosphere lifted, and the end of the session approached. Once Holford off-drove an overpitched ball from Knight to the boundary, showing that the shots were there if he wanted to use them, but his only other scoring strokes were the two 2s that he started with and two singles.

As Holford grew in confidence Sobers became more and more circumspect, so that a typical shot through the covers, feet too far from the line for mere mortals, and a square cut for which his body was still moving away to make room as he played the shot, became no more than a memory. Few could stand their ground and hit the ball so hard and so safely; but now, eschewing risks, he sought to punish the bad balls only, and at lunch West Indies had reached 122 for five, Sobers 21, Holford 10.

Cowdrey was not worried as yet. He regretted Sobers' change of mood, but West Indies were only 36 in front, and there was a long afternoon ahead in which to work through the tail. If all else failed, some time after tea a new ball would become due. He could envisage being set a target of 150 or so, but his batting was quite strong enough to take care of that.

In the first over after lunch from the pavilion end, Knight drew Holford uncertainly forward to an in-swinger which lifted, and the ball squeezed between Holford's mid-riff and the inside edge of his bat. It went through to Parks at catchable height, but he failed to gather it cleanly and the ball ran away to fine leg. The England players showed no discernible chagrin, and only when the batsmen had run 3 and no signal for byes had been given did anyone seem to realise that Holford had been credited with the runs and a vital chance missed.

Holford, as it happened, hadn't hit it, and he was just as mystified as everyone else at the lack of a signal. But from a distance the deviation looked conclusive, and had Parks caught the ball someone would have been sure to appeal and Holford would have been given out.

If this could be construed as bad luck for England, Sobers was quick to rub salt in the wound by driving Knight like a rocket to the pavilion fence.

Higgs came back for a short spell at the Nursery end, but he could not reproduce the life and movement of the morning and Cowdrey soon rested him, anxious to keep him fresh for the new ball. Higgs in the last instance was his match-winner. Sobers despatched a rare D'Oliveira half-volley for 4, but mostly he was in restrained mood, shunning the flourishes off the back foot that had so encouraged Cowdrey that morning.

While Sobers continued to take all the singles on offer, Holford showed sound judgement in defence and scored mostly by deflections. But when the ball was pitched up he showed again that he too could hit powerfully, an on-drive off his toes to the Tavern that put up the 150 qualifying for the stroke of the day.

Denying Sobers a single towards the end of an over was not always possible, but Holford still got more than his share of the bowling. Yet Sobers scored twice as quickly, reaching his fifty out of 73 in just over an hour and a half with a single off Jones, who had replaced Knight. Jones, however, lacked both fire and control, and at 175 Cowdrey turned for the first time to Titmus. He bowled a maiden to Holford, but soon afterwards Sobers straight-drove him for 4. Then, 70 minutes into the afternoon, a heavy cloud settled over the ground and an appeal against the light was allowed.

The time was 3.20, England had bowled 23 overs since lunch — having bowled 44 in all beforehand — and West Indies at 182 for five were 96 runs ahead. Sobers was 62, Holford 28. A substantial recovery had been effected, and the way Sobers was playing there seemed little hope of getting him out; but England only had to dismiss Holford to win.

After tea had been taken and the players presented to the Queen and Prince Philip in front of the pavilion, the duel was resumed at 4.30. Such ceremonies were generally reckoned to be worth a wicket, and certainly Jones, operating from the Nursery end for the first time, bowled his best spell so far. Bursting through Sobers' defence he hit him painfully on the knee; but the ball was missing leg stump.

Titmus, retained at the pavilion end until the new ball was due, tried every ruse in his repertoire to lure Holford to destruction, tossing the ball high to entice him. For a long time Holford resisted the temptation, but at length the thread of his concentration snapped. The mis-hit that followed trickled clear of the field down to square leg, and Holford, visibly upbraiding himself, settled back into the groove.

34 runs came in 50 minutes after tea, mostly to Sobers, at which point the new ball became due. Higgs from the Nursery end with the new ball had been Cowdrey's ace in the hole all afternoon, and he did not delay. The immediate result was something that neither Cowdrey nor anyone else could have foreseen — a spate of scoring from Holford. At 216 for five the West Indies were still only 130 ahead; yet the new ball, which had quickly ended Holford's stay in the first innings, and was confidently expected to do so again now, acted like a magnet to his bat. In a complete change of temper that bordered on elation he turned Knight off his pads for 2 and then on-drove him off the meat of the bat to the Tavern for 4. He clipped Higgs backward of square to take his score to 49, then ran to his fifty with a single off Knight. He had batted ten minutes under three hours and the ground was alive with West Indians jumping for joy.

Holford rather than Sobers had been the target of the bowlers, and from the start of his innings, when he had seemed out of his depth, he had shown a commendable tenacity. He had not been nursed or shielded, indeed quite the reverse. Wisely, as it turned out, Sobers had left his younger cousin to make what he could of it, and the two had inspired each other. Holford, unlike Sobers, had been given no easy runs, Cowdrey's whole strategy being to keep Holford facing the bowling. Every run Holford had scored had had to be earned.

Sobers had meanwhile moved into the 90s with a fierce cover-drive off Higgs, but in trying to repeat it he got the edge that Cowdrey had been waiting for. The ball flew high and wide to Cowdrey's right at slip, and Cowdrey managed to get both hands to it, but he could not hold on. It was Sobers' first real mistake, and it was a frustrating moment for England. Soon afterwards the crowd erupted again as a searing drive through the covers off Jones took Sobers to his hundred. It was his sixth against England and his first at Lord's.

For most of his innings, defeat had stared Sobers in the face.

Cowdrey had set a defensive field for him. Yet he completed his hundred, with nine 4's, in three hours 48 minutes. The achievement stimulated one of his compatriots to run on to the field, hug him round the middle, and hoist him in triumph. His innings confirmed, just in case anyone doubted it, that his marvellous temperament and technical orthodoxy, his range, fluency and power of shot, and his extraordinary gift for late improvisation, put him in front of any other batsman of his time.

From then on the two West Indians sensibly played for the morrow, and at stumps the tourists were 288 for five off 104 overs, a lead of 202. The partnership had added 193 and was only 18 short of the West Indian record for the sixth wicket. Sobers was 121, Holford 71. Between them they had brought off an epic reversal of fortunes, leaving all to play for on the final day.

The legend that West Indians crumpled up when things went wrong — as a characteristic, and to a greater extent than other races — had been laid for ever. Their nerves in a crisis were as good as the next man's. So were their neuroses, as Holford discovered when he got to the dressing-room dying for a smoke, only to find that his colleagues, in their nail-biting apprehension, had devoured every cigarette in sight.

For Colin Cowdrey it had not been the best of days. West Indies had been on the point of surrender, and England had let them off the hook: that was the unanimous verdict, and accusing fingers were inevitably pointed at Cowdrey. The England seamers had bowled splendidly at first, but once the wicket recovered they had looked disappointingly bland. What, it was asked, had Cowdrey done to maintain the challenge? Higgs should have bowled more, said some, and Sobers should have been confronted with Titmus at once. But to have introduced Titmus when the wicket favoured seam would have been rightly castigated unless — against the odds — it had been successful. The nursing of Higgs, too, looked a reasonable precaution.

It was the basic good sense of giving Sobers a single to get at the weaker batsman that deserved closer scrutiny, time-honoured tactics though they were. Keith Miller, for one, abhorred them.

Holford sweeps Titmus past an apprehensive Milburn . . .

. . . who moves too late as Sobers turns Higgs off his toes.

Others found Cowdrey's failure to pressurise Sobers incompre-
hensible. Among the more understanding critics was Denys
Rowbotham: with the resources Cowdrey had, thought Rowbotham, he could not have done much more than he did. Better
surely to give credit to the batsmen. But few understood Cowdrey's psychology in not crowding Sobers, and the dynamic
gestures that impress spectators were not Cowdrey's way.

The selectors, too, were left with reddened faces when it was
known that one of the men they had left out, fast bowler John
Snow, had been irresistible for Sussex that afternoon — at Leeds,
not at Hove — and taken 10 for 120 in Yorkshire's first defeat
of the season.

The last day very nearly fulfilled its potential, and might well
have done so had not rain reduced the time available. Both sides
had a chance to win when play started, but with the Lord's
wicket playing better every hour, as it was apt to do, a sense of
urgency was required. The old West Indian sixth-wicket record
was duly eclipsed, but when fifty runs had been added in even
time, a shower sent the players off. Holford was then 92.

When the players came back after 35 minutes, Holford progressed to 96 in singles, then produced an off-side stroke off the
back foot of rare quality that raced to the Warner Stand. This
time it was Holford who was lifted off his feet by spectators, but
he recovered to get in a straight drive to the pavilion rails before
Sobers declared at the end of the over. Their unbroken sixth
wicket stand had put on 274, taking the score from 95 to 369.

It was only now that the true value of Holford's innings was
appreciated. Until then, Sobers had been given most of the credit.
'Correspondents, including myself,' wrote Tony Crozier, 'did
not give Holford enough praise yesterday for his part in the fight
back with Sobers.'

England were set 284 to win in four hours, and with Cowdrey
not deeming the task impossible, Boycott and Milburn played
their strokes. But after a second interruption for rain a collapse
followed, and at 67 for four it required a severely handicapped
Tom Graveney, withdrawing one hand from the bat because of
a thumb bruised by Hall in the first innings, to join Colin

Sobers reaches his hundred — and an enthusiastic spectator lifts him off his feet. Umpire Buller tolerates, D'Oliveira applauds.

A handshake for Holford from his captain as Umpire Price signals the 4 off Jones that took Holford in turn to his century.

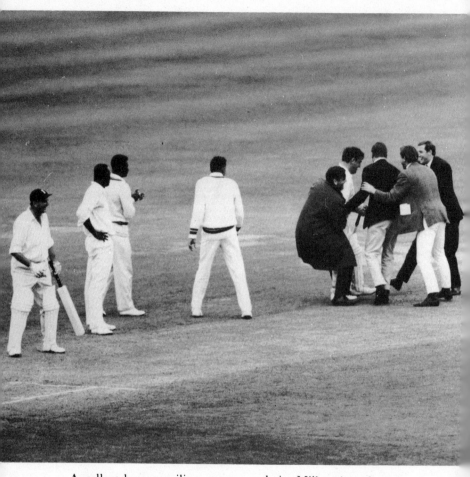

A gallant but unavailing attempt to hoist Milburn's 17½ stone as he completes his century greatly amuses Graveney.

ENGLAND v WEST INDIES 1966 (2nd Test)
at Lords, June 16, 17, 18, 20, 21
Match drawn

WEST INDIES: First Innings

C. C. Hunte, c Parks b Higgs	18
M. C. Carew, c Parks b Higgs	2
R. B. Kanhai, c Titmus b Higgs	25
B. F. Butcher, c Milburn b Knight	49
S. M. Nurse, b D'Oliveira	64
*G. S. Sobers, lbw b Knight	46
D. A. J. Holford, b Jones	26
†D. W. Allan, c Titmus b Higgs	13
C. C. Griffiths, lbw b Higgs	5
W. W. Hall, not out	8
L. R. Gibbs, c Parks b Higgs	4
Extras (B 2, LB 7)	9
Total	269

Fall of wickets: 1-8, 2-42, 3-53, 4-119, 5-205, 6-213, 7-252, 8-252, 9-261, 10-269.

Bowling: Jones, 21-3-64-1; Higgs, 33-9-91-6; Knight, 21-0-63-2; Titmus, 5-0-18-0; D'Oliveira, 14-5-24-1.

ENGLAND: First Innings

G. Boycott, c Griffith b Gibbs	60
C. Milburn, lbw b Hall	6
T. W. Graveney, c Allan b Hall	96
K. F. Barrington, b Sobers	19
*M. C. Cowdrey, c Gibbs b Hall	9
†J. M. Parks, lbw b Carew	91
B. D'Oliveira, run out	27
B. R. Knight, b Griffith	6
F. J. Titmus, c Allan b Hall	6
K. Higgs, c Holford b Gibbs	13
I. J. Jones, not out	0
Extras (B 7, LB 10, NB 5)	22
Total	355

Fall of wickets: 1-8, 2-123, 3-164, 4-198, 5-203, 6-251, 7-266, 8-296, 9-355, 10-355.

Bowling: Sobers, 39-12-89-1; Hall, 36-2-106-4; Griffith, 28-4-79-1; Gibbs, 37.3-18-48-2; Carew, 3-0-11-1.

WEST INDIES: Second Innings

C. C. Hunte, c Milburn b Knight	13
M. C. Carew, c Knight b Higgs	0
R. B. Kanhai, c Parks b Knight	40
B. F. Butcher, lbw b Higgs	3
S. M. Nurse, c Parks b D'Oliveira	35
G. S. Sobers, not out	163
D. A. J. Holford, not out	105
Extras (LB 8, NB 2)	10
Total (5 wkts dec.)	369

Fall of wickets: 1-2, 2-22, 3-25, 4-91, 5-95.

Bowling: Jones, 25-2-95-0; Higgs, 34-5-82-2; Knight, 30-3-106-2; D'Oliveira, 25-7-46-1; Titmus, 19-3-30-0.

ENGLAND: Second Innings

G. Boycott, c Allan b Griffith	25
C. Milburn, not out	126
K. F. Barrington, b Griffith	5
M. C. Cowdrey, c Allan b Hall	5
J. M. Parks, b Hall	0
T. W. Graveney, not out	30
Extras (B 4, LB 2)	6
Total (4 wkts)	197

Fall of wickets: 1-37, 2-43, 3-67, 4-67.

Bowling: Hall, 14-1-65-2; Griffith, 11-2-43-2; Gibbs, 13-4-40-0; Sobers, 8-4-8-0; Holford, 9-1-35-0.

Umpires—J. S. Buller and W. F. Price

Milburn in a partnership almost as match-saving as that of Sobers and Holford. England lost no more wickets and finished up at 197 for four, Milburn making an exhilarating 126, Graveney an invaluable 30.

When Milburn reached his hundred, a group of Englishmen rushed on the field and tried to hoist him aloft as Sobers and Holford had been hoisted. Amidst great amusement, Milburn's 17½ stone proved too much for them.

West Indies won the third and fourth Tests to confirm their status as World Champions. Then came England's solitary victory at the Oval under Brian Close.

Sobers played so many great innings that to name any one of them as his innings of a lifetime might seem invidious. But we have it on his own authority that he regarded this as the outstanding innings of his career. How much more was this true of Holford, who, despite a distinguished Test record that spanned the next ten years, never again reached these heights.

It was David Holford, that day at Lord's, who bore the brunt of the England attack in the crisis period, and stood firm.

6

ASIF IQBAL

'Son — all I want you to know is that this is the best Test innings I've seen in my life.'
— *Sir Leary Constantine*

When the mid-morning drinks were taken out to the players at the Oval on Monday 28th August 1967, the batting side were in a hopeless position. It was the fourth day of the third and final Test between England and Pakistan, and the tourists were crumbling to defeat by an innings and a great many runs. By lunchtime the Pakistan team would have drunk the cup of defeat to the dregs. For England the beverage would be champagne.

Overnight the visitors had been 26 for four, but their 'Little Master', the 32-year-old Hanif Mohammad, had been one of the not out batsmen, encouraging a grain of optimism. It was Bank Holiday Monday, and despite such rival attractions as the first professional tennis tournament to be held at Wimbledon (the final, between Laver and Rosewall, was to be televised that afternoon), a faithful few, amounting as the morning progressed to about 5,000, turned up to see if Hanif could work the miracle, as he had done a month earlier at Lord's.

Such hopes were quickly proved fanciful. After an hour's play, Hanif was out and Pakistan were 58 for seven.

Shortly before the drinks interval, when the seventh wicket fell, a figure of marked idiosyncrasy, little known as yet on English cricket grounds, emerged from the pavilion. An opening bowler of restless energy who scampered up to the wicket pigeon-toed and slightly bow-legged, he moved the ball about at a lively fast-medium; and he was also establishing himself as a late-order batsman of aggression and panache. Already he had

117

put bat to ball and twice struck Titmus to the ring. A 24-year-old Moslem from Hyderabad (India) whose family had moved to Karachi after partition, his name was Asif Iqbal. But his pugnacity today could be no more than a brief and futile flourish.

This seemed amply confirmed when, almost as the drinks waiters disappeared up the pavilion steps, another wicket fell and Pakistan were 65 for eight. 159 runs were still needed to avoid an innings defeat, and those who had long since written off Pakistan's chances of avoiding this ultimate disgrace, and were congratulating themselves on having stayed at home, were being proved right.

The time was 12.40, and in all probability the game would be over by lunchtime. This meant turning away some of cricket's most loyal followers after less than two hours' cricket on what promised to be a perfect summer's day. It was a farce that cricket's already battered image could hardly stand.

With 22 international players assembled, an exhibition match, of an agreed number of overs, would extend the entertainment through the afternoon and send the crowd away happy. This was the solution arrived at by cricket's administrators. Thus it was that, when the eighth wicket fell, England's twelfth man was offered further employment, this time as a courier, taking a note out to England captain Brian Close.

Brian Close, as it happened, was under a cloud, having just been censured for time-wasting in a county match when skippering Yorkshire; his appointment as captain for the forthcoming tour of the West Indies was in jeopardy. He was not, perhaps, in the best position to argue, supposing he wanted to. For personal reasons he needed a crushing victory, and he was on the point of getting one; but as a professional cricketer he was equally conscious of the importance of the paying public. Already his players were guaranteed a full day to spare on the Tuesday, since five days had been set aside for the game. If the Pakistanis were agreeable, there would be no objection from Close on behalf of his team.

Hanif Mohammad had already been sounded, and, with many Pakistanis present in the crowd, he had proved amenable. An announcement was duly made, and the spectators, resigned to an inglorious finish to the Test Match, looked forward to some spectacular cricket in the afternoon. One-day cricket was in its infancy, the Gillette Cup being in only its fifth season and the Benson and Hedges and John Player competitions being as yet unborn. But exhibition cricket, played with just enough antagonism to satisfy all but the purists, was being popularised by a team of internationals known as the Cavaliers.

The gist of the plot being hatched with Brian Close had been divined soon enough by Asif, and his instincts, as a cricketer and a Pakistani, were deeply offended. No game of cricket was over until the last ball was bowled. What right had anyone to assume otherwise? Talk of an exhibition match was not only premature, it was in the worst possible taste, an insult to the Pakistan players and the Pakistan flag. Throughout the tour there had been times when they had been made to feel like second-class citizens in the cricketing sense, not good enough to take on England at full strength. In the breast of one Pakistani, at least, this was a stigma not to be borne.

Even before going to the wicket he had resolved to achieve something special. Talk of an overs match only stiffened his determination. 'There'll be no overs match if I can help it,' he muttered.

Joining him simultaneously with the arrival of the note was another all-rounder, though vastly different in physique, temperament and style. This was Intikhab Alam, and like Asif he was beginning to make his way in the world of international cricket. In his less volatile way he was equally incensed at the assumption that his team were giving in without a fight. Thus he welcomed Asif's greeting. 'Let's enjoy ourselves,' Asif was saying. 'Let's go for our shots and see what happens.' In situations like this, Asif believed that bold methods were best.

'I've got a stye on my eye,' replied Intikhab. 'I've rubbed some ointment on it and at the moment I can hardly see. But you're playing well. I'll just try to stay here.'

*   *

119

Asif Iqbal was born into a cricketing family. His father, who died soon after Asif was born, had played for Hyderabad, and four of his uncles had played good cricket. One of them, Ghulam Ahmed, had captained India. 'You have the talent,' they told him, 'to become a good cricketer one day,' and without any rigid coaching they inspired him to develop his natural game. With the bat he always hit the ball as hard as he could. With the ball he always bowled as fast as he could.

Cricket for Asif was first and foremost an entertainment, not just for the players but also for the people who came to watch. He wanted to be a cricketer who enjoyed himself and gave enjoyment to others. His heroes were exciting players like Norman O'Neill and Rohan Kanhai, and there were times when he tried to copy their style. Eventually he realised that above all he must be himself.

He played for Hyderabad in the Ranji Trophy at the age of 17, and when Pakistan toured India in 1961 he played against them for South Zone and had a match haul of six wickets. By this time most of his family, as Muslims, had emigrated to Pakistan, and Asif joined his brother, Dr Shahid Iqbal, also a useful cricketer, in Karachi.

The impact of those six wickets followed him to Karachi, and whereas in Hyderabad he had been considered as primarily a batsman, in Pakistan he was treated more as a bowler — a preconceived notion that took him years to correct. He had opened the bowling for South Zone against Pakistan and batted No. 7, and they couldn't forget it. Through college and university, where he graduated in history and economics, the reputation stuck, and since the Pakistan team at that time was stronger in batting than bowling, he made a virtue of necessity, realising that it was as a bowler that he must try to make the national side.

In 1963 the Pakistan Eaglets, a party composed of promising youngsters with a leavening of Test players, undertook a short English tour. Led by Wazir Mohammad, elder brother of Hanif, the party included two younger brothers, Mushtaq and Sadiq, Majid Khan, Intikhab Alam and Asif Iqbal. Batting mostly at No. 8, Asif averaged 29 in his eight first-class innings, but it was as a bowler that he excelled, taking 19 first-class wickets at an average of 14.73, more wickets than anyone except Intikhab, who took the same number at 23.15.

All activity on a cricket field was enjoyable to Asif, but the amount of movement he could get in the air and off the wicket in English conditions was both a thrill and revelation to him. Nothing delighted him more than knocking back Geoff Pullar's middle stump at Old Trafford with an in-swinger (to the left-hander) that the batsman left alone. Outstanding performances were 6 for 45 against Cambridge University and 5 for 103 against Derbyshire, when he bowled 34 overs. *Wisden* could not make up its mind whether to call him Asif or Iqbal, but they made sure of being at least 50% right by calling him Asif in the first instance and Iqbal in the second.

Asif made his first real impact as a batsman in his first international match, when the Australians, returning home from their 1964 England tour, played one Test Match at Karachi. Batting No 10, he joined Intikhab and helped to make sure of a first innings lead after a sudden collapse. According to *Wisden* they 'batted beautifully, playing excellent strokes all round the wicket', and Asif made 41. In the second innings he went in as night-watchman, surely a most curious role for him, and 'played some beautiful shots' in making 36. But any chance of a Pakistan victory was destroyed by tedious middle batting and a second hundred of the match by Bobby Simpson.

Selected to tour Australia and New Zealand in 1964-65, Asif suffered his first major setback — an injury which threatened to end his career. After having no success with bat or ball in the only Test Match played, he injured his back while bowling in a State match, and although the doctors told him it was no worse than a muscular spasm he felt instinctively that it was something more severe. At 5' 9" and 10½ stone he was not really built for fast bowling, and although he was strong and wiry and could hurry the ball through for long periods he was never more than medium fast. It seemed very likely that to stay in Test cricket he would have to make a mark as a batsman.

Continuing to New Zealand, the tourists played three Test

Matches. At Wellington, Asif's back stood up to 25 overs in the New Zealand first innings and he took 5 for 48, but in the second innings the pain returned. He did well with the bat, however, making second top score of 30 in the first innings and the only Pakistan fifty of the match (undefeated) in the second, when he saved the side from what looked like certain defeat. Going in at 64 for six, he saw the last day out to 140 for seven. For the last 35 minutes he was accompanied by Intikhab.

His back recovered sufficiently for him to bowl long spells in the remaining Tests, with outstanding success, but he did nothing more with the bat. Nevertheless that not out fifty had convinced him that he had the ability and the temperament to become a Test batsman.

The opportunity to prove himself came at the beginning of 1967, when the MCC sent an Under-25 team to Pakistan under Mike Brearley, with Les Ames as manager. Asif's potential for leadership was recognised by his appointment as captain, and he did not allow false modesty to impede his chances of staking his claim for the tour of England that year. He did not shirk his share of the bowling, but in the second representative match, when his team were forced to follow on 212 behind, he joined Majid at 124 for four and led the way with a characteristic amalgam of ruthless efficiency and carefree abandon in a stand of 167 in two hours. An attack which included Brown, Arnold, Pocock, Hobbs and Underwood was reduced to impotence, Asif recorded his maiden first-class hundred, and the match was saved.

This innings assured Asif of fulfilling his greatest ambition, a full tour of England. But just before the side was announced he strained his back again in a training session and his prospects looked grim.

At first he was tempted to hide his weakness, and he prayed to be allowed to make this one trip, after which he wouldn't care if he never played Test cricket again. But when he heard that the tour itinerary consisted of 17 first-class matches in ten weeks, including three five-day Tests, he realised that this would be folly. So he owned up, and spent many agonising hours on the physiotherapist's table. 'I'll do my best to get fit,' he promised the selectors, and eventually they decided to take a gamble on his doing so.

In London he was sent at once to Dr. Bill Tucker, famous for his treatment of injuries sustained by professional sportsmen. Of the first eight matches of the tour he played in only four, but one of these was significant in that it provided a pointer to the future. In his first appearance, against Kent, he found that secretary-manager Ames had not forgotten him. He had a mixed game, making 41 and taking 0 for 85 in 25 overs, but in the course of it Colin Cowdrey sounded him about the possibility of a special registration for the county.

Just before the first Test, at Lord's, he went to Dr. Tucker for a cortisone injection. 'You have to be careful,' said Tucker. 'You should bowl only in short spells.' Asif passed this instruction on to Hanif, who was captaining Pakistan, but England reached 280 with only two wickets down and Hanif was obliged to call on him for a sustained effort. From this point on wickets fell regularly, and England were all out for 369. *Wisden* recorded that the landslide was begun by 'some fine pace bowling by Salim and Asif'. Asif in 28 overs took 3 for 76.

The Pakistan party was swollen to 20 by the addition of four players who were fulfilling professional engagements in England — Mushtaq, in his second season with Northants; Khalid Ibadulla, for ten years a Warwickshire regular; Nasim-ul-Ghani, in the Lancashire League; and Intikhab Alam, with West of Scotland. Undoubtedly they strengthened the side, but their 'guest' appearances, mostly for Test Matches only, did not improve team or tour spirit. This was reflected in results, and soon after lunch on the third day of the Lord's Test Pakistan were 139 for seven. At this point Asif, batting later than all four 'guests', joined his captain, and when the weather intervened at five o'clock they had added 94. Hanif had reached his century and Asif, scoring much the faster, was 56.

Here, again at a crucial point, was another convincing demonstration that Asif's place in the order bore little relation to his ability. Next day he and Hanif took their stand to 130 before Asif got out for 76. Hanif went on to make 187 not out, and

Pakistan, once in danger of following on, finished only 15 behind. They went on to reduce England to 95 for four in their second innings, and a declaration, from a more aggressive captain, might well have brought victory. As it was the game petered out in a draw.

The second Test, played at Trent Bridge on a pitch that twice became flooded after water seeped under the covers, produced a wicket utterly alien to the tourists, and indeed Hanif complained at having to bat in such conditions. 'One does not expect that sort of thing,' he said, 'on a Test ground.' Only Ken Barrington, after observing that three great players, Hanif, Cowdrey and Graveney, were caught trying to drive, prospered, and his 109, which came mostly from deflections and pushes and took nearly seven hours, decided the match. Pakistan were all out for 140 in their first innings and 114 in their second, and their capitulation, and especially the conditions that had brought it about, rankled.

One writer at least — Keith Miller — had rated the visitors a well-balanced side, a surprise packet even, and certainly no push-over. Now the comments were less flattering. 'The contest is becoming wholly one-sided,' was one opinion, 'and until such time as these contests are more even, five-day Tests are unnecessary.' Only Hanif's innings, it was suggested, had masked the difference of class between the two sides at Lord's. Three days would be ample for these games: anything more merely slowed down the play.

Asif had bowled 30 overs in England's innings and taken 2 for 78, but like nearly everyone else he had failed with the bat. And after the game his back was so painful that he missed the next two matches. Then came the Oval Test, leaving him no chance of a try-out beforehand. He was getting the most skilled treatment available, but no cure seemed possible, and he had to face the fact that, even supposing he was able to play, this would probably be his last Test and his last tour. As for his chances of playing for Kent, his back would never stand up to four months of county cricket.

He accepted these disappointments, bitter as they were, with the fatalism of his creed. He had wanted two things above all:

124

to come to England on a senior Pakistan tour, and to play at Lord's. He had done both. Even if he played no more cricket, he would have these things to look back on.

His back improved with treatment, but he could still feel it when he tried to bowl in the nets. Nevertheless he was tempted to chance it. For batting he had adjusted his stance, involuntarily at first, so that he was standing much more square on than formerly. This, he realised, had been a subconscious reaction, to reduce bending. His play seemed unaffected.

On the eve of the selection of the side Asif was still unfit, and he knew he had no right to play. He discussed his dilemma with Majid, who was sympathetic. Majid was having a wonderful tour against the counties but a disastrous time in the Tests. 'I don't know if I'll be able to play any more Test cricket,' he told Majid, 'so although I'm not really fit I shan't tell the selectors. I shall just go and play.' The selectors knew he was still having treatment, but they wanted him to play, and he told them he would be all right. It was, as he was well aware, an irresponsible and even a selfish decision. It was to change his whole life.

* *

The morning of the match was sunless and misty. It was only 24th August, but the first whiff of autumn was in the air. The buildings surrounding the Oval were shrouded in haze, and a seasonal dampness could be expected in the wicket. The pitch was hard enough in appearance, but there were well-grassed patches, from which the faster bowlers would get life and movement. It looked a good toss to lose. Indeed when Brian Close won the toss he had no hesitation in putting his opponents in.

Hanif had batted throughout the tour at No. 4 or 5, and in the Test Matches he had invariably come in to face a crisis. He had therefore decided, for the final Test, to go in first himself. Of the previous openers, Ibadulla was left out and Burki was dropped to No. 6, making room for Mohammad Ilyas, a sound player who had missed the first two Tests. It was a move that Hanif was soon to regret. The conditions, exacerbated by indifferent light which twice brought the umpires together in consultation, were expertly exploited by the England opening bowlers. Hanif, deceived by late movement, played on to Ken Higgs, Ilyas and Majid Khan fell to Arnold, and Pakistan were 17 for three.

A minor recovery was effected, thanks mainly to Mushtaq, and when he was sixth out for 66 soon after tea Asif played with equal boldness. He had scored 26 and seemed set to take Pakistan to a more respectable total when his innings was cruelly cut short by a typically blinding catch by Close, in the gully, off a meaty square drive.

All out for 216, Pakistan hit back quickly when Asif had Close, who opened with Cowdrey, caught behind. Cowdrey soon followed, but with the sun shining and conditions much improved for batting, Barrington made 142 and Graveney 77. Even so, England at one point were 276 for six, and for Pakistan a moderate deficit looked possible. But Asif, although outstanding in the field, dared not charge in with his customary zest with the ball, and although he bowled 42 overs including 19 maidens and took 3 for 66, he could not break through the tail. England made 440, a lead of 224, and at five minutes past five on the third day, Saturday, Pakistan were batting again. This time Hanif reverted to No. 5, sending wicket-keeper Wasim Bari in as a makeshift opener with Ilyas. But an inspired spell by Higgs, moving the ball away late and hurrying it off the pitch, cut a swathe through the early batting, and at 5 for three no real recovery seemed possible. Wasim, defending stoutly, was still there, and he was joined by Hanif, but just before stumps Knott caught Wasim off Higgs and Pakistan were 26 for four. This left them with all day Sunday to await their execution. Only another mammoth innings by Hanif stood between them and complete degradation.

The atmosphere in the tourists' hotel next morning was depressing, relieved only by a frivolous challenge by Omer Quarshy, a radio commentator who was also an executive of Pakistan International Airlines. 'If you get a hundred on Monday,' he told Asif, 'I'll fix you a trip to Paris.' At that moment, Paris seemed even further away than Pakistan.

Asif was glad to get away to visit his brother, who was

practising in London and living in a flat in Balham. His mother and sister, too, were on holiday in London and were staying at the flat. After lunch with them Asif switched on the television to find that the Cavaliers were playing at Lord's. At first he was no more than mildly interested. Then a wicket fell and something the commentator said attracted his notice. 'Here comes the great South African left-hander Graeme Pollock. But we must give him time to adjust. He's come straight from a South African winter and hasn't played for several months. It'll be fascinating to see how he copes.'

The way Pollock tackled the problem impressed Asif. Analysing it, he concluded that the South African had resolved above all to play straight. He had never seen a straighter bat. Pollock made a chanceless fifty, and Asif's reaction progressed from admiration to a determination to emulate. If a player could come straight from a winter in the Southern Hemisphere and bat in so commanding and cultured a fashion, simply, as it seemed to him, by concentrating on playing straight, surely he himself, after playing regularly for many weeks, could do the same. The lesson was imprinted on his mind to the point of obsession. 'If only I can play like this guy Pollock,' he told his mother when he left to return to the hotel that evening. 'I'm sure you can play even better,' she said, 'if only you apply yourself and try hard. I shall be praying for you.'

A playback of Pollock's undeviating bat lingered in his subconscious all night and was still within total recall when he awoke next morning. When he got to the Oval he asked two of his team-mates to throw the ball to him, just to practise hitting it straight back. The crowd was a disappointing one for a Bank Holiday, but there were several thousand people present when Hanif Mohammad and Ghulam Abbas, a stylish left-hander, resumed to the bowling of Arnold and Higgs.

On the strength of some good scores against the counties, Ghulam was playing in his first Test. But he had failed in the first innings, and now he was out to the second ball of the day, caught by Knott off Higgs. That was 26 for 5, and the crowd groaned. They would be lucky to get an hour's cricket.

At 11.33 Hanif was joined by Mushtaq, whom he had also held back, and the main fight was joined. That these two brothers were capable of great things in partnership no one doubted, and for the next half-hour they defended stubbornly, bat correctly angled when they played forward, body behind the ball when they played back. Then Hanif, forced to play at a perfectly pitched Higgs out-swinger, touched it to Knott, and that was 41 for six.

Pakistan's lowest-ever Test total was 84, against England at Lord's in 1954. But in that series, thanks to Fazal Mahmood, they had come back to win at the Oval and square the series. Now the last four wickets needed to more than double the score to escape a new and unenviable record.

The shuffling of the batting order had relegated Javed Burki, an Oxford Blue well used to English conditions, with three hundreds against England to his credit, to No. 8. Burki knew the value of patience and application and he began to dig in. The man who lost patience was Mushtaq. Lashing out at Underwood, he was caught off a skier by D'Oliveira at mid-on.

The incoming batsman, sweaterless, shirt open and flapping at the breast, sleeves buttoned to the wrist, mop of jet-black hair overhanging his brow, had already set a new Pakistan record for an eighth-wicket partnership with Hanif at Lord's. At 53 for seven, a repeat performance was desperately needed. This time there was no Hanif; but the man he was joining, Javed Burki, was a fine player. Asif, at least, had not given up hope.

Immediately after the drinks interval Close rested Higgs, who had bowled for an hour; he gave Titmus the task of mopping up the tail. Asif responded defiantly with two straight drives along the ground to the pavilion rails; but there was to be no new record eighth wicket stand. Three overs later Burki was bowled by Underwood's faster ball, and that was 65 for eight.

Serious resistance was over: that was the view of the administrators as they sent the twelfth man out with a message to Close. (The bearer of the note was Surrey batsman W.A. 'Bill' Smith.) There were still fifty minutes to go until lunch, so the plan became that lunch would be taken on the demise of the

Brian Close studies the note taken out to him by 12th man Bill Smith
as the England players look bored and the batsmen peeved.

Pakistan innings, after which the exhibition match would be staged.

So far as the crowd were concerned, further resistance would be frustrating and time-wasting, liable to curtail the afternoon's entertainment. But Asif, eyes flashing with resentment, saw his mission developing into a crusade. For all the passion of his resolve he was inwardly relaxed, and he had been middling the ball from the first. His new partner, Intikhab Alam, might be No. 10 in the order, but more than once the two men had shared match-saving stands.

When Intikhab greeted Asif with the news of his impairment of vision, Asif realised what he had to do. He knew this Karachi-born cricketer as an intelligent all-rounder and loyal colleague, a powerful hitter who was capable in emergency of iron self-control. But because of Intikhab's handicap, he, Asif, would have to farm the bowling, at least for a time. Then Intikhab's vision might clear.

Facing Titmus, Asif took a single off the last ball of the over to keep the strike, and he experienced no problems with Underwood, off whom he also took a single late in the over to take him back to the Vauxhall end to face Titmus. But to achieve his purpose he would have to break up the close field. Dancing in to drive, he lofted Titmus high over mid-on into the pavilion for 6.

Asif's counter-attack found a sympathetic echo in the crowd, as did the scrambled singles, upsetting the field. It would be fun while it lasted; but it couldn't last long.

After the 6 came another scampered single, then a glorious drive through the covers for 4 off Underwood. For all Close's astute manipulation of the field he was again unable to stop the single, and Titmus's next over, forcing Asif on to the defensive despite twinkling footwork in getting to the pitch of the ball, finally brought an improvised stroke that allowed the batsmen to change ends.

The strong Pakistan element in the crowd, silent thus far, now cheered every run. Underwood succeeded in bowling Asif a maiden, and then Intikhab, who had scarcely had to face a ball in six overs, stole a single off Titmus to break his duck amidst a patriotic roar.

Feigning to give Titmus the charge, Asif caused him to drop short, then pulled him to the terraces in front of the gasholder for a second 6. Now the hubbub, becoming more impartial, reached a crescendo. Twenty 6's in an exhibition game could not match these two ripostes to a bowler probing for the kill. Meanwhile the spectre of a new record low total had been laid.

Again Asif managed a single off the last ball, and in Underwood's next over, the 28th of the morning, he pulled him in front of square and drove him straight for 4's that left the fielders standing. He couldn't work the single this time, but Intikhab did so to give him the strike, and again an alert, converging arc of fielders could not stop the single off the last ball. Another boundary off Underwood took the score to 102, and the crowd's delight erupted. Yet they recognised an element of fantasy in the cricket, the fanning of dying embers, the rallying of an innings in its death-throes. What was happening in the middle seemed almost an illusion, yet the scoreboard said Asif was 43 not out.

England's spinners had failed, and Close turned back to Higgs and Arnold for a final fling before lunch. But they could not stop Asif now, and when he drove Higgs for his seventh 4 to reach 50 in 48 minutes, out of only 56 added while he was at the wicket, the cheering reached a new frenzy. The game had come alive and the crowd with it, although feelings were inextricably muddled. Impatience to see the exhibition match get under way competed with a growing conviction that Asif's innings was the real thing, infinitely superior to anything they were likely to see in the afternoon.

Close still kept an attacking field, certain that no No. 9 could go on playing so freely without making a fatal mistake. But Higgs's first over cost seven runs, six of them to Asif, and Arnold, too, in his second over, was struck for 4 and 2. Every shot raised a new clamour, which was extended to a prolonged outburst to signal the 50 partnership. When the players went off for lunch at 1.30 Pakistan were 121 for 8, still hopelessly placed, but with racial pride and self-esteem at least partially restored.

131

Everyone had expected Brian Close to find a way of finishing the game off, but they had reckoned without the cheeky defiance of Asif. The Pakistan crowd had a hero, and they applauded him all the way in.

Congratulations followed all the way to the dressing room. 'Well done,' said the other Pakistan players. 'Keep it going.' But their tone lacked conviction. After lunch Higgs and Arnold, refreshed by the break, would pick up the last two wickets, and the Overs match would begin.

Even more infuriating to Asif was the attitude taken by the authorities. He gathered that sponsored awards, cash prizes presented for the best batsman and bowler on each side, had already been adjudicated. The batting prizes, of £100 each, were to go to Barrington and Mushtaq, and he heard Mushtaq being congratulated. How could they decide such matters before the game was over?

He sought out Omer Quarshy. 'Do you remember your promise? That if I get a hundred, you'll get me a ticket to Paris'?

'Yes, I do,' said Omer, 'and I've already been on the air and told the listeners about it.'

'OK then — just have the ticket ready.'

Asif had scored only one first-class hundred in his life, but he believed he could make good his boast. Meanwhile, too keyed-up to eat, he limited himself to a glass of milk for lunch and relaxed on a dressing-room bench.

He and Intikhab did enjoy one good laugh together. 'What have they decided now?' asked Asif. It seemed that the projected exhibition match had already been limited to a 20-overs game. 'We'll get it down to less than that,' said Intikhab. But Asif's sights were set higher. 'Let's see if we can make them bat again.' They had already put on 54 runs together, but they needed another 103 to do that. So far out of reach did this target seem, as they left the dressing room for the afternoon session, that some of the players, with the manager in the centre, gathered round a television set to watch Laver and Rosewall at Wimbledon.

Asif's devastating stroke-play against Higgs and Arnold before lunch persuaded Close to rely on his spinners, and he reverted to Titmus and Underwood. Giving the ball plenty of air, they aimed to tease the bastmen into what seemed the inevitable indiscretion. But Asif, still thinking of Graeme Pollock, concentrated on playing straight, and on playing himself back in. The cricket during the morning, sombre at first and then almost light-hearted, had seemed strangely unlike a Test Match, but now it was clear that England had a fight on their hands.

For a time the innings was becalmed. Then Titmus pitched one marginally short and Asif cut it to the Harleyford Road boundary. Thus encouraged, Intikhab swept Underwood to the same boundary, and the Pakistan sails filled again as the innings regained its momentum. Titmus and Underwood still bowled with their customary accuracy, but there was no hint of the indiscretion for which Close was scheming, and in the 74th over he introduced Ken Barrington with his leg breaks and top spinners at the pavilion end.

For the two Pakistanis, the situation was deliciously ironic. Meeting between overs, and whenever the ball reached the boundary, they speculated on the calculations that must be going on in the pavilion and chuckled delightedly at their conclusions. 'How many overs now?' 'Must be down to fifteen'. 'Can't be more than fourteen, surely?' 'Perhaps only thirteen.' And then: 'About twelve now. Every over means one less.'

At the Vauxhall end, where he had replaced Underwood, Titmus dropped straight on a length, and of his next five overs three were maidens and the other two yielded only a single apiece. But there was plenty of action at the other end. Intikhab was goaded by the fleet-footed Asif, who had a reputation for lapping his partners, into running a 5, and then two tremendous cover-drives off the same bowler took Asif into the 90s and put up the 100 partnership. As they acknowledged the applause they could not stop laughing. 'It must be down to ten overs now.'

Six overs from Barrington produced 33 runs, and in their primary task, at least, the spinners had failed. But their secondary task of getting through their overs quickly so that the new ball could be taken was achieved. Pakistan were 190 for eight, still

' 'Ere, 'ere, wot's all this?' Asif is chaired by his fellow-countrymen on reaching his century, while a solitary policeman advances, and a subdued Brian Close looks on.

'We did it!'

34 short of making England bat again, Asif was still in the 90s, and the new ball was due.

It made no difference to Asif. He took six runs off Arnold, who was powering in again from the Vauxhall end, and after Higgs had been bludgeoned for 2 and 1 by Intikhab, Asif produced yet another classic drive through the covers, still packed despite the new ball, to reach his century with his fourteenth 4. He had batted only two hours 16 minutes.

'An amazing scene followed,' recorded *Wisden*. The ball was still well short of the boundary when scores of Pakistan supporters streamed in kaleidoscopic profusion on to the field and converged on the batting crease, the vanguard amongst them seizing hold of their light-weight hero and hoisting him shoulder high. Such crowd hysteria in the years that followed would no longer amaze, but this, in the England of 1967, was spontaneous and rare. It seemed indeed that Asif might be crushed or suffocated by the wild enthusiasm of his countrymen, and a single policeman moved somewhat anxiously to his rescue. By the time a space had been cleared Asif was in a state of collapse, squatting on his haunches, head in his hands, completely overwhelmed. But he had not been hurt. His prostration was emotional rather than physical. He had never known such happiness, and in that moment he thanked Allah for it. It seemed to him that he had achieved just about everything in this world that it was possible to achieve.

Straightening himself out and brushing himself down, he found, sticking out of his trouser pocket, a £5 note. Someone from the crowd must have thrust it there during the mêlée. He handed it to umpire Hugo Yarnold. 'Keep this for me, will you?' he asked. 'I'll have it back afterwards.' Five pounds, in 1967, was a substantial sum.

Revived by a drink of water brought out by the assistant manager — Laver and Rosewall having been forgotten — Asif continued, after Arnold had bowled a maiden to Intikhab, to belabour Higgs, two superb drives for 4 taking the score to 200. In the same over a third cover-drive looked a certain 4, but Amiss intercepted it and Intikhab, backing up, was nearly run out. The action continued at three-reeler speed as Intikhab, seeing the ball well now although not always middling it, took eight runs off Arnold, including a thick edge through the slips to the pavilion rails.

Three 4s in four balls by Asif off Higgs — beating first mid-on, then cover, then third man, the last a square cut of dazzling power — maintained the tempo, and Higgs took his sweater. So too, after being square-driven for 4 by Intikhab, did Arnold. The new ball, kernel of Close's strategy for the past hour or more, had been roughened irreparably in the space of six overs, and at 226 for eight the follow on, amidst further scenes of rejoicing, was saved.

Of those 226, Asif and Intikhab had put on 161, and although Titmus, back at the pavilion end for the 92nd over, and Underwood restored a measure of sanity to the scoring rate, three briskly taken singles took the stand to 164 and established a new world record for a ninth-wicket partnership in a Test Match. The initial gloom of the holiday crowd had been dispelled, and they congratulated themselves on their good fortune in having decided, against their better judgement, to turn up.

Englishmen amongst the crowd, enjoying themselves as much as any, were beginning to look speculatively at the clock. The batsmen were taking their singles more sedately now, even Asif walking some of them, and boundaries were less frequent. Yet every run was now on the credit side, setting a target, infinitesimal as yet, for England. At four o'clock, with the tea interval approaching, all thoughts of an exhibition match had long since been forgotten, and the victory that England had seemed certain to achieve with more than a day to spare could no longer be taken for granted.

Ten minutes before tea, in the 100th over, Intikhab, having been dropped immediately beforehand, swung Titmus high to leg for 4 to reach 51. The merit of this innings was hardly less than that of Asif's, and indeed in the circumstances of Intikhab's disability it was almost more remarkable. With this the game reached a new phase, and the batsmen, having achieved their declared ambition of making England bat again, and having each passed a personal landmark, were in need of fresh motivation. They had not yet found their physical or psychological second wind. Sensing this, Brian Close decided to confront them with something unfamiliar, something which might break up the stalemate he felt was developing and induce the fatal error for which he had waited so long.

There was time for another two overs before tea. Desperate situations, he thought wryly, called for desperate measures. He would bowl the penultimate over, from the Vauxhall end, himself.

His first ball was overpitched and Asif struck it for his twenty-first 4 to take his score to 146. It did not escape Close that the temptation for Asif might be to look for another 4 to take him to 150. It was time to toss the ball up.

Everything had come off for Asif throughout his innings, and in his exhaustion he did not see the danger. Close's fifth ball, delivered from round the wicket, was flighted outside the off stump, seductively inviting, a half-volley, thought Asif, if he moved towards it. Thus he took the bait, only to find, as he advanced, that it was shorter and tossed rather wider than he thought. He went through with his shot, failed to connect, and was far out of his crease when he heard Knott's gleeful shout. He had no need to look round for the umpire's verdict.

Few innings can have received such general acclaim, and several people came into the dressing room afterwards to congratulate him. Among them was Sir Learie Constantine. 'Son,' he said, 'all I want you to know is that this is the best Test innings I've seen in my life. And I'm telling you this after seeing the three great Ws.'

It was almost inevitable, perhaps, that Intikhab, who had restrained himself so nobly during two hours fifty minutes of unaccustomed application, should suffer a reaction from the loss of his partner. He swung across the first ball of Titmus's next over and was bowled, leaving England 32 to win.

It was not a stroke he was proud of. Salim Altaf, the No. 11, was a good enough player to have stayed with him and magnified England's target. But his moment of folly was easily forgiven.

In partnership with Asif he had helped to put on an incredible 190, setting a ninth-wicket record for Test cricket that still stands.

Throughout his own innings, which lasted three hours ten minutes, Asif had been unconscious of his back, but now he was feeling it, and he would have been glad of a rest. But when he suggested that a substitute might field in his place Hanif would not hear of it. He must go out with the others; that, after all that had happened, was mandatory. And after Salim had bowled a maiden to Cowdrey, Hanif handed him the ball.

'Do you mind if I bowl off a shorter run?'

'Oh no — that's all right. Do what you want.'

It was not in Asif, when it came to the point, to give of less than his best, and somehow he charged in as though the game could yet be won. But his first over cost six runs, and Salim's second cost eight, plus a no ball. When Close took 2 early in Asif's second over, England were already more than half way to their target. But to Asif's fifth ball, Close reached tentatively forward, and his off stump went down. Was it possible that England, at 17 for one, might be given a fright even yet?

In the previous match, at Worcester, Saeed Ahmed had caused a collapse with his off spin, and now Hanif, with nothing to lose, gave him the ball. He was treated cautiously, and then Asif, in his third over, deceived Cowdrey with a slower ball and had him caught by Intikhab at mid-on.

Now the score-board read 20 for two.

Sent in next, to enlarge his experience, was Dennis Amiss, ahead of Tom Graveney. Amiss's Test Match form had so far been unconvincing, and Asif, forgetting his back, spurted purposefully in. If he could get Amiss at once it would be 20 for three, and England might be put under real pressure. He found the edge of Amiss's bat with an outswinger and the ball flew fast and low to Hanif at slip.

What might have happened in the next few minutes had Hanif held that catch must remain an imponderable. England would still have won, no doubt, but more wickets might have fallen. As it was, Barrington and Amiss took England to within a stroke

ENGLAND v PAKISTAN 1967 (3rd Test)
at the Oval, August 24, 25, 26, 28
England won by 8 wickets

PAKISTAN: First Innings

*Hanif Mohammad, b Higgs	3
Mohammad Ilyas, b Arnold	2
Saeed Ahmed, b Arnold	38
Majd Khan, c Knott b Arnold	6
Mushtaq Mohammad, lbw b Higgs	66
Javed Burki, c D'Oliveira b Titmus	27
Ghulam Abbas, c Underwood b Titmus	12
Asif Iqbal, c Close b Arnold	26
Intikhab Alam, b Higgs	20
†Wasim Bari, c Knott b Arnold	1
Salim Altaf, not out	7
Extras (B 5, LB 2, NB 1)	8
Total	216

Fall of wickets: 1-3, 2-5, 3-17, 4-74, 5-138, 6-155, 7-182, 8-188, 9-194, 10-216.

Bowling: Arnold, 29-9-58-5; Higgs, 29-10-61-3; D'Oliveira, 17-6-41-0; Close, 5-1-15-0; Titmus, 13-6-21-2; Underwood, 9-5-12-0.

ENGLAND: First Innings

M. C. Cowdrey, c Mushtaq b Majid	16
*D. B. Close, c Bari b Asif	6
K. F. Barrington, c Bari b Salim	142
T. W. Graveney, c Majid b Intikhab	77
D. L. Amiss, c Saeed b Asif	26
B. L. D'Oliveira, c Mushtaq b Asif	3
F. J. Titmus, c sub b Mushtaq	65
†A. Knott, c Ilyas b Mushtaq	28
G. Arnold, c Majid b Mushtaq	59
K. Higgs, b Mushtaq	7
D. L. Underwood, not out	2
Extras (LB 4, NB 5)	9
Total	440

Fall of wickets: 1-16, 2-35, 3-176, 4-270, 5-276, 6-276, 7-323, 8-416, 9-437, 10-440.

Bowling: Salim, 40-14-94-1; Asif, 42-19-66-3; Majid, 10-0-29-1; Mushtaq, 26.4-7-80-4; Saeed, 21-5-69-0; Intikhab, 28-3-93-1.

PAKISTAN: Second Innings

Mohammad Ilyas, c Cowdrey b Higgs	1
Wasim Bari, b Titmus	12
Saeed Ahmed, c Knott b Higgs	0
Majd Khan, b Higgs	0
Hanif Mohammad, c Knott b Higgs	18
Ghulam Abbas, c Knott b Higgs	0
Mushtaq Mohammad, c D'Oliveira b Underwood	17
Javed Burki, b Underwood	7
Asif Iqbal, st Knott b Close	146
Intikhab Alam, b Titmus	51
Salim Altaf, not out	0
Extras (B 1, LB 1, NB 1)	3
Total	255

Fall of wickets: 1-1, 2-5, 3-5, 4-26, 5-26, 6-41, 7-53, 8-65, 9-255, 10-255.

Bowling: Arnold, 17-5-49-0; Higgs, 20-7-58-5; Titmus, 29.1-8-64-2; Underwood, 26-12-48-2; Barrington, 8-2-29-0; Close, 1-0-4-1.

ENGLAND: Second Innings

M. C. Cowdrey, c Intikhab b Asif	9
D.B. Close, b Asif	8
K. F. Barrington, not out	13
D. L. Amiss, not out	3
Extras (NB 1)	1
Total (2 wkts)	34

Fall of wickets: 1-17, 2-20.

Bowling: Salim, 2-1-8-0; Asif, 4-1-14-2; Saeed, 2-0-7-0; Hanif, 0.2-0-4-0.

Umpires—W. F. Price and H. Yarnold

of victory, and when Hanif came on to bowl the final over, Barrington made the winning hit. But the time was ten minutes past five, the hours had been filled with competitive cricket, and the final overs had provided a fitting end to an enthralling day.

Asif's back never fully recovered, and it frequently troubled him in later years, preventing him from fulfilling his promise as an all-rounder. But his innings at the Oval secured his future. 'When Asif arrived at the wicket,' wrote Ken Higgs later, 'we all thought the game would be over within the hour. But the longer he stayed the less likely it seemed to us that we would get him out.' Despite his lowly place in the order, here, as was clear to Higgs and many others, was a world-class player, and he duly signed for Kent. When his benefit year came in 1981 he had played for them for 14 seasons, skippering them in 1977 and again in 1981/82.

Between 1964 and 1977, when he retired from Test cricket, Asif broke all Pakistan records by making 45 consecutive appearances. He scored eleven Test hundreds, including three against England and three against Australia. But none of them was quite so dramatic as his 146 that day at the Oval.

Back at his brother's flat that night, Asif was greeted first by his mother. 'Well, you've done it, haven't you,' she said. He enjoyed the promised trip to Paris, and he kept the £5 note as a souvenir, but his mother's greeting was the happiest moment of all.

*   *

One question remains to be answered: how was it that one Basil D'Oliveira, in the moment of England's need, failed to catch his skipper's eye? He had bowled 17 overs in the first innings. Did Brian Close simply forget all about him? Certainly neither man can remember anything about it today. But since they are still speaking it seems safe to assume that D'Oliveira was suffering from a strain.

7

GLENN TURNER

*'We could not get that fellow Turner
out.'*   *— Ian Chappell*

Even for those viewers who adjusted the colour controls on their
TV screens with moderation, the pitch at Lancaster Park,
Christchurch looked more like green baize than a Test Match
wicket, the nap uncropped and luxuriant. When concern was
voiced by those on the spot at its lushness, ground manager Ian
Cromb, himself a former international cricketer, was uncompromising. 'I've issued orders,' he said, 'that it is not to be cut down.'

'Cranky' Cromb, as he was known, was reacting — perhaps
over-reacting — to the placid pitch that had been prepared for
the first Test Match of the series — New Zealand v Australia,
1974 — which had ended in frustration and stalemate. 'This
wicket,' he promised, indeed almost threatened, 'will get a result
in five days.'

At the Basin Reserve at Wellington a week earlier, in only
the second official Test Match between the two countries ever
played in New Zealand, Greg Chappell had scored 380 (for once
out) and his brother Ian 266. Batting first, Australia had declared
at 511 for six, New Zealand had replied with 484, and Australia,
with the wicket still docile, had batted out time with 460 for
eight. It didn't need much crankiness on the part of 'Cranky'
Cromb to plot to prevent a repeat showing.

Two months before that indigestible Wellington Test, the
Kangaroo had at last condescended to meet the Kiwi on equal
terms, granting that much-despised animal — in the eyes of the
Australian Board of Control — full Test Match status. England
and South Africa had been playing official Tests against New
Zealand for more than 40 years, the West Indies, India and

Pakistan for 20: but apart from a single confrontation immediately after the war, the Australians had not deigned to do so. They had treated the New Zealanders as the poor relations of Australasian cricket, the second-class citizens of the Antipodes, to be fobbed off at suitable intervals with a 'B' Australian side. In most other fields, friendly rivalry between these two near neighbours, despite their disparity in size and population, was intense. But in a cricket sense the Australians had turned up their noses, evincing a hurtful and uncharacteristic snobbery. This left both teams, in those early months of 1974, with something to prove — Australia that her judgement had been right, New Zealand that it had been utterly wrong.

Australia was the strongest of all cricketing nations, stronger even than England or the West Indies; that much, in New Zealand at least, was accepted. Indeed Australian supremacy was greatly admired. But that supremacy had not stopped Australia from playing official Tests against South Africa, India and Pakistan, and at various times all these countries had emerged victorious. Australian ostracism of New Zealand in international cricket looked very much like fraternal jealousy, the reluctance of the older brother to enter into direct competition with the younger. Australian superiority, although real enough, should be put to the test; it should not be used to avoid the risk of defeat.

No one resented the Australian attitude more than a 26-year-old New Zealander who had already been playing for his country for six years. He did not accept that he and his team-mates were not good enough for the Australians. And he was a young man of some determination. As a youth in Otago he had worked nights in a bakery to save the passage money for a trip to England to take up the offer of a trial with Warwickshire. He had been about to leave for England when Mike Smith, the Warwickshire secretary, warned him that his county's allowance of overseas players was complete. Despite this shattering intelligence the young man took the gamble, Warwickshire recommended him to other counties, and he accepted the first offer that came. The county was Worcestershire, the name of the immigrant Glenn Turner. He was then just 19.

Within a year he established himself in county cricket, returning each winter to his homeland, either to play in club matches
and for Otago in the Plunket Shield, or to tour with the national
side. Playing in England did not blunt his patriotism, rather it
sharpened his perspective, so that he saw the more clearly the
arrogance of Australia in denying New Zealand Test status. He
felt that his countrymen acquiesced in this rejection all too
readily. New Zealand had beaten every other cricketing nation
except England, and even that was a consummation that could
not be long delayed.[1]

Compounding his anger was the meek way the New Zealand
administrators accepted invitations to take part in Australian
one-day competitions on an equal footing with the State sides.
They even seemed grateful to be asked. Admittedly New Zealand
were suffered to come in at the semi-final stage, after two of the
five States had been eliminated, but this was no more than a sop
to their pride. Turner felt that by taking part in Australian
inter-State one-day cricket they were in danger of surrendering
their national identity.

One of the reasons for accepting the invitation, so it was said,
was to prove their ability. But they had done that already, in the
West Indies, in India, and in Pakistan. Playing in this competition
they were in a Catch-22 situation. If they won, then so they
ought to. If they lost, then their claims for parity were exposed.
In any case, to put their cricketing reputation on the line in a
one-day match, which any well-organised side might win, was
self-destructive.

However much Turner's view may have been a minority one,
he was not alone in looking forward eagerly to the first full tour
of Australia, arranged for the season 1973-74, and the return visit
to New Zealand by the Australians that was to follow. Although
Australia, as undisputed world champions, unbeaten in 14 Tests,
would be doubly determined not to submit, the New Zealand
players, their confidence bolstered by the recent tour of England,
believed they could win.

[1] It came at Wellington four years later, in 1978.

That 1973 tour had been an extraordinary one for Turner, starting as it did with an outstanding personal triumph, the unique feat in post-war English cricket of scoring 1,000 runs in May — or more correctly, before the end of May, since a third of the runs were scored in April. It ended with over 1,000 runs for Worcestershire in the last six weeks, from mid-July to early September. But sandwiched between these two substantial chunks of run-getting was the thinnest of Test Match spread, and it was these failures which made the biggest impact back home. He had peaked too early, and by the end of May he felt flat. When the first Test came along in June — one of the truly great Tests, in which New Zealand, chasing 479 to win, lost by 38 runs — he was mentally tired, unable to rekindle the motivation. Had he made any sort of contribution in either innings New Zealand must surely have won. In the second (drawn) Test he failed again, and in the third and final game he failed in the vital first innings, when Congdon at last won the toss. His second-innings 81, not one of his best, came too late to redeem his failures. His Test average of 23 was in striking contrast to his overall tour average of 62 and his subsequent average for Worcestershire of 74, and his dedication to New Zealand cricket was questioned. He had never made a Test hundred in front of his home crowd, he had suffered much at the hands of New Zealand commentators for slow scoring, and he felt less the local boy who had made good than the prophet who was not appreciated in his own country. This was something he was determined to redress in the coming New Zealand season.

Repenting of past churlishness, the Australian Big Brother had recanted handsomely in agreeing to six Tests, three in each country, starting in Australia. New Zealand opened their tour campaign with matches against all four eastern States, and then came the first Test, staged at Melbourne. But meanwhile, in the second State match, at Sydney, Turner was fielding at slip when one of the New South Wales openers top-edged a ball from Richard Hadlee which flew like an arrow at his head. Misjudgements of pace and height on Australian wickets had been general among the New Zealand slip-fielders, and Turner was no exception. In trying to take the catch he moved his head, lost the flight, and broke the knuckle-joint of the little finger of his right hand. The hand was put in plaster, he took no further part in the match, and his absence helped the State side to record an easy victory. He then missed the next two State games, both of which were lost. This calamitous start to the tour provided an 'I told you so' corroboration for Australians, at the same time increasing the pressure on Turner, not yet completely recovered from his injury, to play in the Melbourne Test.

Even in the first match, against Victoria, Turner had failed to find his touch, and that was three weeks earlier. With no match practice since then, and with his knuckle still tender, he expected to stand down. But partly because several top players, for business reasons, had been unable to make the trip, Turner's position in the side was crucial.

For all the resolute play of the captain, Bevan Congdon, Turner was potentially New Zealand's top batsman, one of only two players around whom a big score was likely to be built. Although modest and unassuming off the field, Turner had no false modesty about his ability on it, and in addition to outside pressure he had his own conscience to satisfy.

The particular hazard facing opening batsmen in Australia was extra bounce, which meant that rapped knuckles were to be expected. Turner would have liked to wait for the second Test, which followed directly after the first, giving his finger another week to heal; but with medical advice favourable, the pressure on him to play became irresistible. Without mincing words, he was talked into it.

The Australian opening bowlers at Melbourne were Tony Dell and Gary Gilmour, both left-arm fast-medium, and Dell especially, from his height of 6' 4", extracted considerable bounce. After Australia had declared at 462 for eight, Turner was hit almost at once on his injured hand by a rising ball from Dell, shaking up the injury so that he could scarcely hold the bat. He knew he would eventually have to retire for repairs, but first he conceived it as his duty to see off the new ball. If he did no more than that he would have contributed usefully, and he might be able to come back later. But soon another kicker from Dell had him caught at first slip.

One look at his damaged hand was enough. Back it went into a splint, and there was no question of his batting again. New Zealand lost by an innings, which after their showing against the State sides looked about par for the course. The only encouragement was the batting of wicket-keeper Ken Wadsworth, who carried the fight to the enemy in an innings of 80.

The three days between the defeat at Melbourne and the start of the second Test at Sydney gave Turner no chance of recovering, and as a result he missed a game which, with one day to go, looked certain to provide New Zealand with the much-desired first victory. Then the weather intervened. Australia, facing the last day 425 behind with two wickets already gone, were saved by the rain.

An interlude in Tasmania gave Turner a chance to play himself back into form, but against more demanding opposition in Perth he was twice dismissed cheaply by Graham McKenzie, and he played little part in the tourists' first win. Nevertheless he was included in the side for the final Test of the series in Adelaide.

Turner himself, as vice-captain, had a voice in that selection; he knew he had to play. This was the crucial game. His teammates had given the Australians a fright at Sydney, and a victory at Adelaide would square the series, giving New Zealand cricket an important boost. Yet he could not share in the general enthusiasm, could not find the motivation. The thought of Adelaide alone was bad enough. The prospect of three more Tests in New Zealand appalled him.

*   *

After the 1971–72 tour of the West Indies, when he had made four double hundreds, including two in the Tests, Turner had returned to the English season with misgiving. Then, as now, cricket had meant everything to him, it was his whole life. There were no questions in his mind about whether or not he wanted his entire horizon to be dominated by cricket; he took that for granted. Questions of that nature were to come only later. But at that time, too, he had felt stale, mentally and physically drained, and he had thought he needed a break. That hadn't been altogether true; he had kept on playing, and gradually, almost without noticing it, he had found he was making runs and enjoying his cricket again. That regeneration, indeed, had been a watershed in his development as a player.

Just as New Zealanders in international cricket tended to think negatively, avoiding losing rather than going all out to win, so Turner had based his game on a watertight defence and the elimination of risk. This had been the foundation of his success in the West Indies. But his marathon innings there had given him neither enjoyment nor satisfaction. Safety-first methods, when adopted by both sides, produced a war of attrition. He didn't mind grinding away for hour after hour when circumstances demanded it, but he was beginning to realise that he lacked both the mental and physical stamina to continue such methods throughout his career.

This first became apparent to him in the West Indies, when he found it impossible to sleep properly after a long innings, especially when not out at close of play. Alcohol didn't relax him. It sent him into a drugged sleep from which he awoke in the middle of the night with no hope of sleeping again. Relaxation had to come from the game itself.

The demands of one-day cricket in England, and especially of the 40-over Sunday League games, where shots had to be played from the start, had already revealed an unsuspected brilliance in his play. It was this side of his game that he resolved to emancipate. When necessary he would still graft as hard as the next man, but otherwise he would go for his shots. Thus in 1972 he became a much more exciting player, finding just the right blend of concentration and aggression. *Wisden*, at the end of that year, while ranking him among the world's top three opening batsmen, was anxious that its rating should not obscure his 'carefully planned switch from painstaking defence to stroke play of immense vision.' They added the opinion that no player in the world could have bettered the effortless flow of off-side strokes which helped to bring him three hundreds in four days against Warwickshire at Edgbaston, two in the county championship and one in the Sunday league. Mike Smith, who fielded out to the two championship hundreds, must have watched ruefully.

That exciting season, together with the triumphs and disappointments of the 1973 tour of England and the traumas occasioned by his recent injury, were things of the past. Somehow he had to revitalise his approach for the Adelaide Test. But in both innings of that game he played a loose shot when he was going well. He was not one to look for excuses for dismissal, believing that most batsmen got themselves out, but here his failures seemed more than normally self-inflicted, inexplicable lapses when he was set. Contributions of 20 and 34 were little help in answering an Australian score of 477, and again New Zealand lost by an innings. Australians, seldom guilty of taking reputations on trust, dismissed Turner as much over-rated.

The advantage Congdon's men had established in the second Test, however, had gone some way to curing the diffidence that had so often assailed New Zealanders at the highest level, and they were by no means downcast. Under their own conditions, with most of their missing players available, they would redeem themselves. Yet for home series they suffered from a unique disadvantage. The Plunket Shield matches were concentrated into a three-to-four week period either side of Christmas, and they were already over. The Adelaide Test did not finish until the end of January, and only those players engaged in the four warm-up matches arranged for the touring Australians would get proper match practice. About half the side benefited from these games, but Glenn Turner was not among them. His only innings after returning to New Zealand were in a club match, when he scored 3, and in a charity match, when he scored 7.

Turner knew from experience that if he could have kept on playing the old enthusiasm would almost certainly have returned. What effect the further lay-off would have on him was problematical. There were some who had written off his chances already. Invited to be a guest on a sports talk-back programme,

answering listeners' questions, he was interrogated by a caller
who claimed to be speaking for many New Zealand cricket fans.
'You may be able to do all right in provincial and county
matches,' suggested the caller, 'but you're no good in Tests.
That's what they're saying. What do you say to that?'

Turner admitted that he had had an unhappy series in Australia.
'What about the series in England?' pressed the caller. It emerged
that a friend of his had wagered a substantial sum that Turner
wouldn't total a hundred runs in the series, and he had only
narrowly lost the bet. Turner objected that it was unfair to take
a short period of his career in isolation, and his commentator
host, Alan Richards, intervened to remind the caller of Turner's
overall Test Match average of 45; but the riling did Turner's
motivation no harm.

In the first of the three home Tests, at Wellington, the
Australians, as already recorded, made 511 for six before declar-
ing. They made the runs quickly, and they aimed to bowl New
Zealand out twice. Turner, preparing to open, was still concerned
about his mental approach. 'I knew I wasn't as sharp and as
keyed up as I felt I ought to be.' The danger of the more relaxed
approach he had cultivated in 1972 was that it could degenerate
at times into light-heartedness and even frivolity. He had to
reassert his old ability to graft: that was what was wanted now.
In fact he made 79, and in the eyes of his critics he batted
beautifully; but it was in his new style rather than his old. He
was reasonably but not wholly satisfied. In that situation he
should have got a hundred, then started again, planning his
innings from session to session as he had done in the West
Indies. Fortunately Congdon and Hastings both got centuries,
and long before the final day deadlock was reached.

The preliminaries to the second Test, to be played on 'Cranky'
Cromb's greentop at Christchurch, were no more propitious. It
was the Australians who got the star billing and the most modern
and fashionable hotel; that was inevitable. But the favouritism
did not end there. There had been heavy rain at Christchurch,
and when the New Zealand team arrived at Lancaster Park to
practise they found the Australians had been given the only dry

net. No doubt it was right that the visitors should have first go, but nothing had been arranged for the home side and Congdon and his men had to be content with fielding practice. Experiences like this could only aggravate any complexes that remained.

An early morning drizzle on the first day, Friday 9th March, saturated the outfield and delayed the 11 o'clock start, but when the covers were removed at 11.30 the wicket rolled out green and playable. None of the rain had got under the covers, but those who knew the Lancaster Park wicket were astonished at its texture. There was a lot of moisture in it, and it was so heavily grassed that it looked as though it would never dry out, anyway without several days of sunshine. But the atmosphere was damp, and such sunshine seemed unlikely. 'What a wicket!' said Turner, when he got back to the dressing room. 'It's going to seam all over the place.' For this he was quietly reprimanded by Congdon. 'That may please the bowlers, but suppose we have to bat first? It's bad psychology.' Turner knew Congdon as a hard man, but he knew he was right, and he shut up.

Play was to start at 2.20, and Congdon, debating with vice-captain Turner whether to bat or to field, called Brian Hastings into their discussions; Hastings had played a lot of his cricket at Lancaster Park. Temptingly green though the pitch was, it looked to Turner as though it wouldn't change much all through. Congdon wasn't sure how much help his bowlers would get, but he wanted to give them every chance. 'Our attack is based on pace. I think we should bowl first.' Hastings agreed. Turner, still doubtful if the toss would prove crucial, reminded Congdon of his habitual ill-luck with the coin. 'You don't need to worry anyway,' he joked. 'You couldn't win a toss if you tried.' Congdon promptly went out with Ian Chappell, proved Turner wrong, and invited the Australians to bat.

Lancaster Park, like most of the major cricket grounds in New Zealand, was basically a rugby ground, enclosed by stands and terraces and capable of holding some 50,000 people. Despite its size it boasted an intimate atmosphere, ideal for cricket, largely because of a trick of acoustics. Sound seemed to echo back from the stands and reverberate, bringing the spectators closer to the game. A good attendance for a Test Match might be no more than ten or fifteen thousand, but it gave the illusion of a full stadium.

There were 3¼ hours left for play when the left-arm Collinge opened the bowling from the southern end — the end opposite the pavilion — and he soon bowled Stackpole with an in-swinging yorker which the batsman deflected on to his stumps. Thus at 8 for one Redpath was joined by his captain. Sharing the attack was Richard Hadlee, the younger of the two Hadlee brothers in the New Zealand side. (The other was Dayle, while a third, Barry, was twelfth man.) But Hadlee failed to find his rhythm or direction, and neither bowler made the best use of the undoubted life and movement in the pitch. Even so the batsmen — especially Redpath — were continually playing and missing. Ian Chappell's technique looked the sounder, but at 45 Richard Hadlee held one back and Chappell, going back and across, missed an intended pull and was bowled behind his legs.

Although neither bounce nor movement was excessive, the wicket continued to assist the bowler, and Greg Chappell, then the world's top batsman, spent 89 minutes reaching 25. Then he slashed at the slow-medium short-of-a-length dribblers of Congdon, and Howarth in the gully brought off a spectacular one-handed catch. Richard Hadlee returned to get the 20-year-old Ian Davis lbw, and with the first ball of the last over of the day he brought one back between bat and pad to bowl Walters. At 128 for five, with Redpath, the only surviving specialist batsman, 55 not out, Congdon's decision to field had been well rewarded.

Aggression next morning by Marsh started an Australian fight back, but after helping to add 53 with Redpath he went down on one knee to sweep Congdon and was bowled. Then Collinge took a superb return catch to dismiss Redpath. Two more wickets fell cheaply, and Australia with nine men out were still four short of 200. Then their opening bowlers, Walker and Dymock, added 27 for the last wicket, taking the total to 223. Congdon had kept his fast attack — Collinge and the Hadlee brothers — going throughout, apart from eleven overs from himself, and he had not used the slow-left-arm Howarth at all. He, Collinge and the younger Hadlee had each taken three wickets and Dayle Hadlee one.

By playing two spinners, Kevin O'Keeffe and Ashley Mallett, Australia had gone for the more balanced attack, but this resulted in the exclusion of Gary Gilmour. It elevated Greg Chappell to third seamer, with Doug Walters as an occasional stand-breaker with his medium-paced out-swingers. This placed a considerable burden on the two faster men, Max Walker and Geoff Dymock. Both were young and strong, and it is true that Greg Chappell, with his high action and extra bounce, was an underrated bowler who had finished third that season in the Australian averages. Without being more than medium pace he bowled a good bouncer, which batsmen learned to look for, and this deterred them from getting onto the front foot. A tendency to play half-forward to him could be fatal when he got the ball to swing away. But it was to Walker and Dymock that Ian Chappell would look to work their way through the hard core of the New Zealand line-up.

Max Walker had been Australia's leading bowler in the 1972-73 tour of the West Indies, and with Lillee injured and Massie ineffective he had taken 26 wickets in the Tests and bowled his side to victory. 6' 4" tall, he specialised in big looping in-duckers that were quicker than they looked. In spite of his in-swinging action he could also make the ball hold its line and occasionally leave the bat off the seam. An awkward, almost wrong-footed delivery did not reduce his stamina, and he was a genuinely attacking bowler who aimed at the stumps. His opening partner, the consistent Geoff Dymock, bowled left arm over and aimed to slant the ball across the right-hand batsman to a packed slip and gully field. This was only his third Test, all against New Zealand, but he had finished second behind Ray Bright in the Australian averages that season and had been the only bowler to take 50 wickets. These were the men whom Turner and his opening partner, John Parker (also of Worcestershire), faced when they began the New Zealand reply 45 minutes before lunch on the second day.

Turner was not too worried about not having had a net

between the two Tests. In the nets he tended to play freely — too freely — and he was then apt to carry that freedom with him into the middle. On this wicket it was going to be difficult to eliminate error, but he was determined to restrict his back-lift, to play close to himself, and to leave everything alone that he didn't have to play.

The atmosphere was still damp, the wicket showed no signs of drying out, and the ball was continually deviating. A rash of playing and missing disturbed and inhibited both batsmen, and Turner, scratchy and out of touch, took half an hour to open his score. Then he got going with a square cut and a straight drive for 4 and a steer through gully for 3. Despite magnificent seam bowling by Walker, with Dymock scarcely less menacing, the batsmen somehow survived until lunch, when New Zealand were 21 for nought. An Australian break-through in this period could have been impossible to repair.

Nothing seemed more unlikely, in these opening overs, than that the opening stand would reach 50, but after lunch the score was taken to 59, albeit precariously, before Parker was lbw to Dymock for 18. John Morrison helped to add another 31 before being undone by Greg Chappell's high bounce, and when Congdon was caught at slip off Walker, New Zealand were 104 for three. Brian Hastings, always an attacking player, went for his shots, and another 32 were added before he flicked once too often at Walker and was caught by Marsh.

The next man in was the 21-year-old Jeremy Coney, who had joined the New Zealand touring party in Australia as a reinforcement when Turner was injured and shown such a good temperament that he had kept his place in the home series. Walker and Greg Chappell were relieved by Dymock and Walters, and another 35 were added before Coney fell for Dymock's away slant. Everyone was contributing usefully, but with the fourth innings to face New Zealand needed to make at least 300. 171 for five, still more than 50 behind, was not enough.

Throughout these partnerships Turner was playing what one writer described as 'an astonishing innings'. He was, said the writer, 'quite unlike his careful, cultured self, playing and missing

153

quite regularly.' *Wisden* believed that this infirmity was 'as much a tribute to the antagonistic and skilful bowling of Walker and Dymock as it was a reflection of his [Turner's] own frailties.' Turner wasn't playing as he had hoped, but he was determined not to let it upset him. In conditions like this one couldn't possibly middle the ball all the time. He had seen the same thing happen to Redpath.

The difference between Turner and the other New Zealand batsmen was that they were eventually getting a touch whereas he was either middling the ball or missing it altogether. He claimed no credit for this, but he knew he had to fight his way through it. 'Even if it takes me all day,' he said to himself, 'I'll keep going until it comes right.'

The pressure exerted on Turner was not confined to hostile bowling and thoughtful, aggressive field-placing. Australian exasperation at Turner's survival went far beyond mere gestures of frustration. They missed no chance of letting him know, by a stage-whispered barrage of disparagement, how lucky he was. This 'sledging', as it was called, may not have had anything vicious about it, but it was deliberately aimed at discomfiting Turner and undermining his confidence and concentration. This was the further test they were putting him to, and later in his career he would learn to sledge back. But now he preferred not to get into a slanging match, lest it affect his composure. The more they got at him, the more he gritted his teeth. And as time passed he began to feel they were helping him, bringing the best out of him. Suddenly he was hitting the ball in the middle, and when the flaxen-haired Ken Wadsworth joined him with half an hour to go he was 85 not out.

He tried to forget about the hundred, but when a single in the penultimate over of the day took him to 99 he could hardly do so. He had a whole over from Dymock — they were eight-ball overs — to reach his hundred that night, and the crowd-noise accompaniment was fluctuating like the dark and light passages of a symphony. Determined to foil the achievement, or anyway to delay it until the morrow, Ian Chappell moved a slip to

'Whatever happened to that one?'

reinforce the cover cordon and beckoned everyone up to save one.

Dymock bowled, Wadsworth backed up enthusiastically, and several times both batsmen moved yards out of their crease as the fielders closed in. The batsmen seemed like puppets, manipulated on the string of crowd hysteria, but in fact neither was every really committed, and they were always able to scramble back. With the last ball of the day Dymock dropped short outside the off stump, perhaps deliberately, and Turner flailed, getting the ball full on the meat. But the shot went straight to backward point and there was no chance of a run. Thus the second day ended with New Zealand 194 for five, Turner 99, Wadsworth 9.

No player could claim to be accustomed to being 99 not out overnight, although strangely enough Turner had had the experience before, in a Test Match too, against Pakistan at Dacca in 1969. On that occasion he had safely completed his first Test century next day. Now, with his side still 29 behind, he had to do much more than reach three figures. Prospects of getting the substantial lead they needed rested largely on him.

Turner had never been one to dream beforehand of success, to visualise the magic figures on the score-board, and to anticipate the acclaim. Obviously it was better to leave the field with a hundred than with 99, but he slept well that night. 'I shan't take any chances,' he told himself. 'It'll come.'

On that Sunday morning — the third day — Ian Chappell did all he could to ensure that it didn't. The longer he could keep Turner on 99, the more likely it was that he would make a rash shot, or go for a run that wasn't quite there. Chappell tried every conceivable trick, slowing the game down, adjusting the field, playing on Turner's impatience by instructing his bowlers to aim down the leg side and wide of the off stump, with a ration of bouncers just out of safe reach. While the rest of his side fielded like terriers, he himself crouched close in at silly mid-off.

It seemed to Turner, in the agonising half-hour that followed, that every bad ball within reach of the bat went to Wadsworth.

He was thankful to Wadsworth, though, for keeping the score moving. That relieved some of the pressure.

The tension in the ground had reached unbearable proportions the previous night, but then, as each threat of a run-out abated, it had been relieved by laughter. Now the atmosphere was suffocating.

Every time Turner faced the bowling the crowd held its breath. He had been batting for 36 minutes, and had received 35 balls, when at last Greg Chappell strayed from a strictly defensive line and length and Turner's forcing stroke eluded the field. There was time, as the fuse burnt through and the ground exploded, to run 2.

He had completed his first Test hundred before his own countrymen, and they were making it plain that they had never really meant to belittle him, that past disappointments were forgiven, just as they in their turn looked for forgiveness from him. New Zealand were still 10 behind, and many more runs were wanted, but this, for Turner, was a moment to savour. He had scarcely extinguished the glow of achievement when a shortish ball from Greg Chappell, wide enough to have left alone, found him playing too far from his body. The ball lifted, he got an edge, and he watched it carry to Stackpole's right hand at second slip. There it stuck, and he was out for 101.

One correspondent described Turner's innings as 'the worst century he has probably made'. But this scarcely took account of the wicket and the bowlers who exploited it. Not every great innings need be chanceless, masterly, studded with glorious strokes, tearing the bowling apart. Dismissed for an inadequate total, Ian Chappell's Australians had done all they could to get back into the game, using every weapon to hand. The focus of their hostility had been Turner, and he had made a hundred. It might not have been a match-winning innings, but it had kept New Zealand on terms.

The total at that point was 213 for six, and the tail added another 42, taking the score to 255 and giving a slender lead of 32. Wadsworth was second top scorer with 24, and Richard

Hadlee made 23. Apart from Turner, none of the specialist batsmen made 20.

How Ian Chappell judged the wicket is illustrated by the bowling figures. All but three of the 71 overs of the innings were bowled by seamers. Mallett was the exception, and O'Keeffe did not bowl at all. Even at this stage the omission of Gilmour looked a critical error.

By lunchtime that Sunday Australia in their second innings were eleven for nought, slowly working their way towards clearing the deficit. But soon after lunch Stackpole, sadly out of touch in what was to prove his last series, was caught on the leg side from the finest of deflections, and Australia were 12 for one. Redpath was not far from being out in the same way, and then Ian Chappell, moving too far across his stumps in aiming to turn Collinge to the on, got so far inside the line that he missed the ball altogether and was bowled leg stump by what was virtually a yorker. It was a dreadful stroke in any circumstances, and no one looked more disgusted with it than Chappell. As he stamped off to an unsympathetic reception the score-board read 26 for two.

With Redpath and Greg Chappell together the arrears were cleared. But only just. At eight minutes past two, with the score at 33, Richard Hadlee moved one away from Greg Chappell, who followed it trance-like, apparently trying to cut. So sure had Coney's catching been at first slip since his hurried introduction to Test cricket that Hadlee shouted his appeal as the ball left the bat. Coney made no mistake, and Australia with three wickets down were only one run ahead.

The contrast between the performance of the Chappell brothers at Wellington and at Christchurch was extraordinary. 646 between them for three times out at Wellington, 52 for four times out at Christchurch. Only a side of exceptional batting strength could withstand such a slump.

Coming in to face the crisis was the 20-year-old Ian Davis, lucky to be persevered with after an impetuous start in Test cricket which had brought him only 88 runs in six innings. Undisturbed by the uproar, he batted with sensible restraint, and with Redpath cautious but determined a fight-back developed. Redpath, looking much safer than in the first innings, pushed for ones and twos, seeking the gaps, and gradually Davis became more adventurous. Redpath reached his fifty, and the hundred partnership came in two hours. Two minutes later Davis completed his maiden Test fifty, and the see-saw nature of the contest had taken yet another alternation. Then came a bizarre incident which disturbed the balance yet again.

Glenn Turner has recorded that Richard Hadlee had a habit, when he bowled a bad ball, of emitting a groan of chagrin and remorse which often carried to the wicket-keeper and the slips, as it did on this occasion. The ball was a long hop, outside the off stump, and Redpath, mistaking Hadlee's snort for a shout of no-ball, cut it as hard as he could. The ball flew straight to Howarth in the gully, and Howarth held on.

Redpath, a noted walker, stood his ground. Surely the umpire had called no-ball. Umpire John Hastie, shaking his head, decided that the spirit of the laws had not been infringed, and he gave Redpath out.

This maddening misfortune was followed by two brilliant catches, swinging the game perceptibly New Zealand's way. Davis pulled another long hop from Richard Hadlee with tremendous force towards the fence, and it was not until the boundary had been scoured for the ball that the crowd realised that Congdon had pouched the catch at mid-wicket. 139 for four with the departure of Redpath had become 142 for five, and when Marsh crashed a full toss from Dayle Hadlee straight back over the bowler's head and Hadlee, following through and off-balance, stuck out a hand and found he had caught it, Australia were 160 for six. That was only 128 in front, and at least another hundred were needed to make a game of it.

All day the ground had simmered with excitement, and now, with a home win becoming a probability, crowd involvement became partisan to the point of ill manners. Good-humoured banter directed at the Australians degenerated into ridicule and abuse, becoming especially offensive from a hooligan element in the No. 6 Stand at the southern end. The police, thinly spread, could do little but tolerate the throwing of beer cans and the brawling and skirmishing of rival groups as the barracking became raucous.

If there was one man not likely to be intimidated by the situation it was Doug Walters; he had come in at No. 6 and seen first Davis and then Marsh lose their wickets. Because of his known frailty outside the off stump Walters on this wicket seemed vulnerable, but he was not the sort of player to be affected by theory. Joined by Kevin O'Keeffe, he made 48 runs in the next 84 minutes, far and away the fastest scoring of the match so far, silencing the larrikins and re-establishing the Australian foothold on the tightrope. By stumps Walters (52) and O'Keeffe (6) had put on 51, and Australia at 211 for six were 179 in front. This was more like it. Another 60 or 70 next morning would complete the transformation and set New Zealand a formidable task.

In fact the following day, Monday, was a rest day, giving both sides ample time to work out their methods of salvation. The captains agreed that Tuesday morning's cricket was likely to decide the issue. The key figure was obviously Walters. 'If we can get 250 on,' said Ian Chappell, 'we'll be right in the game. There'll be a lot of pressure on New Zealand chasing that many runs. I think we could bowl well enough to prevent them getting them.' Bevan Congdon didn't want to have to face a target of more than 200, but he felt the dénouement would depend not so much on how many runs were required as on how his team handled the sort of pressure the Australians would apply. The New Zealand record in such crises was poor. 'If we can handle the pressure to make 200,' thought Congdon, 'we could probably handle it for more.'

When play resumed after the rest day, Congdon sprang something of a surprise by opening the attack with the Hadlee brothers, keeping Collinge in reserve. The wicket, although drier, still favoured the seamers, but Walters, playing with the same authority as before, began with two 4's, and O'Keeffe, too, was middling the ball with stubborn application. Between them the Hadlee brothers stemmed the early flow of runs, but the necessary 21 to give a lead of 200 were confidently added. The target of 250 that the Australians were seeking had begun to look attainable when, in Dayle Hadlee's fourth over, Walters attempted a leg-side flick through mid-wicket. The ball kept low, Walters failed to make contact, and umpire Monteith gave him out lbw. The lead remained at exactly 200. Walters had batted six minutes short of two hours for his 65 and hit ten 4's.

The choice of Dayle Hadlee to open the assault proved an inspired one. In a twelve-ball burst he followed up his trapping of Walters by getting Walker caught at third slip and Dymock caught behind. From 232 for six the score plunged to 239 for nine, and only a stubborn last-wicket stand between O'Keeffe and Mallett adjusted the scales. They added 20 precious runs before Richard Hadlee returned with the new ball to get Mallett caught at the wicket. The total of 259 was the highest of the three innings so far, and the target of 228, roughly half-way between the hopes and fears of the two sides, might have been set by computer. 228 did not sound too daunting a total; but it was more than New Zealand had ever made in a fourth innings to win.

None of the New Zealanders harboured any illusions about the magnitude of their task. With the best part of two days to go there were oceans of time, but it might be that there was too much time, encouraging too defensive an attitude. The runs still had to be got, and with the ball still seaming around it was essential to tackle the task in a controlled but positive manner.

'Can Congdon and his men do it?' This was the question posed by the midday placards as Turner and Parker emerged from the pavilion. For the third time on three successive playing days, opening batsmen had to face a brief but tense pre-lunch period. This one was due to last forty minutes, in a highly-charged atmosphere, with the fielders boosting the bowlers almost every ball with extravagant praise as they threw everything in for the break-through. Somehow lunch was reached without mishap — indeed almost without alarm — at 21 for nought, Turner 12, Parker 6. That was the first hurdle cleared.

Turner shared two priceless virtues with another great opening batsman, Len Hutton. First, he played uncompromisingly straight. 'He is one of the few players in the game who picks up his bat straight and brings it down the same way,' wrote Tom Graveney. Second, he was never stroke-bound. Many fine players, having resolved to concentrate on defence, have been apt to get into a groove, from which they could not break out. Their strokes atrophied and they were unable to middle the loose ball when it came. Like Sir Leonard, Turner was never completely becalmed. He could always play shots.

In resolving to revert to his pre-1972 style, Turner was putting no extra pressure on his partners, as he had sometimes done in three-day cricket. If the Australians were going to win, they must be made to earn their victory: that was his attitude. Let's make damn sure we don't give it away.

Both men continued in confident style after lunch, and with Parker scoring slightly the faster, they registered their second 50 partnership of the match, just the foundation that Congdon had hoped for. But Walker, in a superbly hostile spell, was still posing all sorts of problems, and at 51 he produced a ball which held its line and perhaps moved fractionally away, and Parker edged it fatally to Marsh.

John Morrison, who came next, found Walker's line difficult to judge. It was not an uncommon experience against this bowler. Determined to leave the ball alone whenever he could, he shouldered arms in Walker's next over and as the ball seamed back viciously off the wicket he was trapped in front. That was 55 for two.

On the tour of England, Congdon had been his country's premier batsman in the Tests, and he played himself in carefully now. He had been in half an hour without quite establishing himself when Turner drove Walker fractionally wide of Redpath's left hand in the covers. It was a brisk but not dangerous run, and he called Congdon to come. Turner set off at once, but Congdon, not quite so sure of the angle, said 'No.' The refusal came late, Turner was committed, and Redpath was gathering the ball. 'Come on!' yelled Turner, and then, with Congdon still hesitating, '*You must come!*' It was a despairing cry, and Congdon, greatly to his credit, answered it, to be run out by yards.

Feeling that Turner was in and he was not, Congdon had sacrificed his wicket. But he could not suppress a tortured look at Turner as he passed. All the advantage of the good start had been dissipated, and at 62 for 3 the New Zealand goose, if not yet cooked, was ripe for the plucking.

The next man in, Brian Hastings, although not of robust physique, was a fine stroke-player who liked to attack. With the inexperienced Coney at No. 6, followed by Wadsworth and the bowlers, a challenging fourth-wicket stand looked like New Zealand's last chance.

Although a nervous starter, Hastings, like Turner, played admirably straight and was in many ways a model cricketer. Cheerful and sociable off the field, where his ability to relax with a gin-and-tonic after the game was a byword, he had shown an innate toughness during his Test career, belying his gentle exterior. The manner of Congdon's dismissal had upset Turner, and it was up to Hastings to try to assuage in Turner any sense of guilt. Who had been fundamentally at fault didn't matter; for the moment it was better to let Congdon take the blame. 'What did he do that for?' asked Turner, looking for sympathy, and Hastings provided it. Turner, he knew, was not an emotional person, and the main thing was to steady him down. 'Let's forget about it,' said Hastings. 'We've got a job to do.'

Walker's post-lunch spell was his best of the match so far, and he never looked like being mastered. But the batsmen kept him out, and eventually he had to be rested. The nasty lift and bounce that Greg Chappell extracted was studiously avoided, and when Mallett bowled, his off-spin was easily smothered. It was not a spinners' wicket, and as the partnership developed, with Turner the senior partner and Hastings giving his fine attacking shots freer rein, Turner reached his half-century and the stand, too, passed the 50 mark. That left 116 to win.

The Australian out-cricket never faltered, and although Chappell kept up the pressure with an attacking field, many of the batsmen's most flowing square and cover drives were cut off, the young Ian Davis, patrolling the backward point area, saving many runs. Turner was playing beautifully now, rarely missing an opportunity to push the score along, and both he and Hastings cultivated an aggressive attitude which did not always bring runs but which wrested the initiative from Chappell and his bowlers. These two were doing for New Zealand what Redpath and Davis had done for Australia the previous day, and the more they asserted themselves the more the Australians had to put up with taunts from the crowd.

Chappell's lack of a third seamer was never more regretted than now. He was obliged to use Mallett again. With twelve minutes to go Hastings, stepping in to drive the off-spinner, suddenly lifted him over the top — a vast, soaring blow wide of mid-on. Turner, aware that there was no one out there, did not need to run, and instead he followed the flight of the ball. It landed just inside the boundary and ricocheted first bounce into the lower tiers of No. 6 Stand. It was from this area that the beer cans had been thrown earlier in the game, and it may have been no more than alcoholic exuberance — or myopia — that prompted the enthusiastic signalling of a 6.

Umpire Monteith, unsighted, accepted the signal and passed it on to the scorers, but Turner, having followed the flight, knew better. 'Did you lose sight of that one, Bob?' he asked.

Monteith, momentarily confused, but anxious to correct an error if one had been made, answered with some asperity. 'Why, why, why?'

'Actually it bounced inside the boundary.'

'Oh — thanks very much.'

Monteith was about to correct his signal when Ian Chappell, sprinting up from slip, intervened. From a distance it must have seemed to him that in the signalling of 6 Turner and Monteith were in agreement, even possibly collusion, and with the game in the balance, Chappell, not renowned for keeping his cool, exploded. Whatever had happened it had nothing to do with Turner, and to that extent Chappell was in the right. But without stopping to enquire further he rounded on Turner and told him, with suitable embellishments, to keep his nose out of it. When

Turner tried to explain that the mistake had been sorted out and that Monteith was about to signal 4, Chappell became abusive. The mistake was duly corrected, but even when Turner got down to the striker's end and tried to explain to Rod Marsh what had happened, Chappell let fly with such a torrent of abuse that Turner walked away from the wicket, refusing to take guard until he stopped. This calmed things down and the game proceeded.

Whether this incident had any bearing on what followed is an imponderable. But in the last over of the day, when Hastings had added 115 with Turner and the game seemed all but won, he advanced again to Mallett but this time failed to get quite to the pitch. He went through with his shot, the ball eluded his wild, despairing swing, and he was bowled. He did not blame the fracas of a few minutes earlier, however, putting it down to the rush of blood under pressure which all cricketers know. 'I don't know why I did it,' he said, 'but I just did.'

New Zealand thus ended the day 177 for four. The Turner/Hastings stand had lasted 2½ hours, Hastings had made 46, and Turner was not out 85. With six wickets in hand New Zealand needed 51 to win, and they had a whole day to get them; but soon after the start of play next morning a new ball would be due.

Turner made it plain that he expected an apology from Chappell for the personal abuse he had been subjected to, and Congdon put this to Chappell. 'We don't expect politeness in a Test Match,' Congdon was quoted as saying, 'but that was beyond the limits.' Chappell replied that he would not be apologising. 'I believe what happens on the field should stay there.' Congdon felt that while the incident had undoubtedly affected Turner, it had 'probably made him all the more determined.'

Turner himself would have agreed with that. So far as he was concerned, nothing had changed. They were on the brink of victory, but it wasn't going to happen unless they made it happen. The job still had to be done. Australia needed something dynamic, even with a new ball, to win, but they would strain every sinew to produce it. No amount of 'sledging', and no 'incidents', would deflect him from his purpose.

There was a natural apprehension that such a redoubtable enemy, facing defeat, might pull out something special. But in the New Zealand dressing room on that last morning there was an atmosphere of confidence. Australians, it was said, never knew when they were beaten. They were going to know it now.

It had always been felt that New Zealand cricket wouldn't come of age until the team had beaten England. But to beat the world champions, and especially Australia, was surely as good. Indeed it was probably more important to New Zealanders to beat Australia than anyone else.

Whatever happened, there could scarcely be more than two hours' cricket, and gate charges were reduced to encourage a sizeable crowd. There were 7,000 people in the ground when the game restarted, by which time all roads led to Lancaster Park.

Coney had two balls to face of Mallett's over, and off one of them the batsmen ran a leg-bye. That left exactly 50 to win. The wicket, if not as lively as on the first two days, was still seaming, and the batsmen survived repeated appeals, none of them dangerously close. While Walker bowled two maidens to Coney, Turner took a 2 and a 3 off successive overs from Mallett to take his score to 90. In between overs he advised and encouraged Coney. Then Walker, in his third over of the morning, took the new ball.

Turner padded up to Walker's first delivery, just as Morrison had done the previous day, and the corporate appeal penetrated to the crowds still hurrying into the ground from home and office, spurring them on. One man was in such a hurry to know what had happened that he stopped his car outside the main gate and ran into the ground, leaving the engine running.

John Hastie, the umpire appealed to, had a heart-stopping habit of raising a hand as he counted each ball. For a moment it seemed that he was allowing Walker's appeal. Then he returned his hand to his pocket, steadfastly unmoved.

Unruffled by this escape, Turner steered Walker for 2, then whipped him off his toes for 3 to take his score to 95. Coney, whose classic back-foot defensive shot, body behind the line, was loudly applauded ball after ball though it brought no runs, did not open his score for half an hour. But he was batting intelligently, and he betrayed no anxiety at the run-drought. Eventually he glanced Walker for a single to get off the mark.

Turner, like Coney, was in no hurry, but a wristy stroke off his left hip backward of square brought him to 97. Then Coney, after batting forty minutes for three, hammered a short ball from Dymock through the covers for 4. Growing in confidence, he chopped Walker past point for 2 in the next over and then thumped him to the cover fence to put up the 200. Turner had meanwhile stolen a single to take him to 98.

Walker, who had bowled for 50 minutes, was replaced by Greg Chappell, and Turner, with another single, moved for the second time in the match to 99. This time there could surely be no interruption, no distraction, apart from the inevitable tactical irritations masterminded by Chappell. But Greg Chappell got the last ball of his first over to lift nastily and Coney, trying to avoid it, felt the ball brush his glove. The appeal was almost half-hearted, but umpire Hastie rightly gave Coney out. He had batted for a vital 56 minutes while 29 runs were added, his own share being 14. Thus Turner still languished on 99; but only 22 were now needed for victory.

As Wadsworth replaced Coney, people were still flocking into the ground, intent on seeing the final overs, hungry to see Turner get his hundred.

Dymock had been plugging away all morning with no luck, beating the forward defensive stroke occasionally and sometimes rapping the pad but appealing in vain. Now, with the field brought in for Turner to save the one, he dropped a trifle short. With a square cut that was four all the way Turner completed a superbly disciplined century, sending the crowd into paroxysms of delight. He had batted nearly six hours and had been on the field for all but 68 minutes of the game.

Turner thus became the first New Zealander to score a hundred in each innings of a Test Match. He may well have played greater single innings, but these two centuries may perhaps be aptly described — using innings in its plural sense — as innings of a lifetime.

Being no hypocrite, Turner would have relished this personal triumph whatever the result of the game. But victory, too, was at hand. Cricket was a direct clash of individual skills, batsman versus bowler, man against man, and whereas the bowler was supported by fielders the batsman was alone. Yet it was also a team game, and to enjoy such a triumph and at the same time make a major contribution to the winning of a Test Match against Australia was the ultimate felicity.

Chappell did not put on a 'rabbit' bowler to concede the last few runs, and he earned respect for that. Ignoring the derisive singing of 'Waltzing Matilda' by the larrikins, he fought against defeat to the end. Eventually Wadsworth, moving down the wicket to Greg Chappell, pierced the cover field to make the winning hit, and as the players ran for safety the crowd streamed on to the field. Turner was 110 not out, and New Zealand had won by five wickets. It was an occasion for national pride and rejoicing, and a notice of motion was tabled in the New Zealand Parliament that afternoon congratulating the team on its success.

Most eagerly awaited of all was the reaction of the Australians, and especially of the Australian captain. It was the old story of Jack the Giant-Killer, of David and Goliath, and the Australians weren't going to like it.

No one could have set more snares or employed more stratagems to prevent a New Zealand victory than Ian Chappell, and indeed some thought his gamesmanship, especially his attempts to needle Turner, went beyond acceptable limits. Distaste for 'incidents', too, was not confined to New Zealand, the *Sydney Daily Telegraph* commenting that it was not the first time Chappell had lost his self-control on the field. 'And if the rest of the world believes we are a nation of squealers,' they added, 'who can blame them?'

Others tried to put Chappell's behaviour in perspective. 'Ian Chappell, it turns out, swears,' said the *Sydney Morning Herald*. 'Well, well. How naughty of Australia's Test cricket captain to use rude words in the heat of a Test Match, and to one of those nice New Zealand fellows at that. England's Freddie Trueman would never have done such a thing. . . .'

Chappell himself, so far as incidents on the field were concerned, was as good as his word. And he offered no excuses. 'You blokes bowled pretty well, we played some bad shots, you made some fine catches. We never had enough runs in either innings to look at this Test Match with confidence.'

What about the umpiring? Should the dismissal of Ian Redpath in the second innings have been allowed to stand? The laws of the game gave the umpires discretion when a batsman's concentration was upset by the fielding side. What about the preparation of a green wicket, avowedly deliberate? Chappell was not to be drawn. 'I was always happy with the umpiring. This has been a good cricket wicket.'

What had he to say about Glenn Turner, whose two centuries had overshadowed all else? Would the Australians now accept that he was in world class? Pinpointing the Turner/Hastings stand as the decisive nail in the Australian coffin, Chappell admitted: 'Turner was our stumbling block in both innings. We could bank on getting a wicket at the other end, but never him.

'I am not one to rate batsmen as Nos. 1, 2 or 3, but Turner is a fine batsman and his two centuries foiled us. We could not get that fellow Turner out.'

Tim Caldwell, chairman of the Australian Cricket Board, called the result 'the greatest thing that has ever happened in New Zealand cricket. You won because you played hard cricket, the way it should be played, against hard opponents. In beating Australia you have earned an indisputable place in international cricket. The "poor relation" tag has gone for all time.'

It only remained for someone to say something nice about the Australians — even, perhaps, about Ian Chappell — and Bevan Congdon, himself described by Turner as a 'hard man', duly did so. 'Throughout the Test series relations between the two teams have been excellent,' he said, 'due in no small way to Ian Chappell.' Both captains described it as about the best Test Match they had played in.

If Chappell had wanted to make excuses he could have found

them in plenty, and high on the list would have been the omission of Gary Gilmour from the Australian side. On that Lancaster Park wicket as prepared under 'Cranky' Cromb, the preferment of Kevin O'Keeffe seems an unaccountable blunder; he didn't bowl a single ball in the match. Greg Chappell and Doug Walters, useful bowlers though they were, never looked the part of a third seamer, and it might well be said that it was the omission of Gilmour, rather than any contribution from Turner, that was at the root of Australia's first-ever defeat by New Zealand.

Such a verdict, understandably, does not meet with the approval of the hero of this story. 'We'd have stuffed them anyway,' he says.

NEW ZEALAND v AUSTRALIA 1974 (2nd Test)
at Christchurch, March 8, 9, 10, 12, 13
New Zealand won by 5 wickets

AUSTRALIA: First Innings

K. R. Stackpole, b Collinge		4
I. R. Redpath, c and b Collinge		71
*I. M. Chappell, b R. Hadlee		20
G. S. Chappell, c Howarth b Congdon		25
I. C. Davis, lbw b R. Hadlee		5
K. D. Walters, b R. Hadlee		6
†R. W. Marsh, b Congdon		38
K. J. O'Keeffe, c Wadsworth b Congdon		3
M. H. N. Walker, not out		19
A. A. Mallett, b Collinge		1
G. Dymock, c Congdon b D. Hadlee		12
Extras (B 1, LB 6, NB 12)		19
Total		223

Fall of wickets: 1-8, 2-45, 3-101, 4-120, 5-128, 6-181, 7-190, 8-194, 9-196.

Bowling: R. J. Hadlee, 14-2-59-3; Collinge, 21-4-70-3; Congdon, 11-2-33-3; D. R. Hadlee, 12.2-2-42-1.

NEW ZEALAND: First Innings

G. M. Turner, c Stackpole b G. Chappell		101
J. M. Parker, lbw b Dymock		18
J. F. M. Morrison, c Marsh b G. Chappell		12
*B. E. Congdon, c I. Chappell b Walker		8
B. F. Hastings, c Marsh b Walker		19
J. V. Coney, c Marsh b Dymock		15
†K. J. Wadsworth, c Marsh b Mallett		24
D. R. Hadlee, c Marsh b Dymock		11
R. J. Hadlee, lbw b Walker		23
H. J. Howarth, c I. Chappell b Walker		0
R. O. Collinge, not out		1
Extras (B 4, LB 8, NB 11)		23
Total		255

Fall of wickets: 1-59, 2-90, 3-104, 4-136, 5-171, 6-213, 7-220, 8-241, 9-242.

Bowling: Walker, 19.6-5-60-4; Dymock, 24-6-59-3; G. S. Chappell, 20-2-76-2; Walters, 7-1-34-0; Mallett, 3-1-3-1.

AUSTRALIA: Second Innings

K. R. Stackpole, c Wadsworth b Collinge		9
I. R. Redpath, c Howarth b R. Hadlee		58
I. M. Chappell, b Collinge		1
G. S. Chappell, c Coney b R. Hadlee		6
I. C. Davis, c Congdon b R. Hadlee		50
K. D. Walters, lbw b D. Hadlee		65
R. W. Marsh, c and b D. Hadlee		4
K. J. O'Keeffe, not out		23
M. H. N. Walker, c Howarth b D. Hadlee		4
G. Dymock, c Wadsworth b D. Hadlee		0
A. A. Mallett, c Wadsworth b R. Hadlee		11
Extras (B 16, LB 4, NB 8)		28
Total		259

Fall of wickets: 1-12, 2-26, 3-33, 4-139, 5-142, 6-160, 7-232, 8-238, 9-239.

Bowling: Collinge, 9-0-37-2; R. J. Hadlee, 20-2-75-4; D. R. Hadlee, 18-5-71-4; Congdon, 9-3-26-0; Howarth, 11-2-22-0.

NEW ZEALAND: Second Innings

G. M. Turner, not out		110
J. M. Parker, c Marsh b Walker		26
J. F. M. Morrison, lbw b Walker		0
B. E. Congdon, run out		2
B. F. Hastings, b Mallett		46
J. V. Coney, c Marsh b G. Chappell		14
K. J. Wadsworth, not out		9
Extras (B 4, LB 14, NB 5)		23
Total (5 wkts)		230

Fall of wickets: 1-51, 2-55, 3-62, 4-177, 5-206.

Bowling: Walker, 28-10-50-2; Dymock, 25-5-84-0; G. S. Chappell, 15.6-5-38-1; Mallett, 13-4-35-1.

Umpires—R. L. Monteith and J. B. Hastie

8

DOUG WALTERS

'Who better than Doug Walters when the mood is on him? If he ever played a dull innings I've yet to see it.'
— *E.W. Swanton*

The pale, spare, wiry figure watching the cricket from the visiting players' balcony at the Oval was standing wistfully, almost forlornly alone. His appearance on that balcony in mufti green blazer and grey flannels marked him as a man apart. Yet the role of spectator at a Test Match was so unfamiliar to him that even his former team-mates were uncomfortably conscious of his presence.

Hailed, like Ian Craig and Norman O'Neill before him, as a new phenomenon, the natural successor to Bradman, he had failed, just as they had done, to justify that extravagant label. Spectacular success had been his; but now, for the first time since he had burst on the international scene seven years earlier with centuries against England in each of his first two Tests, he had been dropped.

He had, of course, expected it. But that didn't soften the blow. Nothing had gone right for him in this 1972 series, and after failing in the first three Tests he had scarcely expected to be picked for the fourth Test at Leeds. As it turned out it would have been better if he hadn't been. On a turning wicket which had been unfit for a Test Match, all the Australian batsmen had struggled against Underwood and Illingworth and the game had been lost. For him, two more failures had meant that for the one match above all others in which he would love to have played, on the ground where the wicket would suit him better perhaps

172

than any other in England, he was denied the chance to redeem himself.

He was a man who could put himself in the other fellow's shoes, and he remembered how Norman O'Neill had reacted when he, Doug Walters, had replaced him in the Australian eleven. It was Norm's telegram of congratulation, among the many he had received, that he had treasured most. At Brisbane in that 1965-66 series against Mike Smith's team he had made a century in his first Test, eight days before his 20th birthday, and he had made another immediately afterwards at Melbourne. At once he had become the magnet for youthful autograph hunters, scores of them, but he did not simply sign a couple of books and brush the rest aside, as some of his contemporaries did. Again it was a question of the other fellow's shoes. 'I've asked for too many myself not to know how they feel.'

He had understood how Norm must have felt even then. And he knew how Ian Chappell, skipper of the 1972 side, must have felt when he faced the task of breaking the news to him now. So he did his best, when Ian approached him, to hide his disappointment and to make it easy for him. Everyone knew his weakness for sleep, and he made a pretence of relief. 'Beaut! Now I shan't have to get up early for nets!'

He had a reputation for being a sportsman in the old-fashioned sense, a good loser, unassuming but with no false humility, treating the crests and the troughs much the same. There was nothing studied or affected about it. It was mostly a natural consideration for others. Even in his fondness for practical jokes he was never unkind.

There was one species of being, though, for whom he showed no consideration at all. Bowlers. He was still only 26, and he was going to get back at them from his present nadir. Seven innings in a series for an average of 7.71 was something he would have to live down.

He had suffered set-backs before and surmounted them. Soon after that story-book start to his Test career his name had come out of the ballot of National Servicemen to serve two years in the Australian army, and he had accepted the misfortune philosophically. There was nothing he could do about it, he decided, short of joining the draft-dodgers, and 'that wouldn't be fair'. He was only one of many, and he asked for no special treatment. He hadn't particularly enjoyed the experience, but he had met some good blokes and had some good times.

He had been sorely missed on the 1966-67 tour of South Africa, where Australia lost the Test series 3-1, but by saving up his leave he managed to play in two Tests against India in 1967-68 and top the averages. His military commitment discharged, he was free for the 1968 tour of England.

In that appalling summer, batting all too often on suspect surfaces that were entirely foreign to him, he nevertheless scored 349 runs in the series and averaged 38, third behind Bill Lawry and Ian Chappell. He had had his moments of brilliance, but only in the first Test at Old Trafford, with 81 and 86, did he dominate. Back in Australia, however, with 699 runs from six Test innings against Hall, Griffith, Sobers and Gibbs, he averaged 116, this time out-scoring Lawry and Chappell. The following year in South Africa, where Australia fell foul of Peter Pollock and Mike Procter and lost four Tests out of four, he played a substantial innings in each of the first three Tests and was one of only three Australians to average more than 30.

So far in his career Walters had played the faster bowlers well, and he did not admit to more than an average dislike of the bouncer. 'If anyone says that bouncers don't worry them, I think they might be having a bit of a line at themselves.' Bouncers might not worry you one day, but next day they could make cricket seem a different game. It certainly seemed a different game when England under Ray Illingworth toured Australia in 1970-71 with John Snow as spearhead. Even an inveterate hooker like Ian Chappell was unsettled by Snow's persistent short-pitched bowling. 'I'd like to see how some of you fellers would get on against this stuff,' he muttered to the close fielders during one of his innings. Four years later he was to get his wish.

Walters, as usual, took the rough with the smooth. When Illingworth's team regained the Ashes in the final Test of that series, Walters was the first in the English dressing room to congratulate them.

For Walters that 1970-71 series had been a mixed one, alternately sparkling and streaky. Even in the few years in which he had played first-class cricket he believed the game had become more scientific. Teams had always sat down together before a match to analyse opposing players, but not in his experience to the extent they did now. An important factor was the greater number of Tests being played and televised, bringing a much fiercer exposure.

If anyone was going to work out the weaknesses of Australian batsmen it was Ray Illingworth, and although Walters got his share of bouncers, it was his vulnerability to the gully catch off the straight ball going away short of a length that was chiefly exploited. Although in most respects his technique was good, he was like many other top players in that he didn't pick his bat up straight, and he was apt to follow the ball with an angled bat and give catches to gully. Others, Richie Benaud among them, believed it was the bouncer that was basically his undoing, ruining his game, so that when the short-of-a-length ball came along near the off stump he wasn't in position to play it.

On one point all his critics, Benaud included, were agreed: whatever his faults he was just as likely to come out next day and paste the fastest bowlers in the world all over the park. Walters himself was of the same opinion. Thus he did not worry overmuch about failure. He was reputed, too, when his side were batting, to take little interest in the play outside his knock. One story, surely apocryphal (though it comes from Henry Blofeld), has him playing cards in the dressing room when suddenly it was his turn to bat. He laid his cards face downwards on the table and his cigarette in the ash-tray, picked up his bat, went out to the wicket, got bowled first ball, returned to the dressing room, picked up his cards and his cigarette and continued as if there had been no interruption. His explanation, so it is said, was that he had a good hand at the time. Apocryphal or not, the story illustrates — and no doubt exaggerates — an aspect of the Walters temperament.

Walters liked to get on with the game; that was what he was there for. If a ball was anywhere near hitable length, and he thought he could get away with it, he hit it. Even if the ball was not quite there he would still have a go. This was why he was such an exciting player. It was also one of the reasons for his comparative lack of success on English wickets. But he accepted his reverses phlegmatically, as natural hazards of his approach to batting, and he made enough runs to persuade him to stick to his last. His special value was his ability and readiness to hit the ball that wasn't quite a safe shot for 4. 'He's the one fellow whom I reckon you always have to pick,' was Rod Marsh's verdict, 'because he's one of the few batsmen in the world who can win a Test Match for you off his own bat.'

In that 1970-71 series Walters was successful enough, making 373 runs in the six Tests and averaging 37. But he was lucky to do so, being missed several times and getting far too many of his runs off the edge. A splendid series against a World Eleven in which he averaged 71 followed, and his place on the 1972 England tour was never in doubt. Yet he remained an enigma, a player of extremes, one day playing and missing, the next day a match-winner. 'If asked to pick an Australian side,' said Ian Chappell, captain for the tour, 'Doug Walters would be one of the first names on my list.'

That opinion made it all the more difficult for Chappell when he reached the conclusion, before the 1972 Oval Test, that Walters would have to be dropped. But easing his embarrassment — in addition to Walters' considerate reaction — was the certainty that Walters would be back. And back he came in thrilling fashion with the best innings of the series in the third Test against the West Indies in 1973 at Port of Spain. Here he exploded the myth that the wicket was not one for stroke-play by making exactly 100 in a session — between lunch and tea — a rare feat in a Test Match. 'By any standards it was a magnificent innings,' said *Wisden*. For once he had the privilege of batting No. 4, instead of his usual 5 or 6.

A man of less carefree temperament than Walters might have worked on his game after the 1972 tour of England and changed his whole style and approach, tightening up weaknesses but destroying the individual flair. Those who saw his innings at Port of Spain were glad he had not. So were those who saw his 81 in this series at Georgetown, where his footwork against the spinners, according to *Wisden*, was a 'a joy to watch'.

Most astonishing of all was his 104 not out, coming in at 37 for four, against New Zealand at Auckland in the third and deciding Test of 1974, on a treacherous surface where eighteen wickets fell in the day. 'By all the norms,' wrote Richie Benaud, 'no batsman should have made 30.' It was unwise to be dogmatic about the technique of a man who could do that.

Thus it was that when Mike Denness's side arrived in Australia in October 1974, Doug Walters, still two months short of his 29th birthday, was potentially at his peak. But he still had some unfinished business with English bowlers. For all the rise to power of other cricketing nations, for an Australian it was beating England that counted for most.

Yet in the early weeks of that season his form was so poor that it seemed doubtful whether he would play in the Test Matches at all. 10 and 2 against Queensland, 48 and 6 against Western Australia, 16 and 4 against the tourists for his State, and 11 against Victoria, added up to form that, allowing for the traditional lack of sentiment of Australians towards their ageing stars — and by Australian standards Walters was almost a veteran — threatened banishment not only from the Test side but also from the State side as well. He himself had first played for New South Wales at 17, and in that State particularly there were always young players coming along.

When the side was picked for the first Test at Brisbane Walters was in it, but the England players reckoned they knew how to get him out. His past discomfiture against the short-pitched ball meant that Willis, who was bowling when Walters went in at 197 for four, was bound to test him with a brace or two of bouncers, and after one good hook Walters tried to repeat the shot to a ball of too full a length and lofted it tamely to mid-on. 'Walters at his worst,' was one comment. Any other player must have wished the ground would open under his feet and swallow him up after such a shot, but Walters' temperament excluded such fancies. Adjusting his sights, he focused on doing well enough in the second innings to hold his place for the second Test at Perth. He had missed the best wicket of the 1972 series in England, and he was determined not to miss his favourite wicket at Perth.

After Australia had made 309, Greig saved England with a rumbustious hundred, and Australia went in again with a lead of 44. The need, when Walters went to the wicket, was for consolidation, and he forsook his cavalier approach and grafted for runs. Later, when Denness took the new ball, he despatched three short balls from Willis to the boundary with relish — all along the ground. He had redeemed that first-innings failure, and when Chappell declared he was 62 not out.

Bowled out by Thomson (6 for 46), England failed to save the game, and with Amiss and Edrich suffering hand injuries it was England who had to make changes for the second Test at Perth. Nevertheless there were harsh words from some critics when the Australian side was announced. The omission of Rick McCosker, who unlike Walters was in the runs, was denounced by Keith Miller as 'mad, nuts, berserk'. The player he would have left out was Walters.

McCosker had been batting No. 3 for New South Wales, and with the Chappells at 4 and 5 and Ross Edwards at 6, the line-up would have looked impressively solid. But Walters as a No. 6 was unique. He was also a much underrated bowler, in the opinion of some, though not of Walters himself. 'On a good flat wicket with the old ball, if I get a wicket it's someone else's fault.' Anyone who underestimated his speed and throw in the field, however, paid the price. In his way Walters, more so perhaps than any other post-war Australian batsman, was irreplaceable.

Walters rejoiced at his reprieve. The wicket at Perth suited his style of play better than any other wicket in the world. It was hard, fast, and true and the bounce was predictable. You knew exactly how high the ball would get up. If you couldn't pull or hook with safety you could duck an eighth of an inch just by a nod of the head, or sway fractionally out of the way and watch the ball go by. At Sydney, say, the bounce of the ball varied and you could duck straight into it.

With the England side in disarray through illness and injury, and Colin Cowdrey drafted in within four days of answering a panic call for a replacement, Ian Chappell kept up the pressure on his opponents by putting them in. Lillee, Thomson and Walker broke up the early batting, Walters picked up two wickets in the middle (Knott and Titmus were the batsmen 'at fault') and England were dismissed for 208. Then, in the single over there was time for before stumps, bowled by Willis from the southern (Swan River) end, Wally Edwards (no relation to Ross) was hit on the head and Redpath offered a difficult chance to Fletcher at slip which went down.

England could not lose this match and still have any realistic chance of retaining the Ashes. To come back from two down against Lillee and Thomson was something they knew was beyond them. Somehow they had to bowl Australia out for a moderate score and then do far better in their second innings.

Neither Willis nor Arnold had much luck when play restarted at eleven o'clock next morning, Redpath nibbling dangerously and Wally Edwards, playing in his second Test (he had also opened at Brisbane) enjoying a charmed life. After ten overs Denness — a much more confident captain in this series than in the West Indies the previous year, though still not a lucky one — tried a double change, Old for Willis, Greig for Arnold. Greig was able to extract some life from the wicket, and he got Edwards caught behind for 30 with the score at 64.

Greig came in for severe punishment from Edwards' replacement, Ian Chappell, and at 12.47 he was succeeded by Titmus. Meanwhile Old, bowling eight overs for 16 runs, was effectively closing the southern end. But it was Titmus who got the wicket, Redpath being stumped for 41. When Arnold, taking over from Old after lunch, separated the Chappell brothers by getting Ian caught behind, Australia were 113 for three and England were hauling themselves back into the game.

Joining Greg Chappell was the upright, rugby-scrum figure

of Ross Edwards, and between them they gave England an
unprofitable afternoon. Titmus, in fact, bowled beautifully, vary-
ing his pace and flight, and puzzling both batsmen with his
away-swinger, which neither seemed to detect. Whenever he
beat the sweep his lbw appeals were refused, and the nearest
England got to a wicket was a concerted appeal for a bat/pad
catch from Greg Chappell off Titmus, scooped up by Knott
falling forward, which was rejected. The players near the wicket
believed Chappell was out, but there was no walking in this
series.

After Old's long bowl of the morning Denness rested him
through the afternoon, dividing the work from the southern end
between Arnold, for the first hour, and Willis. Titmus mono-
polised the northern end, apart from one over from Greig,
making skilful use of the 'Freemantle Doctor', as the cooling
south-west breeze off the Indian Ocean was known. His afternoon spell of 13 overs cost only 31 runs. But none of the bowlers
had any luck until shortly before tea, when Willis, having posted
two gullies for Greg Chappell, had him caught off a ricochet
from one to the other for 62. The partnership had added 79 runs
and taken the score to 192 for four.

Walters was next, and then would come Marsh and the
bowlers. They were not rabbits, far from it, but Max Walker
at No. 8 meant a longish tail.

As Chappell passed the incoming batsman he said playfully;
'There you are, Doug — I've set it up for you. Now you can get
a hundred in the last session!' Walters' achievement in the West
Indies was still fresh in the mind. In fact Chappell had exposed
Walters to a precarious seven minutes before tea, and his chal-
lenge was in lieu of an apology.

Willis had been bowling for nearly an hour, but he always
fancied his chance against Walters. Chappell had got out to the
last ball of an over, but Willis would get one more over in before
tea. The batsmen took five runs between them off Titmus, the
effect of which was to bring Edwards down to face Willis.
Edwards, well established now, was careful to keep the strike,
and Willis was denied the torrid welcome he had planned for

180

Walters. At the break Australia were in a strong but by no means unassailable position at 201 for four, seven runs behind. Edwards was 31, Walters 3. An inspired over, or a few moments of carelessness or over-confidence by the batsmen, could still restrict Australia's lead.

Who, in the period immediately after tea, was available to bowl such an over? Denness was criticised afterwards for not confronting Walters with Willis directly after the break, but the most cursory re-cap of the afternoon's play stamps this as unfair. Willis had bowled the last seven overs from the river end before tea, and they were eight-ball overs. Near the end of that spell he had dismissed Greg Chappell. An hour after tea the new ball would be due, so Willis had to be rested, as also Titmus, who had bowled 13 overs in the afternoon. Unless Arnold were to be given a brief spell now — and he was Denness's best new-ball bowler — the combination would have to be Old and Greig.

Greig was a genuine all-rounder, capable of taking four or five wickets at the highest level, albeit at greater cost than the specialist bowlers. He had got Walters out in a Test Match before, he had taken a wicket with his off-cutters that morning, and if he could extract his usual bounce he might well get another. Old had bowled a magnificent spell in the morning and had been rested since then. It was a combination in which Denness was entitled to have every confidence.

Comments of leading Australian critics at the time make it clear that English optimism was no mere wishful thinking. One more wicket at this stage, with the new ball on the way (noted Richie Benaud), and England could be gathering themselves for a great fighting triumph.

All these reflections, like trees mirrored in water, trembled and muddied and dissolved under the first leaf-stirring gusts of the tornado that was about to break. The 'Freemantle Doctor' seemed to freshen in sympathy, and Greig, bowling into it, and trying for lift on and outside Walters' off stump, pitched too short, to be pulled and cut with a savagery not yet seen in the series. Eight runs came off Greig's first over, seven of them to Walters, a pull and a leg glance for 3 which put Australia into the lead and took Walters down to face Old. When Old pitched a full length he was driven superbly for 4.

A slight but never diminutive figure, Walters in this hawk-eyed mood approached the limits of human precision. His appetite had been whetted, and already he gave the impression of looking for a hundred by nightfall. An uncanny ability to pull anything the least bit short, however wide of the off stump, to mid-wicket was varied by wristy whip-drives and murderous square and back cuts. The 50 partnership came in 38 minutes, and in the next over Walters overtook Edwards as he moved through the 30s, having given him one and three-quarter hours' start. In the eighth over after tea he put up the 250 with another boundary off Old, making 51 runs since the break, 43 to Walters and 8 to Edwards. Under this devastating assault the ground fielding wilted, and returns to the wicket became ragged.

Brian Luckhurst, another victim of a lifting ball from Thomson, was off the field with a swollen hand, and the substitute was Derek Underwood. How Denness must have sighed for a containing spell from Underwood in that crucial post-tea period.

Greig's four overs had cost 31 runs and he had to come off. Another four overs separated England from the new ball, and Titmus came on at the northern end, but this time he couldn't apply the brake. His first over cost ten runs, nine to Walters, made up of a drive and a pull that both sped to the fence and a single. The first of these boundaries took Walters to his fifty in 48 minutes off 50 balls, five before tea and 45 after.

Throughout this onslaught Old was never collared, somehow restricting the batsmen to no more than two scoring strokes an over. Titmus could not always achieve this, nor could he prevent Walters monopolising the strike. By the end of the 65th over, when the new ball became due, Walters in the hour since tea had scored 66 runs to Edwards' 9. 75 runs had been added since tea and Australia were 276 for four.

At this point drinks were taken, after which Denness allowed Titmus and Old to continue, on the basis that the interruption might be worth a wicket. If that happened, Arnold and Willis would have one end open for the new ball. But the ruse failed, and after one more over from each end the new ball was taken. Walters was on 72 and Edwards 47, and 84 had been added since tea.

Arnold came on at the northern end at 5.07; if he and Willis ran true to form they would bowl five overs each in the time that remained. Walters needed 28 for his century and 31 for his hundred in the session, which in the context of his progress so far was not out of the way. Arnold and Willis with the new ball, bowling as it seemed for the match, were a tough proposition, and if they once got a break-through they might run through the side, restricting the lead to under a hundred: but Walters was seeing the ball so well that he would go on playing his game.

Arnold sent down three looseners with the old ball, from the first of which Walters took a single. The first delivery with the new cherry was a no-ball, which Edwards played off his toes for 2; and another 2 off the next ball took him to 51. First with Chappell and then with Walters he had adopted the unselfish role of anchorman, and although he had batted 174 minutes he had done what was wanted. He took a single at the end of the over and thus kept the bowling.

Now it was Willis, thundering in from the river end and carrying on his shoulders, with Arnold, all England's hopes. Edwards got a run off the fourth ball to put up the 100 partnership in 80 minutes, Walters kept the score moving with another single, but Edwards took another off the last ball and again kept the strike.

There was no question at this stage of either batsman manipulating the strike. The new ball was scarcely deviating, but both were under fierce and determined attack, by bowlers who knew that this partnership absolutely had to be broken.

Five more singles came off Arnold's second over, the odd single going to Edwards, who was thus left to face Willis. It was entirely involuntary that of the 14 runs that came off the first three overs with the new ball, Edwards' share was 10 and Walters' 4.

A leg-bye off Willis put up the 300 and gave Walters the strike. He got a single next ball, taking him to 77, but he was left inactive at the non-strikers' end while Edwards, under pressure, played out the over.

Six overs to go.

Walters did better off Arnold, forcing him for 2 and 1 off the third and fifth balls, inflating the crowd's expectations. Edwards took one off the sixth, Walters another off the seventh, and there were feverish cheers as Edwards took 2 off the last ball. Thus Walters kept the strike.

81 to Walters. Five overs to go.

A leg-bye off the first ball of Willis's third over lost Walters the strike right away, to the dismay of the crowd. He did not regain it. Profiting from a misdirected attack on his leg stump, Edwards took 2's off the second, fourth and fifth balls and a single off the last. Walters, with four overs to go, remained at the non-striker's end, still on 81.

Edwards was actually overhauling Walters now, introducing an intriguing counter-plot, a competitive element between the two batsmen which the crowd did not resent, since Edwards was a Western Australian. When Edwards took 2, 4 and 1 off the first three balls of Arnold's penultimate over he moved to within seven runs of Walters. But three more singles off the over, two of them to Walters, meant that Walters would face Willis. Edwards was on 75, Walters 83.

Willis was still banging them in just short of a length, certain he must soon find the edge. He did not scruple, either, to make free with the bouncer. The best Walters could do was a 2 off the second ball and a single off the fifth, taking him to 86. Edwards was pinned down for the rest of the over.

With 14 still wanted and only two overs to go, Walters' chances of reaching his hundred before stumps were now slim. The field, if not wholly defensive, was well spread. The most he had scored in any one over since the new ball was taken was four, and he hadn't hit a boundary for nearly an hour. The crowd, bubbling with interest throughout the session and still simmering, had been tantalised enough. Their excitement must surely subside as all hint of the chase was called off.

Arnold's fifth and last over, however, rekindled the blaze as

Walters stroked 2's off the second, third and fifth balls to take him into the 90s. A run off the seventh ball was cheered ecstatically, but then came a full-throated groan as the last ball gave Edwards a single.

There was never any question of refusing runs. Both batsmen were looking for all the runs they could get, for Australia first, and then for themselves.

Walters was on 93, but there was only one over to go and he was not even facing the bowling. He was fighting off an attack of cramp in one hand, which caused a burdensome delay, one finger refusing to stop twitching. When at length the rock-like Edwards took 2 off Willis's first ball, and the batsmen ran with no more than normal urgency, it seemed that the absorbing melodrama of the last hour had been based on little more substantial than crowd hysteria.

Walters, however, had not given up. And when Edwards took 3 off the second ball, and Walters scampered home, leaving six balls to go, the open WACA ground, pleasantly situated but not normally renowned for its atmosphere, became charged with an ambience so stifling that it boiled like a cauldron.

Walters had six balls to get seven runs — or ten, if that hundred in a session was still on. Flexing his hand, he took up his stance. Willis, as *he* saw it, had six balls to get Walters out. He had worked up to top pace in this spell, and now he was gripped by a wild notion that he was going to get Walters out every ball. Indeed he believed he could *bounce* him out. He had posted two gullies, and he had a man on the square leg boundary and another on the edge at long leg. He was flat out to get Walters that night, not so much to stop him getting a ton as to stop him from getting another tomorrow.

Willis at this period of his career was not the mature cricketer of later years. But he was quick, and he had his heart in what he was doing. His first ball to Walters was a bouncer, and Walters was expecting it. Even so, as he went to hook it, he was just a shade late. The result was a thickish top-edge — and he turned to see the ball sail high over Knott's head for 4.

97. Five balls to go.

'It had to be the bouncer. Walters knew it, Willis knew it too.'

The morning after — caught by Fletcher off Willis's second ball.

Walking back to his mark, head down, ignoring the hubbub, Willis decided to pitch further up, aiming for those gullies while retaining the element of shock for a well-disguised bouncer. Walters, expecting another bouncer, moved on to the back foot to prepare for the hook and was left with nothing to offer but a defensive prod to keep Willis out.

Three balls, four balls, and Willis kept him playing, with no chance to score. He might have tried to push for one, but he was no longer interested in singles.

Very few of the crowd were aware of the target of a hundred in a session. All they were looking for was the hundred. That, for them, was enough. For Walters, too, on 97 with one ball to go, the hundred had become the goal.

Willis had been bowling three bouncers an over just now. Surely after that top edge he *must* try another.

With the crowd consciously willing the perfect climax to the day, Willis pounded in to bowl the last ball. It *had* to be the bouncer. Walters knew it, and Willis knew it too.

No use to worry about those men on the fence, thought Walters, or the miss-hit to mid-on, or the skier to the wicket-keeper. He was going to crack it, whatever. Backing away in anticipation, he judged the bounce perfectly, pivoted on his toes, and swung as hard as he could to mid-wicket.

It was one of those lucky occasions when the ball hits the bat in the right spot at precisely the right moment. The ball soared like a bird towards mid-wicket, leaving square-leg back-pedalling helplessly. As for Walters, as soon as he struck it he knew it was 6.

103! A hundred in a session! He could hardly believe it! But a swarm of youngsters racing towards him from the pickets confirmed that he'd done it.

Only Bradman before him had scored a hundred in a Test Match session more than once. Walters' hundred had come off 117 balls.

Mobbed and cheered all the way to the pavilion and until he vanished from sight, Walters had a surprise awaiting him when he got to the dressing room. His team-mates, getting back at him for his practical jokes and his habit of not watching the play, had disappeared into the showers. Pretending they had seen nothing of the climax, they had left the dressing room empty, denying him the boisterous welcome he expected. Soon, however, they had to steal back and peep in, to congratulate him and savour the joke.

It was just as well Walters got his hundred that night. Next morning, after Ross Edwards had taken ten runs off Arnold's first over, Willis found just the ball he'd been urging himself to bowl the previous evening, a sharp lifter that cut away late. Walters played and missed; but having found perfection once Willis found it again, and this time the ball nicked the edge and Fletcher at slip took the catch. Walters had not added a run to his overnight score.

He and Ross Edwards had put on 170, and although England fought to the end they lost by nine wickets. They drew the third Test with credit, but they lost the fourth to surrender the Ashes.

When Doug Walters retired from first-class cricket after missing selection for the 1981 England tour, he was 40 runs short of 5,000 runs in Tests, a target reached by only five Australians — Bradman, Harvey, the Chappell brothers, and Bill Lawry. His Test average of 47.69 places him ahead of all past Australian batsmen bar Bradman, Harvey, Ponsford, and McCabe.

AUSTRALIA v ENGLAND 1974-75 (2nd Test)
at Perth, December 13, 14, 15, 17
Australia won by 9 wickets

ENGLAND: First Innings

D. Lloyd, c G. Chappell b Thomson	49
B. W. Luckhurst, c Mallett b Walker	27
M. C. Cowdrey, b Thomson	22
A. W. Greig, c Mallett b Walker	23
K. W. R. Fletcher, c Redpath b Lillee	4
*M. H. Denness, c G. Chappell b Lillee	2
†A. P. E. Knott, c Redpath b Walters	51
F. J. Titmus, c Redpath b Walters	10
C. M. Old, c G. Chappell b I. Chappell	7
G. G. Arnold, run out	1
R. G. D. Willis, not out	4
Extras (W 3, NB 5)	8
Total	208

Fall of wickets: 1-44, 2-99, 3-119, 4-128, 5-132, 6-132, 7-194, 8-201, 9-202.

Bowling: Lillee, 16-4-48-2; Thomson, 15-6-45-2; Walker, 20-5-49-2; Mallett, 10-3-35-0; Walters, 2.3-0-13-2; I. Chappell, 2-0-10-1.

AUSTRALIA: First Innings

I. R. Redpath, st Knott b Titmus	41
W. J. Edwards, c Lloyd b Greig	30
*I. M. Chappell, c Knott b Arnold	25
G. S. Chappell, c Greig b Willis	62
R. Edwards, b Arnold	115
K. D. Walters, c Fletcher b Willis	103
†R. W. Marsh, c Lloyd b Titmus	41
M. H. N. Walker, c Knott b Old	19
D. K. Lillee, b Old	11
A. A. Mallett, c Knott b Old	0
J. R. Thomson, not out	11
Extras (B 7, LB 14, NB 2)	23
Total	481

Fall of wickets: 1-64, 2-101, 3-113, 4-192, 5-362, 6-416, 7-449, 8-462, 9-462.

Bowling: Willis, 22-0-91-2; Arnold, 27-1-129-2; Old, 22.6-3-85-3; Greig, 9-0-69-1; Titmus, 28-3-84-2.

ENGLAND: Second Innings

D. Lloyd, c G. Chappell b Walker	35
M. C. Cowdrey, lbw b Thomson	41
M. H. Denness, c Redpath b Thomson	20
A. W. Greig, c G. Chappell b Thomson	32
K. W. R. Fletcher, c Marsh b Thomson	0
A. P. E. Knott, c G. Chappell b Lillee	18
B. W. Luckhurst, c Mallett b Lillee	23
F. J. Titmus, c G. Chappell b Mallett	61
C. M. Old, c Thomson b Mallett	43
G. G. Arnold, c Mallett b Thomson	4
R. G. D. Willis, not out	0
Extras (LB 4, W 1, NB 11)	16
Total	293

Fall of wickets: 1-62, 2-106, 3-124, 4-124, 5-154, 6-156, 7-219, 8-285, 9-293.

Bowling: Lillee, 22-5-59-2; Thomson, 25-4-93-5; Walker, 24-7-76-1; Walters, 9-4-17-0; Mallett, 11.1-4-32-2.

AUSTRALIA: Second Innings

I. R. Redpath, not out	12
W. J. Edwards, lbw b Arnold	0
I. M. Chappell, not out	11
Extras	0
Total (1 wkt)	23

Bowling: Willis, 2-0-8-0; Arnold, 1.7-0-15-1.

Umpires—R. Bailhache and T. F. Brooks

9

DENNIS AMISS

*'There are not many better sights in
English cricket than Amiss in full
flow.'*   *— Michael Melford*

At four minutes past six in the evening, after a long day in the field, the batsmen on their way to the crease, booked for a brief but intimidatory barrage of pace, were on a hiding to nothing. Yet for one of them, a Test Match discard whose failures against fast bowling had become an embarrassment to him, this early-season MCC game against the tourists at Headquarters, before the Test series began, was likely to be his one chance of proving the selectors wrong.

To survive for a few awkward minutes at the end of a day's play was no more than the average bowler sent in as night-watchman might be expected to do. But the last 26 minutes of this particular session, with one of the fastest attacks in the world fleetingly on view, promised to be more than usually tempestuous.

Even for recognised batsmen, early dismissal, as bowlers slipped into top gear in the knowledge that they had only a few overs to bowl, might be shrugged off as a natural hazard of their calling. It was, after all, for this very burst of speed with the new ball that a declaration had been applied. But for the man taking strike, the normal excuses were unlikely to be offered or accepted. It was now or never.

Dennis Amiss, the batsman on trial, had been blasted out of Test cricket twelve months earlier by the Australians Lillee and Thomson. Could he put that traumatic experience behind him? Many people doubted it. The challenge to English cricket, in that season of 1976, came from the West Indies, and rumour had it that they had a young fast bowler of almost unbelievable velocity, faster even than Lillee and Thomson.

It was this young fast bowler, the 22-year-old Michael Holding, who now stood more than 60 yards distant from Amiss, silhouetted against the shadowy pavilion background, marking the extremity of his 40-yard run as Amiss took guard.

Until this match, begun at 11.30 that morning, Saturday 22nd May, Holding in England had been under-exposed. This was partly deliberate, to save him for the Test Matches, and partly of necessity, since he had not been fully match-fit. He had played in only one first-class match, at Southampton, and bowled only 24 overs in Hampshire's two innings. It had not yet been possible to judge his potential. During a tour of Australia that winter he had been timed as faster than either Roberts, Lillee or Thomson, and he had played in five of the six Test Matches; but his ten wickets in the series had cost 61 runs each. It was not until the four-match series at home to India in March and April of that year that he had been spoken of as a great fast bowler.

It was exactly a month since the last and deciding game of that series, which Bishen Bedi, the Indian captain, had described as a 'war'. It was nearer a massacre. Two Indian batsmen retired hurt in the first innings and a third fractured a finger when he was caught off the bat handle — all when facing Holding. When bouncers were bowled at the tail-enders, Bedi declared the innings closed with only six wickets down — 'in disgust', as he said afterwards, and to save himself and Chandrasekhar, India's two key bowlers, from bodily harm. In the second innings the Indians subsided at 97 for 5, ostensibly all out because of further injuries, leaving the West Indies 13 to win.

'Cause of the bitterness', wrote Tony Cozier, 'was the bowling of Holding, the tall, athletically-built Jamaican who was as fast and as dangerous as any I have seen.' This was the bowler who now sprinted in light-footed, his long, supple limbs achieving a gliding, rhythmic grace, to deliver the first ball of the MCC innings to Dennis Amiss. It was a confrontation that even old hands behind the bowler's arm leaned forward to watch.

For Amiss, a fighting knock of no more than 30 or 40 could

191

win him back his place in the England side. For Holding, a quick dismissal could put this dangerous run-getter, the scourge of the Caribbean little more than two years earlier (before the emergence of either Roberts or Holding), out of the current series and very probably out of Test cricket for good.

Even supposing that the batsman survived Holding's opening assault, there would be no respite from the other end, where Andy Roberts, another bowler of blistering pace and aggression — with a reputation already made — would take up the challenge. What shape was the 33-year-old Amiss in to resist this two-pronged bombardment?

He had begun the season in tremendous form, scoring over 500 runs in six innings by mid-May. But he had not yet had to face an attack of this calibre. And during the day, for no reason that he could think of, he had felt jaded. Perhaps he had got too many runs in the first few games. I'm not quite right for this match, he thought, not quite in the right frame of mind. That sort of feeling came along sometimes, when unaccountably one felt below par. (It was Ted Dexter who said of the county circuit that if the cricket did not tire you out the travelling would.) Yet as a professional opening batsman he couldn't get out of it by saying that he didn't fancy it today, that he'd leave it until Monday and bat lower down. The next 26 minutes would have to be endured. All right, he said to himself, we'll have a bash.

Twice in Holding's first over he connected sweetly and the ball raced to the boundary. It was going to be all right. But two points registered. The pitch was slow; but Holding was quick.

In his first two overs Holding bowled him two or three short ones. Some got up and some didn't, but he kept his eye on them and avoided them. No more chances came along to score, apart from an occasional leg bye, and at 6.23, when Holding began his third over, it was certain that this would be the last over of the day from that end.

Amiss played the first four balls safely enough. The fifth was banged in short, and instead of watching it he took his eye off it — or lost it in the pavilion background. Anyway he turned his head away and ducked. But the ball didn't get up. Instead, it hit him in the back of the head, just above the nape of the neck. He was not wearing a cap, there was nothing to absorb the impact, and he stumbled away from the wicket towards square leg, head down. He thought he would be able to continue and indeed was determined to do so, but then he saw that his right hand, where he had rubbed the bruise, was smeared with blood. The blow had cut his head open and would need stitches. There was no possibility of carrying on, and with the characteristically purposeful Amiss gait reduced to a plod he trudged off. The time was 6.27.

The absence of Geoffrey Boycott, who for the moment had opted out of Test cricket, had left Amiss as England's premier batsman. Although he had fallen from grace, he had hoped to rehabilitate himself. He was by no means the only top-class batsman forced to retire temporarily after being hit by the fast men of the time, and in normal circumstances the incident would have been soon forgotten. But in this instance, the sight of this popular player trooping ignominiously off the field was unbearably poignant. For the selectors it was proof positive that Lillee and Thomson had broken his spirit. For Amiss himself it was the final humiliation.

The switchback career of Dennis Amiss had begun eighteen years earlier, in 1958, when, at the age of 15, encouraged by a club-cricketer father, he joined the Warwickshire junior staff. Coached without undue pedagogy, he was allowed to develop as a natural player, and he made his championship debut against Surrey at the Oval two years later, in 1960. This was the match in which Norman Horner and Khalid 'Billy' Ibadulla set up a Warwickshire record by amassing 377 runs for the first wicket, both undefeated, and Amiss was one of the nine who did not get to the crease. A week later he played at Coventry against Notts and was run out without facing a ball.

Surmounting these early disappointments, he played in seven championship matches in all as a 17-year-old and averaged 22; but in ensuing seasons he failed to take advantage of the opportunities he was given in the senior side. Indeed the point came when his performance at first-class level deteriorated. In 1962 he played eleven innings and averaged 27, but this fell to an average of 19 in fifteen innings in 1963 and a disastrous season in 1964 when in four championship matches he went to the wicket eight times and averaged 7. In the three matches when he went in first he scored 11, 7, 3, 13, 34 and 3, and his pretensions to being considered as an opening bat, fostered by his performances in the second eleven, were ruthlessly exposed by top-class swing bowling.

This dismal regression inevitably inspired a stocktaking. He had begun on the Warwickshire staff as an all-rounder, a right-hand batsman who bowled left-arm at above medium pace. A slipped disc sustained at soccer, although not affecting his batting, had ended his aspirations as a bowler, and with John Jameson, two years his senior, establishing himself in the county side there was no room for another batsman. Amiss was marked as one of those players who scored heavily for the Seconds but was quickly found out at top level. After his sequence of failures in the first team in 1964 he began to think seriously of joining his father in the family tyre business.

News of the impending retirement of Norman Horner and Ray Hitchcock, however, changed the picture. He was still only 22. And at the start of the 1965 season he was promised selection in the first six matches, which instilled just the right mixture of controlled relaxation. In his first three-day match, against Scotland, he top-scored with 68, drawing a compliment from *Wisden*. 'Amiss was the only batsman to score with any freedom,' they said.

After a duck against Surrey he pulled the game round against Somerset when Brian Langford threatened to go through the side. He did not quite maintain this ascendancy through the season, but he played in all 28 championship matches, scored over 1400 runs in all games, and averaged 28. The confidence the Warwickshire committee had placed in him at the start of the season was thus amply rewarded. 'He possesses a correct technique,' said *Wisden*, 'and can shrewdly mix aggression with caution.'

Throughout the 1966 season Amiss scored steadily if not

heavily, batting mostly at No. 3. Nevertheless it was something of a surprise when, as one of six changes in the England side after the rubber against the West Indies had been lost, Amiss was chosen for the final Test at the Oval. He had not yet scored a championship hundred, but he justified the selectors' foresight by opening the innings for Warwickshire against the tourists two days before the Oval Test and scoring 160 not out.

This was Brian Close's first match as captain, and under his inspiration some of the reverses of the summer were redeemed; but Amiss played only a minor part in England's victory. Coming in when three wickets had fallen for 85, he shared a stubborn stand of 41 with John Edrich but was then lbw for 17. He had not done himself justice, as his critics were quick to point out. Although now 23, he was abashed and even overawed by the exalted company he found himself in at the Oval and felt he could never be as good a player as men like Cowdrey and Graveney. England recovered to make 527 and win by an innings, so he got no second chance.

A successful tour of Pakistan with the MCC under-25 team that winter under Mike Brearley led to further representative honours against India in 1967, but big scores eluded him and he was dropped after two matches. He only got into the sixth and final Test of the summer, against Pakistan, because Cowdrey and Milburn were not available and Boycott was unwell. Again his performance was pilloried, adjectives like 'stilted' and 'apprehensive' being ruthlessly applied, and in his three Tests that summer, according to one critic, he 'pottered around for not very many'. He had given himself no chance of a place in the party that toured the West Indies that winter.

In the following year, 1968, came his infamous 'pair' against Australia, in the first Test at Old Trafford, which England lost by 159 runs. Finding himself at No. 5, more or less as a replacement for an injured Ken Barrington, he resolved to graft to make up for Barrington's absence and again paid the penalty for not playing his natural game. Worse was to come. 'Old Trafford burst out laughing', wrote one unkind critic, 'when Cowper bowled him in the second innings.' Cowper was a genuine all-rounder, with good performances as an off spinner in Test cricket, and the ball was turning, but for sections of the crowd to guffaw at a player's discomfiture is not, perhaps, anything new.

The Test Match career of Dennis Amiss was in eclipse, and in 1969, inhibited by a weakened Warwickshire batting side, he concentrated too much on survival and averaged no more than 30. But in 1970 the return of Mike Smith from temporary retirement allowed him to bat more freely, and before the end of the season he had forced his way back into the reckoning for the tour of Australia under Ray Illingworth. Chosen for the final Test against the Rest of the World instead of Basil D'Oliveira to give him a chance of winning his place (D'Oliveira's being already booked), he fought hard in both innings, but scores of 24 and 35 were not good enough in a high-scoring game. He was still to some extent overawed, unable to reveal his true self when batting at the highest level, and once again his critics were ready to write him off as an international player. 'Unfortunately,' said *Wisden*, 'he failed again to reproduce his best form under the pressure of the big occasion.'

The same critic did not spare him at the end of the 1971 season, after a moderate series against Pakistan and a failure against India, following which he was dropped. 'Amiss, after an encouraging start, did not have a good year,' said *Wisden*. 'He fell away after the distraction of trying to establish himself in the England side.' *Wisden* added a final dismissive aphorism. 'His four appearances seemed to confirm that he does not possess the temperament for the highest level of the game.'

The England selectors concurred, and they did not pick him for any of the Tests against Australia in 1972, nor did he expect them to do so. After failing against the two Universities at the start of the season, he even lost his place in the Warwickshire side. With Alvin Kallicharran having qualified and batting No. 5, after Whitehouse, Jameson, Kanhai and Mike Smith, Amiss found himself, at the age of 29, with nine England caps, reduced to second-team cricket for the first time in eight years. This was the second major crisis in a chequered career, and it looked very much like the end of the road.

He did nothing outstanding at first for the Seconds, nor when he was recalled for the occasional first-team game. Some of the batsmen who replaced him were performing no more than moderately, but he accepted that they had to be given a reasonable run. Knowing that the only way back was on a tide of big scores, he swallowed his resentment and got down to the business of run-getting. But when he scored a hundred for the Seconds it made no difference, and he seriously considered leaving Warwickshire and moving to another county. The only alternative seemed to be to give up the game, but he loved it too much to do that.

Bearding Alan Smith, who had succeeded Mike Smith (again no relation) as captain, in his office, he pointed to his recent record and to the modest performances of Jameson and Whitehouse. 'I've missed several games,' he said, 'and they've had a fair crack. Now I'd like a chance to open.'

'You want to open?' Smith's surprise was plain. He hadn't thought of Amiss as an opener. It happened that John Whitehouse was injured and that there was a vacancy for an opening batsman in the next home game, against Middlesex. 'O.K.,' said Smith. 'You can open.' Amiss proceeded to play the innings he had been mentally preparing for. He was lucky early on when he played and missed once or twice to John Price, but he batted for 6¾ hours and made 151 not out, out of a total of 334 for 4 declared. Even then some of the praise was grudging. His marathon innings, said *Wisden*, had allowed Mike Smith and Alvin Kallicharran to make 'more positive contributions'.

The runs did not flow immediately, but within a few games he made scores of 154 and 192 not out, developing his stamina for the big innings. For the series of one-day Prudential Cup matches at the end of the season the selectors turned to Amiss, and in the first match, on the same ground — Old Trafford — where four years earlier he had recorded his notorious 'pair', he won the match for England with a sparkling 103. From second team cricket only ten weeks earlier he was England's batsman of the Prudential series and richly earned his place in the tour to India and Pakistan that winter.

New to Indian conditions, the England batsmen were soon ill-at-ease, disturbed by a succession of grassless wickets on which the ball turned from the start. The Indian spin bowlers, Bedi, Chandrasekhar, Prasanna and Venkataraghavan, were great practitioners of their art on any wicket, and these wickets, where at times the ball jumped and turned almost square, were made for them, literally as well as figuratively. Within three or four overs the spinners were on, and England had no one of experience to counter them. A left-hander might have helped, but the touring party had been put together without one.

Bedi, with his silken left-arm spin and arm-ball, proved scarcely less mysterious than the top-spinners and googlies of the guileful Chandrasekhar. Amiss was one of those who tried to block it out, but with the prehensile Solkar lurking at his elbow he couldn't get his mind off the bat-pad catch, and as often as not he worried himself out. He was not the only one: Solkar took twelve close catches in the first three Tests. But even when he tried to get after the spinners he failed, and with his opening partner Barry Wood in similar travail, both were dropped for the fourth Test. Thus they missed the best wicket of the series at Kanpur, where the ball didn't turn, and could only watch with admiration in the fifth Test at Bombay as Tony Greig and Keith Fletcher showed belatedly but convincingly how to deal with Chandrasekhar and Bedi. If the ball beat the bat they forgot about it. They attacked when they could, and when they defended they simply didn't worry about the bat-pad catch, hoping that if it came it eluded the close fielders. They put on a record 254 for the fifth wicket and got a hundred each; but Amiss was left with a Test Match aggregate of 90 runs in six innings.

Criticism of the England batsmen was tempered by appreciation of the conditions that had produced them. Years of stereotyped cricket against seamers were no kind of preparation for taking on spinners like Chandrasekhar and Bedi. 'Constant playing of seam bowling produces only good players of seam bowling,' wrote Clive Taylor in *Wisden*. Greig and Fletcher had eventually triumphed, but a question mark remained against Tony Lewis and Mike Denness, and there was no disputing who were the failures. Most disappointing of all was Dennis Amiss.

No one was more conscious of this than Amiss himself, but at this latest nadir in the graph of his career it was hard to foresee any compensating peak. To liken his career to a switchback was to assume an impetus in the downward swing that would lift it to a fresh summit. But where was this impetus to come from?

It had to come, as Amiss knew, from within. But he needed help. And help, from a totally unexpected source, was at hand. It came from the very men who had been his tormentors. He was discussing his failures with some of the Indian players during the final Test when three of them, Abid Ali, Bishen Bedi, and Venkataraghavan, suggested that it might help if they bowled to him in the nets when the Test was over. Thus it was that a strange spectacle, staged in a deserted arena, was presented at the famous Brabourne Stadium. There were no nets available so one was set up in the middle, and for an hour or more the three Indians, bowling to an aggressive but imaginary close field, tried their hardest to bring about Amiss's presumed downfall, probing his weaknesses and appealing vociferously for anything that they thought might be a catch or might be adjudged lbw. They then assumed the role of umpires, and told him whether he would have been out or not. It gave him an insight into the problems posed by spinners on turning wickets that he could have gained in no other way. He could feel his technique maturing ball by ball, and when the session ended he felt liberated. Such was the fillip to his confidence that his whole approach to Test cricket, he believed, had been invigorated.

The result was an avalanche of runs in the next twelve months that has only twice been exceeded in Test cricket. In the three-match series that followed in Pakistan he scored 406 runs, including a century in each of the first two Tests and 99 in the third. Whereas he had been bottom of the averages in India, apart from two of the bowlers, he was now easily top with an average of 81. In the summer of 1973 he had a satisfactory three-match series against New Zealand and a moderate one against the West Indies, and he was surprisingly left out of the two Prudential matches at the end of the season; but then came the 1973-74 tour of the West Indies.

Apart from the final Test, when Geoff Boycott excelled, Amiss was incomparably England's leading batsman, and he scored 663 runs in the five-match series and averaged 82. Outstanding was his 262 not out in the second Test at Kingston, when he saved the game despite a barrage of bouncers, and he also made 174 in the first Test and 118 in the fourth. There was an inevitability about his run-getting in this series that marked him as a great player, and *Wisden* reflected that it was 'impossible to realise that an allegedly flawed temperament had once restricted his appearances for England'.

Now 31 and at the peak of his career, Amiss returned to England for the 1974 season an automatic choice for his country. He had become, according to one former critic, 'a reassuring figure in any side,' his cover-drive 'one of the most glorious strokes in contemporary cricket.' This stroke, and the stroke off his legs to mid-wicket, were angled through a wide arc which readily found gaps in the field, and he struck the ball with devastating power and certainty, derived from beefy biceps and forearms in an otherwise average figure. His appetite for runs, and his penchant for big scores, were now proven, and his ability to destroy an attack without descending to slogging made him supreme in the one-day game too. A hidden strength, perhaps, and one that he shared with an earlier Denis, Denis Compton, was exceptional strength in the top hand on the bat. Both batted right and bowled left.

Another successful summer was the preamble to the greatest challenge of all. With Boycott abstaining, he was England's No. 1 batsman in the quest to regain the Ashes under Mike Denness that winter. Opposed to them would be the great Dennis Lillee. Jeff Thomson, as yet, had scarcely been heard of.

On a grassy wicket of unpredictable bounce against Queensland immediately before the first Test, Greg Chappell deliberately under-bowled Thomson, who delivered only 21 overs in the match and took one for 22 and one for 29. Both times his victim was Amiss. Then came the Test Match, played on a hastily prepared pitch, again of uneven bounce, following a storm that flooded the ground 48 hours before the start. In the first innings Amiss was caught in the gully for 7 off a lifter — a brute of a ball that cut back chest high off a length and smashed into his thumb. In the second innings, batting in some pain, he was one of only three in the side to get into the twenties before being caught at slip off the bat handle when a good length ball lifted. In these two innings, with the ball rising unpredictably at a great pace, Amiss felt he was facing the most frightening fast bowling he had ever seen. His thumb proved to be fractured, and Edrich, too, had a bone in his hand broken by another explosive delivery. Thus England went into the crucial second Test at Perth without their two leading batsmen, and after a great hundred by Walters[1], they could not escape going two down in the series.

Back for the third Test at Melbourne, where England were put in to bat, Amiss was undone by the last ball of Lillee's first over, which started on the leg stump. He played it with the face of the bat shut towards mid-on but it swung late, caught the bat shoulder, and flew to gully, where Walters, unsighted until after the ball left the bat, made a miraculous catch. The ball seemed to have passed him, but he recovered to snatch it from somewhere behind him.

Judges as knowledgeable as Stuart Surridge and Ian Chappell were now saying that Lillee and Thomson, and especially Thomson, were bowling as fast as was humanly possible, and that they had never seen any combination to compare with them for speed. *Wisden*'s verdict was more controversial. 'Never in 93 years of Test cricket have batsmen been so grievously bruised and battered by ferocious, hostile, short-pitched balls.' The one player who looked capable of asserting himself was Amiss, and for one glorious morning, in the second innings at Melbourne, he dictated the play, driving, cutting, glancing and slashing his way to 41 of the first 50 runs in even time on a pitch that was never completely true. Seven overs from Thomson produced 46 runs,

[1] As related in Chapter 8.

the close field scattered, and the 100 came up in 95 minutes at the rate of five runs an over. David Lloyd, aided by some luck against Lillee and Thomson, helped put on 115 for the first wicket, and Amiss had reached 90, needing only three runs to equal Bobby Simpson's record of 1,381 runs in a calendar year (since eclipsed by Viv Richards), when he tried to steady down as wickets around him fell and got himself out. One of the bowlers opposed to him that day — Max Walker — called it a 'great innings'. The match was drawn.

The Australian close catching was electrifying in this series, and Amiss continued to be one of the chief sufferers, falling to a wonderful left-handed catch by Mallett in the gully in the fourth Test. This was followed by a freak dismissal in the second innings, after he and Lloyd had given England a useful start. They had weathered an overnight barrage, leaving England to bat through the last day to leave them with an outside chance of squaring the series. But disaster came at 70 for 1, with Amiss, having played as well as he had ever played considering the life in the pitch, on 37. Lillee, bowling his fastest of the series, sent down a shortish ball outside the off stump. Amiss, intending to leave it alone, lifted his bat, but the ball ducked in at him off the seam and climbed alarmingly. He avoided it as best he could, arms raised, but the ball brushed his gloves and Marsh made the catch. England failed to last out the day, *Wisden* exempting only Edrich, Amiss and Fletcher of the batsmen from blame.

In the fifth Test, with Thomson injured, Amiss recorded his second 'pair' against Australia, defeated both times by Lillee. In the sixth, which England won by an innings, Thomson was still absent and Lillee broke down after bowling six overs — but he got Amiss first. Even *Wisden* was agape at how it was done. Lillee sent down two huge outswingers, followed by a wild and wayward delivery down the leg side which Marsh dived for in vain. Then for his fourth ball he bowled the perfect fast break-back, which 'not surprisingly', as *Wisden* charitably put it, Amiss played outside. That was three ducks in a row, all against Lillee, who limped off soon afterwards, leaving Edrich, Denness,

Fletcher and Greig to play while the cats were away. All four deserved their luck — but it was galling for Amiss.

No one, then, had a more convincing hard-luck story than Amiss at the end of that tour, nor more sympathetic advocates to relate it on his behalf (he made no excuses himself). But hard-luck stories at cricket rarely survive close scrutiny. Selectors soon conclude that something must be wrong with the method, or the temperament. When Amiss failed in the first two Tests against the Australians that summer, the selectors despaired of him. Amiss in fact was jaded, after three consecutive winters on tour and five successive Test series, culminating in the phenomenal pace he had recently been exposed to as England's No. 1, and he had thought of asking to be rested. But it needed more courage, he found, to ask to be left out than to battle on. Thus he was one of the many who were caught on a rain-affected pitch at Edgbaston after Denness had put Australia in, while in his anxiety to redeem himself after a first innings duck at Lord's (lbw to Lillee), he chased a wide one from the same bowler in the second innings and was caught. In that match the grey-haired, bespectacled David Steele made his first appearance for England at the age of 33. Amiss at 32, with scores of 0, 0, 0, 4, 5, 0 and 10 as his immediate past record, was surely out of Test cricket for good.

Then came the visit of the West Indies in 1976, and the final humiliation at Lord's. International cricket was suddenly studded with great fast bowlers and there was no escape from them. At county level, too, every medium-pacer who thought he could extract a bit of lift got the message and started bouncing them at him. He must find some way of eliminating his weakness or get out of the game.

It had been easy for the critics, watching the inept display in Australia of one England batsman after another, to blame faulty technique and to urge the obvious remedy of getting the body behind the ball. Against such pace, on the wickets prepared for that series, no batsman in the world could have coped. 'Not even God could play that stuff,' was the verdict of West Indian Lawrence Rowe in the following year. But some adjustment must surely be possible. Always ready to examine his technique — as he had with the Indian spinners — Amiss took Ian Chappell as a model, recalling how the Australian captain moved back and across to fast bowling before the ball was bowled. Reg Simpson, one of the great players of fast bowling, was reputed to have done much the same — although Amiss could not remember seeing him play. Even Colin Cowdrey, in that 1974-75 series, had adjusted his method to the extent of leaving his leg stump open on one occasion and being bowled behind his legs.

It was a technique that would need practice. He couldn't try it in the middle until he had confidence in it. What he wanted was not fast bowlers slinging them down and trying to knock his hob over, but medium-pacers against whom he could perfect his footwork. He not only had to get behind the short-pitched ball, he had to be properly balanced to play all his shots.

Two young second-team players, both useful net bowlers, Andy Lloyd and Chris Maynard — the one primarily a batsman and the other a wicket-keeper — bowled to him tirelessly, and at length his faith was sufficient to take his new technique into the middle.

The obvious danger, as he moved back and across and faced the bowler almost square on, lay in the out-swinger. His strength off his legs was such that he was not so worried about the in-swinger or the break-back. 1976 was the hottest and driest summer for many years, wickets were hard and true, and it may be that conditions were abnormally unresponsive to swing and seam bowling. But for whatever reason, Amiss found that the experiment worked. Going back, he gave himself more time to play. Going across, he got well behind and even inside the line of the short-pitched ball.

In mid-July Amiss completed his fifth hundred of the summer. All his old composure had returned. Against the West Indies for Warwickshire he was bowled by Holding for 24, so the ghost was not quite laid, but he was scoring so heavily day by day in the county game, and showing such confidence, that only his past record against fast bowlers — and the West Indies had a glut of them — kept him out of the England side. In Holding,

Roberts and Daniel they had three hostile bowlers who were all genuinely fast, with Holder and the left-arm Julien to back them up. Big scores in county cricket were one thing: what use was it, argued some, to recall the discredited Amiss against such an array?

Rumours of his new method, however, filtered through the county scene. The best England side, as the selectors knew, must include Boycott and Amiss, and Amiss, unlike Boycott, had never opted out. After drawing the first two Tests England were outplayed and indeed outclassed in the next two, and if Amiss really had solved his problems and regained his serenity the selectors wanted him back for the final Test at the Oval, to help salvage something from the series. But was he really ready?

One man with a vested interest was the England captain, Tony Greig. Disillusioned with some of the players who had been selected so far, he admitted to being stuck for a batter for the final Test, and his thoughts turned to Amiss. The fourth Test ended on 27th July, and next day Amiss made 80 against Lancashire and then 92 in the second innings, helping Warwickshire to a narrow victory. At that point Amiss had amassed 500 runs in eight days. It so happened that on 4th August Warwickshire were due to play Sussex at Hove in the quarter-finals of the Gillette Cup, giving Greig a chance of a close-up view.

John Snow, England's leading wicket-taker so far in the series, could still bowl uncomfortably fast for a few overs, and Greig told him to give Amiss a good working over, bouncers and all. Amiss, guessing he might be on trial, got his head down, coped with everything that was hurled at him, and made 87. Later that week, at his home in Birmingham, he had a phone call from Greig. 'I thought you played John Snow pretty well down at Hove the other day,' said Greig. 'How do you feel about taking on the West Indies again in the last Test at the Oval? I want you to play if you're in the right frame of mind.'

Amiss's reply was an eager affirmative, and when the names were announced on the Sunday he was in the side. He learned of his selection during a Sunday League game against Northants at Wellingborough, where he was soon buttonholed by the Press. 'I'm very happy to be asked to play again,' he said, 'and I'll be even happier if I get some runs. In the last couple of years I've got into trouble against the fast stuff — I've been hit a few times and that's set me back a bit. But I've scored runs against fast bowling before and I want to kill this story about not being able to play it now. A few runs will put that right once and for all.'

What about his repeated failures against Lillee and Thomson? 'I like to feel that I'm playing the quicker bowlers better now,' said Amiss, 'and that's the important thing. I've changed my technique a little — not going on to the front foot so often. But basically it's a matter of confidence.'

'And you feel confident?'

'Yes.'

He admitted that he'd been relieved when he'd been dropped twelve months earlier, that at that stage he couldn't have taken much more. 'The thrill and the fun had gone out of the game. It was becoming a chore. If you're not giving your full attention to playing fast bowling you're likely to find yourself in trouble. That's what was happening to me.' Now he was enjoying his cricket again, and looking forward to playing in this game at the Oval.

Leading cricket writers greeted Amiss's selection with a mixture of astonishment and outrage. 'The England selectors have made three changes,' noted John Arlott in the *Guardian*, 'one of them amazing.' There were regrets for the three discarded batsmen, Edrich, Close and Hayes. Amiss had been lucky to escape the onslaught Edrich and Close had faced at Old Trafford, while to pick Amiss in place of Hayes was illogical. Arlott even accused the selectors of insensitivity: choosing Amiss was as surprising as it must be embarrassing to himself and his friends. Recalling the blood-letting at Lord's, when Amiss was hit on the head, Arlott pictured Amiss obliged to face a new nightmare before he had properly recovered from the old. Sustained fast bowling had betrayed Amiss into an appalling awkwardness against the short-pitched ball, wrote Arlott, forgetting perhaps that such awkwardness need not result in dismissal and failure, as Ian Redpath had shown against the same attack that winter in Australia. The West Indian fast bowlers would pile on the agony, exploiting Amiss's technical and temperamental problems to the full.

Arlott did not allow his strictures to be moderated on account of his personal liking for Amiss. 'He is one of the most straight-forward, courteous and popular players in the county game.' But here was a player who had been completely unsettled by boun-cers, and it did neither him nor his side any service to expose him to them again.

All this was neatly counter-balanced on the same page by two short sentences from Frank Keating. 'It made my day to hear Dennis Amiss had been recalled. It couldn't happen to a nicer chap.'

John Arlott, however, was not alone. 'One feels both pleased and sorry for Amiss,' wrote John Woodcock in *The Times*. Pleased, because Amiss had forced his way back by sheer weight of runs, sorry because he now had to face the type of bowling which had still been agony for him only a few weeks earlier. He had cut such a miserable figure at Lord's that he must have thought his Test career was finished. 'All things considered,' concluded Woodcock, 'I thought it best that it should be.'

Michael Melford in the *Daily Telegraph* found it hard to justify the return of Amiss in preference to the claims of Barlow and Gooch. There were 'not many better sights in English cricket than Amiss in full flow', and he admired the way Amiss had emerged triumphantly from a disastrous start in Test cricket; but his reputation now attracted the maximum permissible ration of fast, short-pitched bowling, which was 'not a pretty sight'.

Alec Bedser, as chairman, felt bound to defend the selectors' choice. 'We think Dennis Amiss is the best opening batsman in the country and we feel he has got over his uncertainty against fast bowling.' The best way to test that belief was to put him in the side. As for choosing a man of 33 who had played in 42 Tests and ended with a shocking run of low scores, instead of blooding a youngster, Bedser bemoaned the absence of real pace in the county game. 'We never see our youngsters against the sort of fast bowling we've met in this series.'

Some sought to devalue in advance any success Amiss might have by reminding their readers that the rubber was decided and that the Oval game would be a half-hearted affair, not a real Test Match at all. This unworthy hedging of bets was derided by both teams. For the tourists there was Greig's famous 'grovel' speech, from which it was inferred that his aim was to make the West Indians grovel. 'I don't know what it did to the rest of the team,' said Alvin Kallicharran, 'but man, it sure affected the bowlers!' Because of the support they would get from a boisterous West Indian crowd, they would be doubly keen to grind Greig and his men into the Oval dust. As for England, they had everything to gain by going all out for victory and nothing to lose. 'Our players need no motivation to do their best,' said Greig. 'A Test Match is a Test Match whatever the state of the series. We will be out to win this one just as much as the West Indies.' But with John Snow unfit, England's chances of matching the West Indian speed attack on a dead wicket looked slim. The West Indies, for their part, chose a quartet of quick bowlers to the exclusion of a spinner or Julien.

So to the Oval, where, the day before the game started, Mike Selvey, the Middlesex fast-medium bowler, could be seen bowling to Dennis Amiss off fifteen yards in a net pitched in the middle, simulating the batsman's time for reaction against Holding and Roberts. Amiss still had to prove to himself that his new technique allowed him to get into position to play his shots against exceptional pace.

The morning of Thursday 12th August duly came, and Amiss, the seventh opener to be tried for England that series, had to wait nearly two days while the West Indies scored a mammoth 687 for eight declared (Viv Richards 291), leaving England no prospect whatever of victory. Greig showed what he thought of the wicket by introducing Underwood after two overs each from Willis and Selvey, and every member of the side except Knott and Amiss tried their luck with the ball. 'This is the slowest wicket I've ever played on,' said Greig. That being so, England would surely have no difficulty in avoiding defeat. But there were many who believed that the West Indian bowlers had the pace and fire to bowl England out twice on any wicket.

Amiss and Bob Woolmer went in to bat at 5.37 on the Friday after two tiring days in the field. It was Lord's and the MCC match all over again. Clive Lloyd, the West Indian captain, had set the scene for a tornado of speed aimed at leaving the England reply in ruins by nightfall. As one section of the crowd sat in silent apprehension, another more colourful section bayed in anticipation. Even after that massive total, England had not yet been made to grovel enough.

These conflicting emotions were rapidly tranquillised as Amiss, his new-style footwork bringing gasps from those behind the bowler's arm, showed the eager activity of a man who has waited too long for his knock. There was no sign of the expected trepidation at having to face a violent 53 minutes against the new ball. While Woolmer defended, Amiss played his shots, showing no trace of the shell-shocked batsman of two months earlier. There was one anxious moment when he played at a ball he should have ignored, but this was his one slice of luck.

Roberts tried a few bouncers, but Holding, bowling very fast, kept the ball up, and Amiss responded with some classic strokes off his legs and through the covers, strokes which sped like cannon across the sunbaked outfield in the evening light. He took a 4 off Roberts' second over, a 2 and a 3 off his third, a 3 off Holding, and then a 4 and a 2 off Holder, who had replaced Roberts at the Vauxhall end. In the last over of the day he pierced the field again off Roberts, now at the pavilion end, to take his score to 22 and the total to 34 off twelve overs without loss. Woolmer had made 6 and the rest were extras.

Amiss slept soundly that night, and on the Saturday morning, as the heat-wave continued, he was in the nets early. Wayne Daniel, who had not bowled overnight, and whom Amiss had not seen before, began the attack, but seven runs came off his first two overs, six of them to Amiss. Then Woolmer, who had hitherto looked safe and unhurried, was lbw on the back-stroke to Holding in the fourth over of the day, palpably beaten for speed. That was 47 for one.

Immediately the atmosphere, heightened and perhaps inspired by the crowd, became charged with expectancy, entirely different from when the West Indies had batted. Then, a big score had seemed inevitable, and the crowd had settled down to cheer their heroes on. Now, on the same slow wicket, the West Indian quick bowlers were firing away with attacking fields as though they expected to take a wicket each ball.

No more reassuring figure, in that mid-Seventies period of English cricket, could have emerged from the dressing room than David Steele. He had not, perhaps, quite fulfilled the promise of his series in 1975 against the Australians and his century in the first Test that year. But he had done better than most, and his only failure had been when the selectors, desperate for a good start, had chosen him to open the innings — something he was not accustomed to. Now, as he crouched over the ball, or tucked it away off his legs, he presented a broad bat that calmed the incipient hysteria.

Meanwhile Amiss exuded confidence, reaching the boundary for the fifth time in Daniel's next over with an off-drive that put up the 50, his own share being 33. His peregrinations before the ball was bowled, and the resultant open stance, were offending and even frightening the purists, who could not make up their minds whether he would get himself lbw, caught at slip, or knocked out. But at the actual moment of delivery his feet were still, so that when the ball was pitched up he was able to come forward with his normal certainty. This had been one of the points he had perfected in practice. And although the bowlers were sparing with bouncers, Amiss with his new method dealt with them safely when they came.

For two overs Steele kept the strike, and then Amiss took two 4's in succession off Holding. Roberts replaced Daniel only to be hit by Amiss for 4 and 1, and then a 2 and a 4 off successive balls from Holding took him to his fifty, made off 77 balls and including nine 4's, an astonishing proportion considering there were no spectators on the grass and the full extent of the Oval was in use. A six-over spell from Holder failed to stem the run-rate, and Lloyd tried the left-arm slows of Fredericks, off whom Steele took nine in the last over before lunch, bringing the score to 137 for one, Amiss 78, Steele 36. The morning's cricket, which had produced 90 runs off 26 overs for the loss of one wicket, belonged to England.

After lunch Holding switched to the Vauxhall end and found he much preferred it. That was the end he bowled from for the rest of the match. Steele took two more 4's off him, then succumbed much as Woolmer had done, lbw to a ball of exceptional pace that moved in off the pitch and kept slightly low. The only difference was that whereas Woolmer was trapped on the back foot, Steele had gone forward. Bill Alley, who gave him out, was not one of those who believed that playing forward bestowed immunity. Amiss and Steele had added exactly a hundred, and England were 147 for two.

Next man in was Chris Balderstone. Dogged resistance in the previous Test, his first, had earned him a second chance, but Holding was producing an occasional ball of phenomenal velocity, and when the next one came the unfortunate Balderstone, still feeling his way, was late on his stroke as the ball burst through his defence and shattered his stumps. Amiss was then 83.

Next came another man new to Test cricket, Peter Willey: like Balderstone the fourth Test of the series had been his first. Willey had taken the fight to the fast bowlers in both innings at Leeds, and now, with England 151 for three, and another 337 needed to save the follow on, much was expected and indeed demanded of him. He proceeded to bat less freely but with similar resolution, while Amiss, to whom the possibility of dismissal did not seem to occur, dominated the strike. Needing seventeen runs for his century, he raced to it in fourteen balls, completing it off Holding with his thirteenth 4. He had actually scored faster than Richards on the first day, though Richards had faced fewer balls.

It was his tenth hundred for England, and this was the one that counted most. This was the moment of achievement, the confounding of the critics, the justification of all he'd been through, and a moment of relaxation might perhaps be forgiven. Also, like the time the previous evening when he had played and missed before he got settled, it was a moment of danger. Once again the slice of luck he needed came his way. Two balls after reaching his hundred he glanced Holding low and hard past leg slip's outstretched hand.

A good over from Daniel, every ball of which he had to play, helped to steady him, but then came a break for drinks. Perhaps his concentration was again affected, because in Daniel's first over after the interruption came the biggest let-off of all. The ball was shortish but straight and he was committed to playing it. But fractionally before he edged it to wicket-keeper Murray came the umpire's shout of 'no-ball'. He looked up and there was Daniel grinning down the wicket at him, his expression saying everything.

It was not Wayne Daniel's day. In his next over he had Peter Willey dropped at first slip.

Suddenly Amiss cut loose again, taking three 4's in four balls off Holder and forcing a bowling change. All four of the West Indies quick men had bowled since lunch without effecting a break-through, and now Lloyd turned to spin. All he had was Richards and Fredericks, but they bowled with economy, against circumspect batting, either side of tea. At the interval England were 230 for three after 66 overs, Amiss 134, Willey 23.

After tea Richards continued a long spell of off-breaks, twelve overs in all, but towards the end he came in for severe punishment from Amiss, who just before five o'clock passed 150 with his twentieth 4. This made the seventh of his ten Test centuries to exceed 150. Holder replaced Fredericks and slowed down the scoring, and then, soon after 5.30, in the 81st over and with the new ball shortly due, Lloyd introduced the medium-paced Collis King for the first time. With the fourth ball of his second over he induced Willey to give a bat-pad catch, Willey showing surprise when Alley gave him out. Deliberately playing the junior partner, Willey had been bogged down for long periods, and there had been some strokes of desperation, but he had fought stubbornly and held on for 2½ hours while 128 runs were added, of which his share was 33. England were 279 for four, and, in partnership with Willey, Amiss had exactly doubled his score, from 83 to 166. The breaking of this partnership was a tragedy for England, and again it was notable that the mistake came immediately after a drinks interval, such intervals evidently favouring the fielding side.

Tony Greig came next, to an irreverent reception that included much gleeful rhetoric on the lines of 'Who's grovelling now?' Holder, straining after Greig's wicket before Lloyd relieved him to take the new ball, helped the score along with two no-balls, and then it was Roberts and Holding. The time was 5.50, forty minutes to go, and both men were fresh. It was three o'clock since either had bowled.

Crowd partisanship came to the boil as Tony Greig, the man at least half of them loved to hate, faced up to the West Indian spearhead. Here was the most prized scalp of all, and Greig, for his part, was out to give the crowd their money's worth. The man to man, gladiatorial element of this contest dwarfed all else for the moment. Holding pitched the new ball up in the hope that it would swing, and Greig struck him arrogantly through extra-cover for 4. At the other end he gave Roberts the same disdainful treatment. Amiss joined in the fun by taking six off an over from Roberts, including his twenty-third 4, and this put up the 300. With 188 needed to avoid the follow on and six wickets in hand England seemed well on the way to saving the game.

The first ball of Holding's third over, however, was possibly the fastest ever bowled. Tony Greig certainly thought so. Moving in to drive, he tried desperately to get his bat down in time as the ball flew past him, brushing his pads on the way. The ball was unerringly straight, and the glancing contact with the pads caused little deviation.

Emitting a rapturous roar when they saw that the wicket was broken, a proportion of the crowd, largely West Indian, teemed off the terraces and stampeded on to the field. 'A disgraceful scene followed,' according to *Wisden*; but nothing could have been more predictable, and the spontaneity of it disarmed condemnation. It was ten years since the sanctity of the square had first been comprehensively breached on an English cricket field, and few inhibitions remained. The invading hordes trampled on the pitch and pulled out the stumps in their ecstasy, and Bill Alley and Dickie Bird took the players off the field. 'We consulted first with Clive Lloyd,' said Bird afterwards, 'as the debris on the pitch made it dangerous.' The time was 6.10.

The last thing the West Indians wanted at this stage was an interruption in the play, but that was the result. Yet when the resumption came, at 6.23, it hardly seemed fair to the batting side. The ensuing seven-minute ordeal, after such an emotional outburst, seemed pregnant with further disaster, but as it happened night-watchman Derek Underwood struck Holding's last ball for a belligerent single and then miraculously survived the last over from Roberts.

The West Indies had bowled 80 overs in the day, off which England had scored 270 runs. Of these Amiss had scored 154. Thus at close of play, after batting all day, he was 176 not out.

Amiss had faced what by general consent was the fastest and most sustained speed attack in world cricket for six hours 47 minutes with scarcely a false stroke. He had scored at a personal rate of just under two runs an over, while his partners struggled. It was an epic come-back, winning both the technical and psychological battles in a triumph of temperament and class. Surely the joy would be unanimous, the praise unreserved. But this was not so.

It was not that anyone sought to belittle or disparage the achievement. It was the nature of the achievement that was questioned. It had been a plasticene pitch, unacceptable, in the opinion of John Arlott, as the basis for a cricket match. While some were satisfied that Amiss had developed a technique that cured his weakness against the short-pitched ball, Arlott maintained that in less favourable conditions it would expose him even further to injury and early dismissal — specifically to the ball that moved away and the one that cut back. Amiss's was a personal triumph, not a technical one. 'His technical approach

spoke clearly of much — perhaps too much — thought,' continued Arlott. 'As the fast bowlers approached, he went into an
elaborate foot-drill which meant that he was no more than partly
balanced, often still moving, and in a grotesquely square-on
position when the ball reached him.' (Amiss, had he read the
match reports — which he never did — would have contested
this.) 'On a wicket of even mild pace the slightest movement
must have cut his defence completely open.' He survived, Arlott
concluded, 'by concentration, determination, and ultimately,
sheer courage — but without proving anything technical.'

Fascinating as this evaluation was, it seemed dangerously near
self-justification after what Arlott had written earlier, and it
hardly did justice to the authority with which Amiss had played.
He had been the one batsman who had invariably middled the
ball that cut back.

Michael Melford was more inclined to suspend judgement.
But he warned his readers, having listened to the chat in the
Press Box, that there would be detractors. 'It will be emphasized
that the rubber was won, the pitch so slow that the rare bouncer
was being gathered chest high by the wicket-keeper, that the
attack was an unbalanced one, and that the ball would turn but
that there was no real spin.' It had been an innings of great
resource and character, and while it might have looked easy for
Amiss, it hadn't for anyone else.

Everyone agreed that Holding had been magnificent — hostile,
accurate, and at times of bewildering pace, as Balderstone and
Greig had discovered. Given such prodigious speed, when the
ball was pitched up the pace of the wicket was irrelevant.

Holding had sought throughout to penetrate, whereas the
English attack, and even Roberts, hitherto the most successful
West Indian bowler, had been content to contain. Under the
conditions obtaining, batsmen who could play fast bowling had
been given a chance, which had not always been so in 1974-75
in Australia. The wicket was a flash-back to the Thirties, and
was perhaps to be welcomed.

The pitch certainly did not meet with unanimous condemnation, John Woodcock noting that it produced some brilliant

cricket — a combination of great batting and great fast bowling, with the lack of top-class wrist-spin, and the limitations of the medium-pacers, mercilessly exposed.

Amiss himself took a view much closer to John Arlott's than might be supposed. In previous weeks he had found that a two-eyed stance provided him with the best answer to short-pitched bowling, but he was aware that there was no 100% technique. The time would come when he would discard his new method and revert to the old. It had been, as he came to recognise, a one-off job. 'The main thing is believing in what you are doing.' It was a question of confidence. Whatever might be said about the method, if it restored his confidence — as it patently had — it was worth more than gold.

When play was resumed on the Monday, England at 304 for 5 still needed 184 to save the follow on. Much depended on Amiss, and it was inevitable that the day should begin with a furious onslaught from Holding and Roberts. With Sunday to think about it, the West Indians had devised a method of countering Amiss's technique. In shuffling back and across, they decided, he must leave his leg stump unusually vulnerable, and they tried attacking his leg stump from round the wicket. But they found it difficult to maintain a line from this angle, while Amiss, as on the Friday evening, began with massive confidence. All that the West Indian bowlers got for their pains was a flow of elegant strokes, two of them clipped off the leg stump for 4.

Holding was still flogging unsuspected life from the pitch, however, sometimes rocking Murray back on his heels. Amiss took a single off the second ball of his third over — still from the Vauxhall end — and the next ball, aimed well up and of terrific pace, flattened Underwood's off stump. That was 323 for 6. But Underwood had played his part, and with Alan Knott safely negotiating the rest of Holding's over, bowled from over the wicket, England still hoped to escape.

Such was the rasping power of Amiss's shots that he was now dealing mainly in boundaries. A thundering straight drive off Roberts took his score to 195, Knott managed a single off Holding to give him the strike, and two more sweetly struck leg-side shots

Amiss moves back and across to get in line to play Holding.

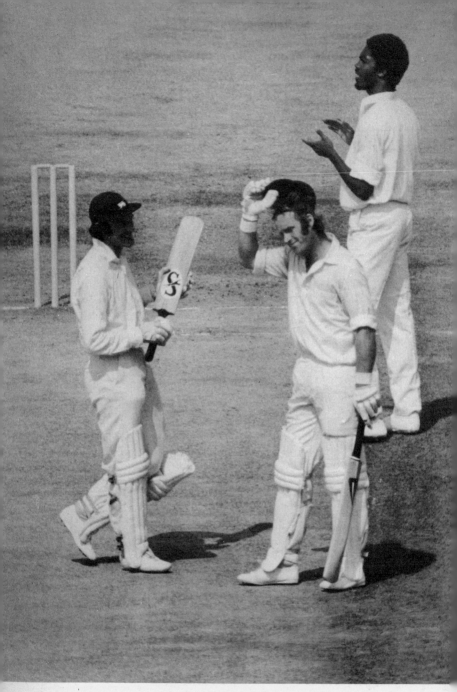

Amiss acknowledges the ovation for his come-back double century
as Knott congratulates and Holding applauds.

that beat the field all the way took him past 200. The second of these was his twenty-eighth 4, and he had scored 27 runs in 35 minutes that morning. The round-the-wicket attack on the leg stump had failed.

Knott took six runs off Roberts' next over, including a leg-side 4 which resulted in an injury to Daniel. Giving chase, he pulled up lame, having strained a hamstring. That was one of the West Indian fast men out of the attack, further enhancing England's chances.

For his next over, to Amiss, his fifth of the morning, Holding reverted to orthodox over the wicket, and Amiss shuffled across, as he had done to all the faster bowlers throughout, whatever their mode of delivery. After blocking the first three balls he aimed to leg glance the fourth. This time he missed.

That Amiss's wicket could ever be broken had seemed beyond imagining. But he had left his leg stump open, and now the bails fell. The shock was such that it was a moment before the crowd reacted. The theory worked out by the West Indians over the week-end had been abandoned, but Amiss had been bowled behind his legs after all.

Amiss had batted for 7½ hours, and his innings had been spread over three days. In scoring 203 out of a total of 342 for seven he had held the innings together, batting with all the grace and conviction of a high-class batsman in form. Indeed he had looked the only class player in the side.

Deprived of the bustling zeal and charisma of Amiss the innings seemed certain to sag, but a spirited partnership between Knott and Geoff Miller, in which Knott reached his 50 in 64 balls, maintained the tempo. Then another interval, this time lunch, proved fatal, and soon after three o'clock the innings subsided, the deficit being 252.

There followed what must surely be the fastest opening partnership in Test Match history. With Daniel injured and Holding, Roberts and Holder needing a rest, Lloyd did not enforce the follow on, and Fredericks and Greenidge made 182 off 33 overs without being separated, all the England bowlers suffering alike. Lloyd then declared to leave England twenty minutes of agony at the end of the day and another six hours after that in which to save the match.

The agony duly came, not in the fall of wickets but in a numbing blow to Amiss's left forearm in Holding's second over. There was a delay while he recovered, and although Woolmer got most of the strike and began by hitting three successive 4's off Roberts, Amiss ended the session by taking nine off the last over of the day. In the five overs bowled, three by Holding and two by Roberts, Woolmer and Amiss actually scored faster than Fredericks and Greenidge had done, making 43 runs (helped by four byes and four wides), an average of more than eight runs an over. Woolmer was not out 21, Amiss not out 14.

It was too much, perhaps, on the final morning, to expect Amiss to settle in yet again, and after taking 2 off Holding's third ball of the day he touched the fourth to Greenidge at slip. Woolmer, Balderstone, Willey and Greig followed cheaply in the first hour, and at 78 for five England seemed to be collapsing without a fight. Then stands of 70 between Steele and Knott and 48 between Knott and Miller (Knott making his second fifty of the match), kept England's hopes of a draw alive, and although this was not achieved face was saved and the end delayed until 80 minutes from stumps. Holding finished with best-ever match figures for a West Indian of 14 for 149, and Greig called it 'the greatest performance I have ever seen by a fast bowler.' He added: 'I do not believe there can ever have been a faster bowler than Holding. On the two occasions in this series when he has been fully fit he was faster than the Australians.'

Jim Laker at Old Trafford had a turning pitch to bowl on. Bob Massie at Lord's had a heavy atmosphere. Against Mike Denness's team Lillee and Thomson were helped by fiery wickets of uneven bounce. But Holding succeeded on a dead, much-maligned pitch on which his pace was so disconcerting that batsmen were glad to get down the other end to face Roberts, one of the greatest fast bowlers of the day.

The stature of Amiss's innings should be measured not against the wicket but against Holding, at the peak of his fitness and strength. It is enough to add that despite the valiant fight put up

ENGLAND v WEST INDIES 1976 (5th Test)
at the Oval, August 12, 13, 14, 16, 17

West Indies won by 231 runs

WEST INDIES: First Innings

R. C. Fredericks, c Balderstone b Miller	71
C. G. Greenidge, lbw b Willis	0
I. V. A. Richards, b Greig	291
L. G. Rowe, st Knott b Underwood	70
C. H. Lloyd, c Knott b Greig	84
C. L. King, c Selvey b Balderstone	63
D. L. Murray, c and b Underwood	36
V. A. Holder, not out	13
M. A. Holding, b Underwood	32
A. M. E. Roberts, did not bat	
W. W. Daniel, did not bat	
Extras (B 1, LB 17, NB 9)	27
Total (8 wkts dec.)	687

Fall of wickets: 1-5, 2-159, 3-350; 4-524, 5-547. 6-640. 7-642, 8-687.

Bowling: Willis, 15-3-73-1; Selvey, 15-0-67-0; Underwood, 60.5-15-165-3; Woolmer, 9-0-44-0; Miller, 27-4-106-1; Balderstone, 16-0-80-1; Greig, 34-5-96-2; Willey, 3-0-11-0; Steele, 3-0-18-0.

ENGLAND: First Innings

D. L. Amiss, b Holding	203
R. A. Woolmer, lbw b Holding	8
D. S. Steele, lbw b Holding	44
J. C. Balderstone, b Holding	0
P. Willey, c Fredericks b King	33
*A.W. Greig, b Holding	12
D. L. Underwood, b Holding	4
†A. P. E. Knott, b Holding	50
G. Miller, c sub (Julien) b Holder	36
M. W. W. Selvey, b Holding	0
R. G. D. Willis, not out	5
Extras (B 8, LB 11, NB 21)	40
Total	435

Fall of wickets: 1-47, 2-147, 3-151, 4-279, 5-303, 6-323, 7-342, 8-411, 9-411.

Bowling: Roberts, 27-4-102-0; Holding, 33-9-92-8; Holder, 27.5-7-75-1; Daniel, 10-1-30-0; Fredericks, 11-2-36-0; Richards, 14-4-30-0; King, 7-3-30-1.

WEST INDIES: Second Innings

R. C. Fredericks, not out	86
C. G. Greenidge, not out	85
Extras (B 4, LB 1, W 1, NB 5)	11
Total (0 wkt dec.)	182

Bowling: Selvey, 9-1-44-0; Willis, 7-0-48-0; Underwood, 9-2-38-0; Greig, 2-0-11-0; Woolmer, 5-0-30-0.

ENGLAND: Second Innings

D. L. Amiss, c Greenidge b Holding	16
R. A. Woolmer, c Murray b Holding	30
D. S. Steele, c Murray b Holder	42
J. C. Balderstone, b Holding	0
P. Willey, c Greenidge b Holder	1
A. W. Greig, b Holding	1
A. P. E. Knott, b Holding	57
G. Miller, b Richards	24
D. L. Underwood, c Lloyd b Roberts	2
M. W. W. Selvey, not out	4
R. G. D. Willis, lbw b Holding	0
Extras (B 15, LB 3, W 8)	26
Total	203

Fall of wickets: 1-49, 2-54, 3-64, 4-77, 5-78, 6-148, 7-196, 8-196, 9-202.

Bowling: Holding, 20.4-6-57-6; Roberts, 13-4-37-1; Holder, 14-5-29-2; Richards, 11-6-11-1; Fredericks, 12-5-33-0; King, 6-2-9-0; Lloyd, 2-1-1-0.

Umpires—W. E. Alley and H. D. Bird

by their later batsmen in the second innings, England, including the 16 contributed by Dennis Amiss, made exactly the same number of runs as Amiss himself had made in the first innings — 203.

10

DEREK RANDALL

'To be chosen ahead of the superb
Lillee [as Man of the Match] was a
feat indeed.'
— *Reg Hayter,* Wisden

The young man from the Midlands was too shy to mix with the immortals, too diffident to join the famous players of bygone years who had gathered in Melbourne to celebrate a hundred years of Test cricket between England and Australia. Amongst the Huttons, the Comptons and the Truemans, the Bradmans, the Millers and the Lindwalls, he felt out of place. Some of the current England side knew many of the older players and had become pleasantly involved in the pre-match festivities. But the long-armed, loose-limbed Derek Randall stayed quietly in his hotel room.

Curiously enough he was quite content to do so. In isolating himself from the carnival atmosphere that permeated the city he was also insulating himself from the pressures of the build-up to the game. There was no more animated, ebullient character in cricket than Derek Randall, but for the moment he was enjoying the pleasures of inactivity and solitude.

It was nearly three and a half months since he had set out as a member of the England touring party for India, Sri Lanka and finally Australia — his first overseas tour. Prior to the tour he had never played in a Test Match, having won his place on the strength of two brilliant displays in the one-day matches against the West Indies at the end of the 1976 season. In India he had played in four of the five Tests, and on his début he had batted well for 37 on an uncertain surface, proving his technique. But

223

this was his highest score in seven Test innings, leaving his temperament and application at international level in doubt.

It wasn't that he had played all that badly. He just hadn't had the breaks. The slow, turning wickets were unfamiliar to him, and despite many hours of practice to get used to them they contributed to his undoing. Then again the slice of luck needed to gain confidence had eluded him, to the extent of marginal decisions always seeming to go against him just as he was settling in. What saved the tour for him was his own cheerful, effervescent disposition and his immense popularity with the vast Indian crowds. Tony Greig, who was captaining the side, never discouraged his antics, since they served two purposes; they kept the crowd in a good humour, and they kept Randall himself in a good frame of mind for the climax of the tour in Australia.

After the long and tiring Indian tour came a fortnight in the steamy heat of Sri Lanka, including eight days' cricket, after which their schedule was disrupted by air traffic delays which compounded their exhaustion, leaving them little more than a day to adjust and acclimatise before playing their only preliminary match in Australia before the Centenary Test — against Western Australia at Perth.

Up to this point Randall and others had scarcely given the Centenary Test a thought. Their minds had been concentrated on the series in India. The Melbourne game seemed far distant, and if they considered it at all they visualised it as some kind of huge jamboree. Ostrich-like, they recoiled from the thought that what really awaited them was a one-shot death or glory confrontation with the full might of Australia.

Illusions were quickly dispelled when they reached Perth. The Australians, fresh from a triumphant series against the West Indies which had left them undisputed world champions, were intent on corroborating their status. They were going to play it for all they were worth, and England had better look out.

If there was one man in the England party who had no doubts about what awaited them in Melbourne it was Tony Greig, and he set to work to re-motivate his team. It looked an impossible task. The process began in the course of the three-day fixture against Western Australia, whose team included Rod Marsh (captain), Kim Hughes, Graeme Wood, Craig Serjeant, Mick Malone, and Dennis Lillee. The jaded tourists were lucky to field first, but when the State side declared at 326 for eight, Amiss's revised technique was cruelly exposed by Lillee, and although the fast bowler was used sparingly with the Test in mind, only Brearley, Miller and Barlow prospered and Greig declared 82 behind. Finally set 301 to win, the tourists slumped to 182 for eight and would have lost but for a stubborn ninth wicket stand between Brearley and Selvey.

The most significant period of the match came when Lillee, who did not open the attack in the second innings, came on after ten overs and bowled off a shortened run. When Miller hooked and glanced Lillee for 4, Marsh moved Wood up from deep square leg to save the one just as Lillee ran up to bowl. Amiss halted Lillee in his run-up to point this out to Miller, and Lillee, enraged at being interrupted, hurled the ball to the ground. Marsh had to run up the wicket to pacify him. Lillee then gestured first, third and fourth slips 30 yards deep and proceeded to bowl short lifters outside the off stump. Miller remained calm, but Amiss, to whom Lillee bowled noticeably straighter, was soon ducking and weaving. Once, when he turned his head away, he was hit in the small of the back. He square-drove a rare half-volley for 4, snicked a lifter over the distant slips to the boundary, and was derisively applauded by Lillee when he missed an intended cut. Flailing yet again at a bouncer, he found his ordeal mercifully ended when he was given out caught by Marsh.

Amiss had played magnificently in India and in the continued absence of Geoff Boycott he was England's leading batsman. But those who maintained that Lillee had broken his spirit against fast short-pitched bowling, and that the technique he had evolved to counter it was irrelevant, seemed distressingly vindicated.

The game only aggravated the headaches of the tour selectors. What to do about Amiss? He must obviously play, but the temptation to drop him down the order to protect him from Lillee's opening assault, already forming in Greig's mind, became irresistible. This meant the inclusion of Woolmer to open.

Woolmer had failed in India, but he had made a useful fifty in the second innings at Perth and the decision was made.

'Dennis is the heaviest scorer in the side,' explained Greig. 'We are nursing him at No. 4 in the hope of a big score. I have always regarded him as a better middle order player than an opener, and I remember reading somewhere that Greg Chappell thought the same.' This was good psychological stuff, aimed at bolstering Amiss's morale, but totally inconsistent with his record. Amiss himself, though, was amenable. 'The more it goes on, the more you think about it,' he said. 'You go in there and something goes wrong and you think "My God, it's happening again." '

The arrangement left two batting places in doubt, Nos. 3 and 5. On the grounds of experience, although he too had had his problems against Lillee, Fletcher was included at No. 5. For all his coolness at Perth, Geoff Miller was hardly an England No. 3, and he was excluded, as was Barlow. Randall had scored only modestly against Western Australia, but he had looked much more at home on the fast, bouncy Perth wicket than in India and the last place went to him.

Amiss, for one, thought Randall deserved it. 'He went into the nets every minute of the day at Perth,' he says, 'and had boys throwing the ball at him from half-way down the wicket, one minute at his head, practising the bouncer, the next minute at his feet, trying to york him — preparing for what he was going to receive in the middle.' Amiss knew because he was in an adjoining net, still trying to work out his problems against the fast lifting ball.

Had the game been played in England, neither Fletcher nor Randall would have been chosen. With Lillee in mind the places must have gone to John Edrich and David Steele.

For Australia there were two notable absentees: Ian Chappell, who had announced his retirement from Test cricket, and Jeff Thomson, whose injured shoulder had not yet mended. This made room for two Garys — Gary Cosier and Gary Gilmour. All was set for what the Melbourne papers described as the match of the century.

Greig maintained that England had a fifty-fifty chance, but he knew the weakness of his batting line-up all too well, and when he won the toss he put Australia in. There was enough moisture in the wicket to justify his decision on tactical grounds, and his side responded magnificently. The bowlers — Willis, Lever, Old and Underwood — attacked the wicket and gave nothing away, every catch was taken, and Australia were bowled out on the first day for 138. The tension of the occasion, and the atmosphere created by the 61,000 crowd, affected the batsmen more than the bowlers, and Australia never recovered from a sensational start in which Ian Davis was lbw to Lever and Rick McCosker gloved an intended hook off Willis to be struck in the jaw, from where the ball dropped on to his wicket. His jaw was broken and he looked to be out of the match.

Urged on by a crowd who, having been glumly silent for much of the day, chanted 'Lil-lee' and 'Max-ie' in vociferous unison as their heroes ran up to bowl, Australia could do no more that evening than dismiss Woolmer. Underwood came in as night-watchman, and the day ended with England apparently well placed at 29 for one.

The illusion of advantage disappeared in the first two overs next morning with the dismissal of Brearley and Underwood. Randall, who had seen Lillee for the first time at Perth, seemed to have plenty of time to play him, and when a bouncer whistled past his ears he doffed his cap and bowed in appreciation, to the delight of the crowd. They were even more delighted two balls later when Lillee bowled the perfect ball, the one Randall knew he had to look out for, pitching off-stumpish and going away, and Randall edged it to Marsh.

The wicket was still green, the England batsmen were even more jittery than the Australians had been, and the Australian catching was no less inspired. Amiss and Fletcher both fell to Walker before settling in, Amiss to a gully slash and Fletcher to a leg-cutter. Greig, not untypically, was bowled off his pads, and the innings collapsed. 95 all out and thus 43 behind, England were dismissed for their lowest total against Australia for nearly 20 years. Jack Fingleton complained that it would have been the dullest Test Match in a hundred years but for the catching.

By the end of that second day, however, a stand between Davis and Walters had taken Australia to 104 for three, the juice had gone out of the wicket, and England faced an uphill struggle to get back into the game. Their most despondent moment came shortly before stumps when Walters gave a straightforward catch to Willis in the gully off Old — strictly according to plan — and the chance went down. It was the first catch to be dropped by either side.

Outstanding incidents on the third day centred around Tony Greig. He got Davis caught behind at 132 for four, and Walters in the same way at 187 for five, giving his bowlers encouragement as well as rest. At this point, 230 behind, and with McCosker not expected to bat, England were in with a chance. The real turning point, in the opinion of the Australian captain, came half an hour later, and again the bowler was Greig. He had tried every trick he could think of to unsettle the 21-year-old David Hookes, a left-hander playing in his first Test, until eventually umpire Tom Brooks intervened. 'Cool it,' he said, 'he's only a youngster.' To Greig this was a *non sequitur*, but soon Hookes cooled him down in thrilling fashion by hammering him for five 4's off successive balls — a lofted on-drive that was nearly a 6, a pull fine of square, a drive through the covers, a clip to mid-wicket, and a drive on the up wide of cover's left hand that was applauded as the stroke of the day. In its context the assault rivalled the six 6's by Sobers off Nash at Swansea in 1968.

Although Underwood got Hookes out in the next over, this aggressive young player had hit 56 off 69 balls and exposed the limitations of the England attack, on a wicket now flattened by usage and sunshine. Australia were 244 for six, the bowlers were tiring, and the beefy Marsh, with his familiar blend of pugnacity and caution, was entrenched.

England wilted as first Gilmour and then Lillee helped Marsh to add another 109 runs by five o'clock, raising the fourth-innings target to just under 400. Then came the final fit of the horrors for England as a Frankenstein monster, face in a sling, unable to speak or hear, and with a runner as warder, appeared in the distance and proved to be the broken-jawed Rick McCosker. To what extent this grotesque apparition inhibited the bowlers is uncertain, but an obligatory restraint against walking-wounded did not long survive the bandaged subject's adhesive intent, Lever trying a couple of bouncers. These so inflamed the crowd that had McCosker been hit again that evening many Australians believed a violent scene would have ensued.

It was announced that McCosker's decision to bat was his own, and surely no one else could have made it for him. Much as such gameness was admired, the ethics of exposing a player to the opposition in such an injured state, submitting to their good-will, came under scrutiny. Under the laws of the game, however, McCosker was perfectly entitled to take his chance, just as the bowlers were entitled to treat him within the same regulations. There was no provision for umpires to intervene to protect a man from further punishment, as a referee can in boxing.

By stumps on that third day McCosker had helped Marsh to add 34 runs in 58 minutes, a wearying frustration for England at the end of a day in the field. Australia at 387 for eight were 430 in front. Marsh, having already — with 91 at Manchester in 1972 — got within one of Don Tallon's record for Australian wicket-keepers against England, was now level on 92. With four catches in the England first innings, he was challenging strongly for the award of Man of the Match.

England's position looked so hopeless that evening that they might well have been glad to get the thrashing over as soon as possible and creep off home. But the following day was a rest day, giving them 24 hours to mull over their plight.

'How Tony Greig's men have become the mugs of Australia,' was the headline in one English newspaper, and the organisers of the game were berated for setting England, straight from an arduous tour of the Indian sub-continent, an impossible task. 'Greig's men who played their hearts out in India are now the mugs of Australia,' repeated Alex Bannister, 'martyrs thrown to the lions.' The Queen and the Duke of Edinburgh were in Sydney and were on their way to Melbourne, with the intention of visiting the ground on the final day. Thus England faced not

only the prospect of overwhelming defeat but also the humiliation
of not being able to keep the game going until the Queen arrived.

'Only Australia can win the Centenary Test,' was another
comment, and John Arlott was not alone in concluding that
England's sole credible hope of saving the game was rain. Others,
wise before the event, criticised the selection of Amiss and
Fletcher. Their nerve was broken, and young players like Barlow
and Miller would have done better. At Perth, Miller especially
had shown the right technique against pace. As for Amiss,
dropping him down the order was a panic measure: he had had
all his success as an opener and if he wasn't going to go in first
he shouldn't have played.

The Australians, for their part, derived scant satisfaction from
the hollow victory that now seemed imminent. The fear on all
sides was that England would go down without a fight. 'If
England have not learnt from Hookes and have not overcome
their obvious discomfiture against Lillee,' wrote Jack Fingleton,
'this game will end tomorrow.' In anticipation of this débâcle a
limited, over match was scheduled if the Test should end on the
fourth day or early on the fifth.

Greg Chappell accepted cautiously that 'changing fortunes
had swung the game almost irreversibly Australia's way.' Even
Tony Greig admitted that Australia had 'a better than even
chance', surely a masterpiece of understatement. 'The time when
we should have got in a winning position was during the first
innings.' But he was quick to put regrets and recriminations
behind him and get on with the job of heartening and re-
animating his team. 'We've by no means written the game off
yet. It has swung back and forth and maybe it will go our way
again.'

He planned no drastic measures for regaining the initiative.
The main thing, he believed, was to get his batsmen into the
right frame of mind, so that they didn't panic merely because of
the size of the score they were chasing.

How were they to achieve the necessary serenity? A spell in
the nets might have helped, but the rest day was marred by
wind-squalls and rain. The players on whom the task would fall

of scoring the best part of 500 runs for victory sat in their hotel rooms, alternately playing Patience, watching television, and snoozing. After the disasters of the first innings, Randall for one was even less ready to mingle with the greats, and he had his meals sent up to his room. Sharing the room with him was Geoff Miller, and the fact that Miller was not personally involved in the game helped Randall relax. Not until four o'clock in the afternoon did he move out, and then it was to stretch his legs and get some fresh air. It seemed to be a rest day for the whole of Melbourne; the streets were strangely deserted. He walked in the opposite direction from the cricket ground, but all the time he was preparing himself mentally for the morrow.

Somehow he had to leave that most dangerous ball of Lillee's, the one that started off-stumpish and at which you were tempted to play, severely alone. The pitch had dried out and on the third day it had been a superb cricket wicket, as the Australians in their second innings had shown. Australian wickets suited him better than most; that much he had already discovered. He knew he was fortunate to be playing, and after his first-innings failure he felt under intense pressure to do well. But in spite of this he felt relaxed and confident. He was in with a chance.

Tony Greig had always led from the front and Randall had a tremendous regard for him. Greig's favourite saying was that a given situation 'would sort out the men from the boys', and he applied it with some aptness to their present predicament. Greig's guiding principle was that they must play positively, and this was in tune with Randall's own temperament. When the last two Australian wickets went down, or when Chappell declared, they were to go out there to win, not to hang about in the hope of saving the game. It was a one-off match, there would be no coming back in a second or third Test, they had to do it now.

The wicket had been covered and when play resumed on the fourth day the pitch behaved as before. The crowd, having had a day to think about it, and perhaps being less volatile at the beginning of a day than at the end of it, no longer resented the occasional bumper that Willis, as well as Lever, now aimed at McCosker. It was no more than McCosker must expect.

The Australians added another 32 runs that morning for the loss of McCosker, caught at mid-wicket. Marsh moved safely to his hundred, and at precisely midday Chappell declared, leaving England fifty minutes' batting before lunch. The target was 463, and they had 590 minutes plus 15 overs to get them. 15 overs in the last hour was in fact a generous allocation; the average through the day was likely to be twelve. For those who bothered to work it out, as an academic exercise, England needed to score at the rate of 3½ runs per eight-ball over for a period of eleven hours to win.

The danger, as Tony Greig had foreseen, was that no one, and especially not the batsmen, would take such a proposition seriously. It was the attitude that all things were possible in cricket that Greig had been working to instil.

Woolmer and Brearley began judiciously to the bowling of Lillee, from the pavilion end, and Walker. After Walker had bowled two overs he was replaced by Gilmour, so that he and Lillee could change ends. Woolmer tucked Gilmour's first delivery, a no-ball, to the square leg boundary. Every time Lillee took the ball the hullabaloo was deafening, and Randall, relaxing in the dressing room with his pads on, decided he'd better see what was happening, get accustomed to the noise, absorb the atmosphere and get the adrenalin going. England seemed certain to come through the pre-lunch session unscathed when, to the second ball of the last over before the interval, bowled from the pavilion end, Woolmer was trapped lbw by a Walker in-ducker. There were less than two minutes to go and Randall did not have to go in. England were 28 for one, Woolmer 9, Brearley not out 14.

With the wicket still fast and true, Greig's greatest fear remained that his batsmen, oppressed by the weight of runs against them, would lose concentration. 'Don't get out when you're 40,' he told Randall. 'Don't get out when you're 60, and don't get out when you're 80.'

After lunch Randall played out Walker's over. He had never felt so nervous in his life, nor more determined. Brearley took six runs off a wayward Gilmour, who could not find his rhythm, and in Walker's next over Randall got off the mark with a single. The more the crowd shouted the more positively Randall played and the more he put bat to ball, radiating the conviction that despite the odds England had a chance.

After turning Walker off his legs for 4 and 1 Randall took eleven runs off Gilmour's next over, which began with a wide. Between stray deliveries and frequent no-balls Gilmour was pitching the right length to give his away swing a chance, but the ball wasn't deviating and Randall drove him fluently through the covers for 3, 4 and 4, Brearley taking a single in between. The runs were coming too fast for Greg Chappell and he tried a double change, bringing Lillee back at the pavilion end for Walker and substituting leg-spinner O'Keeffe for Gilmour. Lillee bowled a maiden to Brearley, but Randall followed his partner into the twenties with a square cut for 2 off O'Keeffe.

Lillee's next over was very nearly the undoing of Randall. He staggered in avoiding a bouncer, and the next ball, an exact replica of the one that got him out in the first innings, found him guilty of the crime he had been nagging himself not to commit — playing and missing. This time the luck was with him and he got away with it. The escape did him good. 'Come on, Rags!' he exhorted. 'Concentrate!' Next ball he drove Lillee for 3 in celebration, then pierced the covers for 4 off O'Keeffe.

In discussions between overs, Brearley and Randall planned to bat in segments of time, cutting up the afternoon into periods of fifteen minutes. If the runs came, fine, but with Lillee tearing in at full bore, which he had not done in his opening spell, and the crowd chanting him on, the most effective counter to the frenetic atmosphere was dogged occupation of the crease. That was the one thing that would damp down crowd hysteria and maintain England's grip on the game. Although on this huge ground the spectators seemed a long way away, no one could forget they were there. It was not a question of going on the defensive, merely that for a couple of overs they would not look to score runs.

Randall's preliminary step in front of the wicket was bringing him in line with Lillee's most dangerous ball, but it did not please the purists, one critic remarking that Randall made 'more movement before the ball was bowled than a clockwork toy'. Continually fidgeting with his cap and adjusting his pads, he looked the most worrying of players. But Randall was not interested in relaxing others. This was his way of relaxing himself.

Chappell continued to use Lillee in three-over bursts, bringing Walker back for the 21st over of the innings. In this spell Walker bowled especially well, moving the ball in the air and off the wicket, and with O'Keeffe bowling his leg- and top-spinners accurately, with slip and short leg hovering near, the run-rate slowed. But Randall's optimism was undimmed. 'Come on, stick at it,' he told Brearley, 'in another fifteen minutes it'll only be fifteen minutes to tea!'

Randall took his score to 30 with a single off Walker's second over, and soon afterwards, with a 3 off O'Keeffe, he crept past Brearley. Then, after four overs' rest, back came Lillee. His first three balls brought a single to Randall, 3 to Brearley, and a magnificently assured pull for 4 by Randall. But to the last ball of the over Randall might have been out. Lillee was bowling at his fastest, and Randall's cut through gully, which went for 4, was 'too rapid to be caught', in the opinion of some. In attempting the catch O'Keeffe bruised his wrist; but catches in the gully off more or less full-blooded hits off Lillee had sometimes been taken.

The two boundaries took Randall to 46, and in the last over before tea he turned O'Keeffe round the corner for a single to reach his fifty. He had batted just under two hours and faced 88 balls. Brearley, on 43, was not far behind, and England at the adjournment were 113 for one. 85 runs had come off 24 overs during the afternoon without the loss of a wicket, and England could hardly have hoped for a better start.

After tea Chappell persevered with Lillee from the pavilion end, and the game had hardly restarted when disaster struck England, Lillee's fourth ball cutting back off the pitch to get Brearley lbw. The lapse may have been partly due to the break, but it was a typical Lillee dismissal. 113 for two, with 350 to get, sounded less hopeful.

Next man in was Dennis Amiss. After all the controversy about where he should bat, he was coming in to face a fresh and rested Lillee with his tail up, the scalp of Dennis Amiss already dangling figuratively from his belt.

The inscribed sheets of bunting which proclaimed 'We luv yer, Dennis,' did not apply to the incoming batsman, except in so far as the authors looked forward to his prompt and predicted degradation.

There can scarcely have been more psychological pressure on any batsman than at that moment, with the huge Melbourne crowd baying for blood. If Amiss was shaking with nerves it was understandable. Even more, perhaps, than at the Oval the previous year, a failure now would be copper-plated indelibly on the parchment of his career.

Lillee came hurtling in at him, menacingly sure of success, and Amiss turned the first ball in the air past short leg for 2. The exercise of running down the wicket, and the knowledge that he might easily have been out, helped to settle his diaphragm, and he got through the rest of the over without mishap. Randall got his score moving again with a square cut for 3 off O'Keeffe, and Amiss off-drove the leg-spinner's fifth ball for 4 and felt infinitely better for doing so.

Meeting in mid-wicket, the two batsmen agreed that the only way they were likely to stop Lillee was to share him as much as they could. If either of them got stuck down that end, Lillee would find a way through. Lillee in this post-tea spell bowled five overs, and the batsmen managed to swap ends with some regularity. After getting Brearley's wicket and greeting Amiss with renewed ferocity, Lillee bowled a maiden to Randall and a maiden to Amiss. In between these two maidens he bowled an over which cost seven runs but in which Amiss had a narrow escape. Randall took a single off the fifth ball, they ran two byes, and then Lillee unleashed his deadly off-stumpish lifter and Amiss steered it through Hookes' hands at third slip for 4. It was the first piece of luck Amiss had had against Lillee in years.

Nevertheless the loss of Brearley and the known vulnerability of Amiss placed an extra burden on Randall, and he responded magnificently. He hooked and cut the short stuff, one tennis-batted bouncer that sped to the mid-wicket fence being a shot reminiscent of Bradman. Whenever Lillee threw a tantrum Randall was ready for him. Typical of the by-play was an lbw appeal of Lillee's which looked patently high but which Randall, balefully glared at by Lillee when the appeal was turned down, dismissed with a gesture as too low.

Whenever Lillee got the better of Randall he would stride down the wicket and glower at him, and Randall, with a 'Well bowled, Mr Lillee', would touch his cap in mock acknowledgement and somehow outface him. No other England player except Tony Greig had ever done this sort of thing and got away with it.

Randall talked a lot, as always, mostly to himself. The Australians, who knew very little about him, could not quite make him out.

When Walker replaced Lillee, Randall hit him for 4, 3 and 1, Amiss keeping things moving with a single after the 3. That was nine runs off the over. Randall's square cutting of O'Keeffe was masterly, and Amiss, his bat now as wide as only his could seem, punished Walker on both sides of the wicket. His only hesitation was against O'Keeffe, whom he did not always seem to read. Twice O'Keeffe might have had him caught off his top-spinner if short leg had dared tuck in closer.

A cover drive off Walker took Randall into the seventies. The runs came so freely in the last hour that the crowd agitated for Lillee, and Chappell felt obliged to call on him for one more effort before stumps. Lillee's first over, his 15th of the innings, was packed with incident. Amiss took a single off the first ball to reach 34, and then Lillee twice pitched short to Randall and each time was pulled firmly for 2. When Lillee reacted with a bouncer, Randall flat-batted it past mid-on for another 2. These three 2's off successive balls raised his score from 77 to 83, and a single off yet another bouncer took him down to the southern end, where Greg Chappell prepared to bowl his first over of the innings. Randall forced him away for 3 to take his personal score to 87 and England's to 191 for two, but at the end of that over,

'Well bowled, Mr Lillee!'

Two ways of
avoiding a bouncer.

at 5.42, the players came off for bad light. There was still a little matter of 272 to win, which meant an average of 90 per session next day — nearly four runs an over — but with eight wickets in hand it no longer looked an impossible target.

England's batting problems had stemmed from the lack of stroke-players who could play fast bowling, and of batsmen who could hook. Right from the start Randall, while looking to bat a long time, had gone for his shots; but he had also displayed the right technique to the rising ball on the off stump. He had found, too, that the eight-ball over helped his concentration. His best shot had been the drive, but what impressed Australians most was his ability and readiness to hook Lillee. Mostly, in fact, he pulled him, square and in front of square. England had done more than discover a batsman, they had found a character, and the Australians took to him.

Greg Chappell conceded that evening that England had clawed their way back into the game. But he had no regrets about his declaration, 'even if the worst comes to the worst. I felt we needed as much time as possible to bowl them out on an easy-paced wicket.' He still had five hours plus 15 overs to do it, and although he agreed that England now had a winning chance he remained confident of victory. 'History is on our side.' The highest score ever made in a fourth innings to win an England/Australia Test was Australia's 404 for three at Leeds in 1948.

With the excitement of the day still on him, Randall retired early, and he was in bed soon after seven, watching television and drinking cups of coffee. He was too tired to dwell on the day's cricket, but when he sought sleep it wouldn't come. It was after midnight before he dropped off, but he awoke clear-eyed and sprightly next morning. By then he was really thinking cricket again, thinking what they had to do to win.

How tremendous it would be to score a Test century! Lying in bed he allowed himself the luxury of savouring the prospect.

After breakfast he went to the ground for an early net. He was the first to arrive, but several of the lads who were playing in Australia on Whitbread Scholarships were there to bowl to him. They gave him a good half-hour's work out, not enough for him to get jaded but sufficient to get his eye in. And the 'scholarship boys' made him concentrate: they included Graham Stevenson, Mike Gatting and Ian Botham.

Even so, when he went in to bat he felt almost as nervous as on the previous day. Normally he would have taken his time early on, accumulating rather than looking to play shots, but with the new ball due after an hour's play, and with his hundred only 13 runs off, he resolved to take his chances.

Chappell called on Lillee for a brief burst from the pavilion end with the old ball, and Randall, who was facing, took a single off the seventh ball. At the other end he was opposed by Kevin O'Keeffe, and off the third and sixth balls he seized the opportunity to sweep and cut at deliveries he might normally have blocked so early in the day. He went for the sweep because O'Keeffe had no one on the 'lap', and he made room for the cut. He middled both shots and they went for 4 and 3, taking him half-way through the 90s.

The second ball of Lillee's next over was short outside the off stump and Randall cut it wide of second slip to take his score to 99.

The third ball hit him on the glove and disappeared down the leg side. He looked up — and there was Amiss, calling him to run. As the magic figures ticked up on the score board he experienced the warmest exhilaration of his life. The cheers that accompanied the achievement were terrific, and when he took off his cap and waved his bat to the crowd the commotion reached a crescendo.

He remembered again what Tony Greig had said. If he mustn't get out on 40, 60, or 80, he certainly mustn't get out on 100. He must start all over again. But despite the hundred, he still didn't feel really settled against Lillee. Lillee was always at you, always trying something. No matter what happened, Randall could see he would never give up.

Amiss took a single off the fifth ball of Lillee's over — Amiss's first run of the morning — and then Randall, with three balls to face, was transfixed by a bouncer bowled wide of the crease

'If he'd hit me anywhere else but on the head it might have hurt.'

which angled in at him and kept on coming. It was a brute of a ball and it left him firm-footed, with no shot to play. Had it not come back at him still further off the pitch he might have avoided it, but as it was there was no escape. It hit him on the left side of the head near the crown, and the impact was sufficient for Lillee to catch the rebound.

Although Randall's cap took the worst of the blow, the direct hit felled him momentarily. Scrambling to his feet, his cap upturned on the ground, he staggered towards square leg rubbing his head.

Perhaps in the euphoria of reaching his hundred he had been guilty of a lapse of concentration. But the ball had beaten him all the way, and as the players gathered round he acknowledged the reverse. 'That was a good one, Mr Lillee.' Then he replaced his cap and shaped up for the next ball.

Although not seriously hurt he was suffering from shock, and he should have taken his time before resuming. The last two balls of Lillee's over went straight through him, over the top of the stumps, and he fished at them both from well clear of the wicket, failing to get into line.

Amiss went down the wicket to talk to Randall and to prolong the gap between overs, giving Randall time to recover. But his plan to farm the strike for a while was foiled by O'Keeffe, who bowled him a maiden.

Chappell, perhaps, did not realise how badly shaken Randall was. Otherwise he would surely have persisted with Lillee. But another five overs from the pavilion end and the second new ball would be due. This for Australia was the anticipated climax, and Chappell wanted Lillee fresh for it. Walker, too, had a long bowl ahead of him, and for the 57th over of the innings Chappell took the ball himself. He was lively enough to bowl a useful bouncer, and he did not ration the short-pitched ball now. Several times Randall failed to move into line and was lucky not to get out.

Amiss, facing O'Keeffe, scored the single that took him to his fifty, and in the next few overs he dominated both the strike and the scoring, giving Randall an essential breather. Whereas Randall had scored the first 13 runs of the morning, Amiss made 19 of the next 22. It was a fine piece of cricket by Amiss, and it wasn't until the 65th over, with a boundary off a Chappell no-ball, that Randall really recovered his poise.

Lillee returned with the new ball fifty minutes before lunch. The sun was hot, and he bowled off a shortened run, but he came pounding in at full throttle. If Randall had ever had any doubts about Lillee's greatness they evaporated now. Lillee's first ball, short of a length, forced Randall to play at it. A shouted appeal for a catch at the wicket was rejected, and Randall held his own in the verbal duel that followed. Lillee went muttering back to his mark, and for the rest of the over Randall let the short stuff alone.

More than once Randall, ducking out of the way of a bouncer, lost his balance, and once he performed a reverse roll as the neatest way of regaining his feet. Lillee, aware that Randall's clowning must have the effect of easing the pressure, took to ignoring him, marching back grim-faced.

Lillee's first two overs with the new ball were maidens, one bowled to Randall and the other to Amiss, who also left the short stuff alone. He was playing his arch-enemy well. Two overs from Walker from the grandstand end cost 15 runs, including a Randall cover-drive eulogised as 'seldom bettered on the Melbourne Club Ground'. Ruling out Gilmour as too erratic, Chappell turned for the first time to the medium-paced out-swingers of Walters. Randall took six off Walters' first over, but then the scoring subsided as lunchtime approached. At the break England were 267 for two, Randall 129, Amiss 63. The morning's play had produced 76 runs, leaving 196 wanted. England might be behind the clock, but with eight wickets standing they could plan for a match-winning acceleration after tea.

That the hour after lunch would be crucial seemed certain, and Chappell kept Lillee going from the pavilion end, taking the southern end himself. After a maiden from either end Randall declared his intentions with a sequence of 4, 2, 4 off Lillee — a drive past extra, a cut, and a hook — and a single to each batsman off Chappell left Amiss with the last four balls of the over to face. With the penultimate ball of this the 80th over of the innings Chappell produced an absolute beauty which nipped back off a length, did not get up, and bowled Amiss through the gate.

With the shine not yet wholly gone, and Lillee still fresh from the lunchtime break, this was a tragedy for England. But the Randall/Amiss partnership had put on 166, saving England's face and opening up the possibility of victory. Against a crushing psychological background, Amiss's innings, though over-shadowed by Randall's, had been a personal triumph.

Fletcher, like Amiss, had suffered many humiliations at Lillee's hands, and like Amiss he could not have come in at a more testing time. In addition he had waited nearly a day for his knock.

From the start the England team had appreciated that they could only win if they kept Lillee at bay, tiring him out if they could. But Lillee, despite a long history of back trouble, always responded vigorously to Chappell's need. Randall hit him boldly for 4 and 2, but between the two shots he played Lillee off his toes and was dropped by Cosier, falling to his left at square leg. A single left Fletcher one delivery to face, which he survived.

A succession of singles off Chappell helped Fletcher to acclimatise, and when Randall saw the chance of a run off Lillee's first ball to reach his 150 he took it. He had batted just over six hours. The next ball, pitching off stump just short of a length and leaving the bat, was too much for Fletcher, and as in the first innings he was caught by Marsh.

England had been only a run short of 280 for two. Now they were 290 for four, with 173 still wanted. Lillee, at one for 79, had been held and even rebuffed. Now, having taken a second wicket, he was metaphorically baring his teeth.

There was only one answer to this, and Greig was the man to provide it. He struck Lillee's first ball defiantly through the covers for 4 — a majestic shot and a grandiloquent gesture. And he slashed Lillee again to the pickets before the over was out. A single off the last ball brought him down to face Chappell, but he reserved his flamboyance for Lillee, treating his rival captain with caution.

Lillee's next over verged on the kaleidoscopic. 3 to Randall, 1 to Greig, 3 more to Randall, 2 and 1 to Greig, 4 to Randall and a final dot added up to 14 off the over. With those two opening boundaries by Greig it was the most belligerent riposte imaginable to the loss of Amiss and Fletcher, and Lillee had to come off. He had bowled ten overs in this spell, five before lunch and five after, and although he had taken an important wicket the ten overs had cost 46 runs.

Such a frenetic pace could not last, and both Randall and Greig steadied down to consolidate as Walker replaced Lillee and Chappell continued to drop on a length. Of the next five overs four were maidens, and Chappell actually bowled four in succession. It was in the fourth of these maidens that Randall, on 161, and with Greig on 23, was beaten by an off-cutter that went through low and wide to Marsh, who scooped up the catch. As he rolled over there was a concerted appeal and the umpire gave Randall out.

Randall, standing disconsolately square of the wicket, could not believe it. Not only was he sure the ball had bounced before Marsh gathered it, he did not think he had hit it.

At this critical point England with six wickets standing needed less than 140 to win. Randall was playing as well as ever, and Greig had established himself after a hectic start. Another half-hour of these two would put England in a winning position. Yet Marsh, leaping to his feet, had no hesitation in rushing down the wicket to Chappell to tell him that the catch had not been properly made. Randall was duly recalled.

As Walker and Chappell continued to share the attack the runs came more freely, one over from Walker costing eleven runs, 4 and 3 to Randall and 4 to Greig. This took Randall to 174, Greig to 30, and England to within 117 of their target.

Having bowled ten overs for 13 runs, Chappell was finding it less easy to contain Randall, and with 17 minutes to go to the tea interval he turned, for the first time that afternoon, to spin.

O'Keeffe's top-spinner, besides puzzling Amiss, had troubled Randall at times, mainly because of the bounce. It was barely a googly. Now Randall, undoubtedly tiring, pushed forward somewhat lazily to O'Keeffe's seventh ball and got the dreaded inside edge on to the pad. Cosier, having replaced earlier short legs who had not cared to field really close, and having juggled more than once with half-chances, dived forward and just clutched the ball in his outstretched left hand.

This was the wicket the Australians desperately wanted, and they shouted in unison. There was no need. Swishing his bat at the grass in vexation, and throwing it up like a juggler, Randall departed, blind to his surroundings, deaf to the tumult. Then, as the tide of emotion turned, the whole ground rose in appreciation. The much-heralded Centenary Test, which had seemed likely to degenerate into a massacre, had undergone a dramatic metamorphosis, evolving into a clash of character and skills comparable with any in the hundred-year saga.

The man who had transformed the occasion was Randall. So far from seeing England crumble, he had batted for seven hours and 28 minutes, hit 21 4s, and brought his side within sight of an astonishing victory. Even more than salving England's pride, he had stirred up the ambivalence of Australians towards the 'Poms' to such an extent that it was not only his countrymen who found themselves moist-eyed at his downfall. The moment was sublimated by a communal catch in the throat.

Randall himself was affected by it, and in his confusion he made his exit through the wrong gate. Suddenly he found himself near the end of a path that led to the specially-appointed Royal Box, where the Queen and Prince Philip were waiting to be introduced to the players at the interval. Discovering his mistake, Randall gave a slight but spontaneous bow to his sovereign before clambering hastily over the public seats and vanishing from view. For some it was the most moving moment of all.

One cartoon, showing two typical Australian 'Ockers' watching the game, caught the mood of the moment. 'First time I haven't had to shout "Have a go, yer mug" at the Poms.'

With the departure of Randall, Chappell immediately called up Dennis Lillee for a final fling. Not once had Chappell fallen back on the defensive, his sole concession to caution being his continued rejection of Gilmour, who had lost his run-up and rhythm. Greig and Knott, now in partnership, gave notice that England, too, scorned to play for a draw but were still going all out to win. They took the score to 453 in the two overs remaining before tea, leaving themselves 109 to get, in a probable 27 eight-ball overs, in the final session. The win was still very much on.

After the two teams had been presented to the royal visitors and tea taken, Chappell put his faith in the combination of Lillee and O'Keeffe. Greig and Knott both threatened in turn to take up where Randall had left off, but an underlying sense of impermanence brought apprehension on the one hand and expectancy on the other. After a brief flourish Greig fell to the O'Keeffe/Cosier trap just as Randall had done, justifying Chappell's faith in the combination, as time began to run out, of speed and spin.

Lillee, whose determination to win the match for his side had never flagged, proved too good for Old, as he had in the past, and O'Keeffe soon accounted for Lever. It was left to Knott and Underwood to revive England's fading hopes by adding 25 runs in 25 minutes for the ninth wicket. But when Lillee bowled Underwood, and last-man-in Willis made his way to the wicket, 53 were still wanted. (The Marsh/McCosker stand, so irksome for England, had added 54.)

Finally Knott, after improvising his way to a personal score of 42, took one liberty too many in Lillee's 35th over, and Australia had won by 45 runs — precisely the margin by which they had won the first of all Test Matches a hundred years earlier.

At the end of that fifth day Lillee was bowling as fast as at the start of the England first innings. Although O'Keeffe had taken two vital wickets — Randall and Greig — Lillee had been Australia's hero, summoning reserves of energy on the final day that placed him on a level with the greatest fast bowlers of Test Match history. His figures of six for 26 in the first innings and 5 for 139 in the second tell the story of the match almost by themselves. Yet the challenge to his and Australia's supremacy would have been sadly deficient but for Randall, who was rightly acclaimed Man of the Match.

In a short speech acknowledging the award, Randall thanked Lillee for the bump on the head. 'If it had hit me anywhere else,' he said, 'it might have hurt.'

Assessment of Randall's innings may best be left to the man who watched it for more than four hours from a distance of 22 yards. 'It was one of the finest knocks I have ever witnessed,' wrote Dennis Amiss recently, 'against Lillee at his best. It must go down as one of the greatest innings of all time.'

AUSTRALIA v ENGLAND Centenary Test Match
at Melbourne, March 12, 13, 14, 16, 17, 1977

Australia won by 45 runs

AUSTRALIA: First Innings

I. C. Davis, lbw b Lever		5
R. B. McCosker, b Willis		4
G. J. Cosier, c Fletcher b Lever		10
*G. S. Chappell, b Underwood		40
D. W. Hookes, c Greig b Old		17
K. D. Walters, c Greig b Willis		4
†R. W. Marsh, c Knott b Old		28
G. J. Gilmour, c Greig b Old		4
K. J. O'Keeffe, c Brearley b Underwood		0
D. K. Lillee, not out		10
M. N. H. Walker, b Underwood		14
Extras (B 4, LB 2, NB 8)		14
Total		138

Fall of wickets: 1-11, 2-13, 3-23, 4-45, 5-51, 6-102, 7-114, 8-117, 9-136.

Bowling: Lever, 12-1-36-2; Willis, 8-0-33-2; Old, 12-4-39-3; Underwood, 11.6-2-16-3.

ENGLAND: First Innings

R. A. Woolmer, c Chappell b Lillee		9
J. M. Brearley, c Hookes b Lillee		12
D. L. Underwood, c Chappell b Walker		7
D. W. Randall, c Marsh b Lillee		4
D. L. Amiss, c O'Keeffe b Walker		4
K. W. R. Fletcher, c Marsh b Walker		4
*A. W. Greig, b Walker		18
†A. P. E. Knott, lbw b Lillee		15
C. M. Old, c Marsh b Lillee		3
J. K. Lever, c Marsh b Lillee		11
R. G. D. Willis, not out		1
Extras (B 2, LB 2, W 1, NB 2)		7
Total		95

Fall of wickets: 1-19, 2-30, 3-34, 4-40, 5-40, 6-61, 7-65, 8-78, 9-86.

Bowling: Lillee, 13.3-2-26-6; Walker, 15-3-54-4; O'Keeffe, 1-0-4-0; Gilmour, 5-3-4-0.

AUSTRALIA: Second Innings

I. C. Davis, c Knott b Greig		68
K. J. O'Keeffe, c Willis b Old		14
G. S. Chappell, b Old		2
G. J. Cosier, c Knott b Lever		4
K. D. Walters, c Knott b Greig		66
D. W. Hookes, c Fletcher b Underwood		56
R. W. Marsh, not out		110
G. J. Gilmour, b Lever		16
D. K. Lillee, c Amiss b Old		25
R. B. McCosker, c Greig b Old		25
M. H. N. Walker, not out		8
Extras (LB 10, NB 15)		25
Total (9 wkts dec.)		419

Fall of wickets: 1-33, 2-40, 3-53, 4-132, 5-187, 6-244, 7-277, 8-353, 9-407.

Bowling: Lever, 21-1-95-2; Willis, 22-0-91-0; Old, 27.6-2-104-4; Greig, 14-3-66-2; Underwood, 12-2-38-1.

ENGLAND: Second Innings

R. A. Woolmer, lbw b Walker		12
J. M. Brearley, lbw b Lillee		43
D. W. Randall, c Cosier b O'Keeffe		174
D. L. Amiss, b Chappell		64
K. W. R. Fletcher, c Marsh b Lillee		1
A. W. Greig, c Cosier b O'Keeffe		41
A. P. E. Knott, lbw b Lillee		42
C. M. Old, c Chappell b Lillee		2
J. K. Lever, lbw b O'Keeffe		4
D. L. Underwood, b Lillee		7
R. G. D. Willis, not out		5
Extras (B 8, LB 4, W 3, NB 7)		22
Total		417

Fall of wickets: 1-28, 2-113, 3-279, 4-290, 5-346, 6-369, 7-380, 8-385, 9-410.

Bowling: Lillee, 34.4-7-139-5; Walker, 22-4-83-1; Gilmour, 4-0-29-0; O'Keeffe, 33-6-108-3; Chappell, 16-7-29-1; Walters, 3-2-7-0.

Umpires—T. F. Brooks and M. G. O'Connell

Index

Abid Ali, S. 199

Allan, D. W. 100, 103

Allen, D. A. 85, 92, 94

Alley, W. E. 211-12, 214

Ames, L. E. G. 122-3

Amiss, D. L. 13-14, 135, 138, 178, 190-222, 225-7, 230, 235-6, 240, 242-5, 248
  two 'pairs' against Australia 195, 202
  help from the Indian spinners 199
  enforced retirement at Lord's 192-3
  revised technique 203-5, 208, 210, 214-6, 225-6

Archer, R. G. 19, 25-6, 28-9, 31

Arlott, John 206-7, 214-6, 230

Arnold, G. G. 122, 126-7, 131-2, 135-6, 179-85, 188

Asif Iqbal 72, 117-40
  inspired by Graeme Pollock 127

Australian Board of Control 141

Bacher, Dr. A. 65-7

Bailey, T. E. 22, 24-7, 31

Balderstone, J. C. 211, 215, 220

Bannister, Alex 229

Barber, R. W. 68-9, 75-96
  and Boycott, as openers 75, 87-8, 92
  moves from Lancashire to Warwickshire 79

Barlow, E. J. 60, 62-5

Barlow, G. D. 207, 226, 230

Barnes, S. F. 25, 31

Barrington, K. F. 41, 55, 72, 83, 94, 101, 124, 126, 132-3, 138-9, 195

Batchelor, Denzil 34

Bedi, B. S. 191, 198-9

Bedser, A. V. 207

Benaud, R. 20, 25-7, 31, 37
  as commentator 69, 175, 177, 181

Benson and Hedges Cup 119

Bird, H. D. 214

Bland, K. C. 61, 63, 65

Blofeld, Henry 175

Bolton, Harry 35, 37

Booth, B. C. 39, 43-4, 85-7

Botham, I. T. 55, 240

Boycott, G. 14, 32, 40-2, 55, 72, 75-6, 80, 82-9, 91-2, 94-6, 100-1, 112, 193, 195, 200, 205, 225
  and Barber, as openers (see Barber)

Brancker, R. C. 97, 99-100

Bradman, Sir Donald 30, 54, 58, 60, 71, 172, 187, 188, 236

Brearley, J. M. 99, 122, 195, 225, 227, 232-5

Bright, R. J. 152

Brooks, T. F. 228

Bromfield, H. D. 61

Brown, D. J. 61, 94, 122

Burge, Joan 34-5

Burge, Peter 34-57, 83

Burge, senior 36

Burki, Javed 125, 128

Butcher, B. F. 97, 102, 105

Caldwell, T. 169

Carew, M. C. 100-1, 105

Cartwright, T. W. 61-9

Cavaliers, International 72, 119, 127

Chandrasekhar, B. S. 191, 198

251

Chappell, G. G. 141, 151-3, 157-8, 163, 167-8, 170, 178-81, 183, 188, 200, 226, 230-34, 236, 239-40, 242-7

Chappell, I. M. 14, 141, 150-52, 154-6, 157-8, 160, 163-5, 167-9, 173-4, 176, 178-9, 188, 201, 203, 226

Close, D. B. 115, 118-19, 125-6, 128-9, 131-3, 136-8, 195, 206

Coldwell, L. J. 39

Collinge, R. O. 151, 158, 160

Compton, D. C. S. 17-18, 20, 22, 24
as commentator 55

Coney, J. V. 153, 158, 163, 166-7

Congdon, B. E. 144-5, 148-51, 153, 159-63, 165, 169

Constantine, Sir Learie (later Lord Constantine) 137

Corling, G. E. 41, 45, 54-5

Cosier, G. J. 226, 244, 246-7

Cowdrey, M. C. 13-32, 36, 40, 65, 71-2, 82-3, 94, 100-110, 112, 123-4, 126, 138, 179, 195, 204
subtle approach as captain 104, 112
tactics of giving the batsman one 106, 110

Cowdrey senior 15-16

Cowper, R. M. 38-40, 44, 88-9, 91-2, 195-6

Cox, G. 58-9, 63, 68

Cozier, Tony 112, 191

Craig, I. D. 36, 172

Crapp, J. F. 71

Cricketer, The 71, 98

Cromb, I. B. 141, 149, 170

Daily Telegraph 51, 207

Daniel, W. W. 205, 209-10, 212, 219

Davis, I. C. 151, 158-60, 164, 227-8

Dell, A. R. 145-6

Denness, M. H. 13-14, 177-82, 199-200, 202-3, 220

Dexter, E. R. 37, 39-41, 43-4, 46-9, 53-5, 76, 78, 192

D'Oliveira, B. L. 100-2, 105-6, 108, 128, 133, 196

Dymock, G. 151-6, 161, 166

Eastern Province Herald 59

Edrich, J. H. 14, 40, 43, 61, 82-3, 92-4, 178, 195, 201-2, 206

Edrich, W. J. 19

Edwards, R. 178-85, 188

Edwards, W. J. 179

Elliott, C. S. 52, 54

Evans, T. G. 16, 27-9, 31

Favell, L. E. 30, 37

Fazal Mahmood 128

Fingleton, Jack 227, 230

Flavell, J. A. 41-2, 46-8, 53, 55

Fletcher, K. W. R. 179, 188, 198, 202-3, 226-7, 230, 244-5

Fortune, Charles 72

Fredericks, R. C. 211-12, 219-20

Freemantle, Doctor 180-81

Gatting, M. W. 240

Gardner, F. C. 60

Ghulam, Abbas 127

Ghulam, Ahmed 100

Gibbs, L. R. 97, 99, 174

Gifford, N. 41-6, 48, 53-4

Gillette Cup 79, 85, 119, 205

Gilmour, G. J. 145, 152, 158, 170, 226, 228, 232-3, 243, 246

Gooch, G. A. 207

Grace, W. G. 18

Graveney, T. W. 100-1, 112, 116, 124, 126, 138, 162, 195

Greenough, T. 78

Greenidge, C. G. 219-20

Greig, A. W. 178-82, 198, 203, 205, 208, 213, 215, 220, 224-32, 236, 240, 244-6

Grey High School 58, 60

Griffith, C. C. 79, 97, 101, 103, 174

Griffith, S. C. 81-2

Grout, A. T. W. 36, 45, 52-4
disdains to run out Titmus 52
Guardian 26, 206

Hadlee, B. G. 151
Hadlee, D. R. 151-2, 159-61
Hadlee, R. J. 144, 151-2, 157-61
dismissal of Redpath at Christ-
church 159, 169
Hall, W. W. 79, 97, 101, 103, 112, 174
Hanif Mohammad 117-18, 123-8,
138-9
Harvey, R. N. 22, 27, 29, 36-7, 188
Hastie, J. B. 159, 166-7
Hastings, B. F. 149-50, 153, 163-5,
169
Hawke, N. J. N. 40-41, 45-9, 51-2,
54, 83-6, 88, 93-4
Hayes, F. C. 206
Hayter, R. J. 223
Hearne, J. W. 31
Hendriks, J. L. 100
Higgs, K. 101-2, 107, 109-10, 126-8,
131-2, 135-6, 140
Hitchcock, R. E. 194
Hobbs, Sir Jack 32
and Rhodes 92
and Sutcliffe 92
Hobbs, R. N. S. 122
Holder, V. A. 205, 209, 211-13, 219
Holding, M. A. 191-2, 204, 208-16,
219-20
Hookes D. W. 228, 230, 235
Horner, N. F. 193-4
Howard, C. G. 16
Howarth, H. J. 151, 159
Hughes, K. J. 55, 225
Hunte, C. C. 97, 99, 101-2, 105
Hutton, Sir Leonard 15-22, 31-2, 71,
162
and Barnett 92
and Washbrook 88

Ibadulla, K. 123, 125, 193
Illingworth, R. 172, 174-5, 196

Intikhab, Alam 119-23, 130, 131-8
Iqbal (see Asif Iqbal)

Jameson, J. A. 194, 196-7
John Player League 119, 147-8, 205
Johnson, I. W. 18-19, 27-9, 31, 36
Johnston, W. A. 26-8, 31
Jones, I. J. 94, 103, 108
Julian, B. D. 205

Kallicharran, A. I. 196-7, 208
Kanhai, R. B. 97, 101-5, 120, 196
Keating, Frank 207
King, C. L. 212
Knight, B. R. 100-3, 105-9
Knott, A. P. E. 126-8, 137, 179-80,
185, 208, 216, 219-20, 246-7

Laker, J. C. 15, 36, 220
Lance, H. R. 62
Langford, B. A. 194
Larter, J. D. F. 62, 66
Laver, R. 117, 132, 135
Lawry, W. M. 39, 41-2, 94, 174, 188
Lever, J. K. 227, 229, 231, 247
Lewis, A. R. 199
Lloyd, C. H. 209, 211-14, 219
Lloyd, D. 202
Lloyd, T. A. 204
Lillee, D. K. 14, 152, 179, 190-1, 193,
200-3, 206, 220, 225-8, 230-36,
239-40, 242-8
Lindsay, J. D. 62-3
Lindwall, R. R. 13-15, 18-22, 24-5,
28-9, 31
Lock, G. A. R. 15
Luckhurst, B. W. 182

McCabe, S. J. 54, 188
McConnon, J. 17
McCosker, R. B. 178, 227-9, 231-2,
247
laws affecting injured batsmen
228-9

INDEX

McDonald, C. C. 36-7
McGilvray, Alan 39
MacKay, K. D. 37
McKenzie, G. D. 40-41, 45-6, 52,
  84-8, 93-4, 146
McKinnon, A. H. 61
McLean, R. A. 61
McMorris, C. A. 100
Maddocks, L. V. 27, 31
Majid, J. Khan 120, 122, 125-6
Mallett, A. A. 152, 158, 161, 163-6,
  202
Malone, M. F. 225
Marsh, R. W. 13, 151, 153, 159-60,
  162, 165, 176, 180, 202, 225, 227-9,
  232, 244-5, 247
  instrumental in recalling Randall
  245
Massie, R. A. L. 152, 220
May, P. B. H. 15, 19, 20, 32
Maynard, C. 204
Melba, Dame Nellie 39
Melford, Michael 190, 207, 215
Menzies, Sir Robert 16
Milburn, C. 101-2, 112, 115, 195
Miller, G. 219-20, 225-6, 230-31
Miller, K. R. 13-15, 18-22, 24-5, 29,
  31-2, 36
  as commentator 110, 124, 178
Mohammad Ilyas 125-6
Monteith, R. L. 161, 164-5
Morris, A. R. 18, 36
Morrison, J. F. M. 153, 162, 166
Murray, D. L. 212, 216
Mushtaq Mohammad 120, 123, 126,
  128, 132

Nash, M. A. 228
Nasim-al-Ghani 123
Nurse, S. M. 97, 101-2, 105

O'Keeffe, K. J. 152, 158, 160-61, 170,
  233-6, 240, 242, 245-7
Old, C. M. 179-82, 227-8, 247
O'Neill, N. C. 37, 39-40, 120, 172-3

Pakistan Eaglets 120
  International Airlines 126
Parfitt, P. H. 41, 48, 55, 61
Parker, J. M. 152-3, 161-2
Parks, J. M. 41, 45, 62, 65, 83, 87, 94,
  101, 103, 107
Philpott, P. I. 85-8, 92-3
Plunket Shield 143, 148
Pocock, P. I. 122
Pollock, A. 59
Pollock, P. M. 59, 61, 72, 174
Pollock, Edith 59, 71-2
Pollock, R. G. 58-74, 86, 91, 127, 134
  advantages of being left-handed 68
  dominant hand at top of bat-handle
  68
  heavy bat 69
  youngest to reach 1000 in Tests 66
Ponsford, W. H. 188
Prasanna, E. A. S. 198
Price, W. F. 52
Price, J. S. E. 197
Proctor, M. J. 174
Prudential Cup 197-8, 200
Pullar, G. 121

Quarshy, Omer 126, 132

Ranji Trophy 120
Randall, D. W. 223-49
  in the nets at Perth 226
  plotting to withstand Lillee 233, 235
Redpath, I. R. 39, 41-3, 55, 151, 154,
  158-9, 162, 164, 169, 179, 207
  freak dismissal at Christchurch 159,
  169
Rees, A. 53-5
Richards, Alan 149
Richards, I. V. A. 202, 208, 211-12
Roberts, A. M. E. 191-2, 205, 208-10,
  213-6, 219-20
Robins, R. W. V. 95
Roebuck, P. M. 97
Rosewall, K. R. 117, 132, 135

254

Rowbotham, Denys 26, 112
Rowe, L. G. 203
Russell, W. E. 82-3, 87
Ruthin School 77

Sadiq Mohammad 120, 205
Saeed Ahmed 138
Salim Altaf 123, 137-8
Selvey, M. W. W. 208, 225
Serjeant, C. S. 225
Seymour, M. A. 76
Shahid Iqbal, Dr. 120
Sheffield Shield 34
Shell Shield 98
Shepherd, B. K. 37
Simpson, R. B. 37, 39-43, 45, 51-2, 55, 75, 85, 89, 94, 121, 202
Simpson, R. T. 203
Sincock, D. J. 85-8, 91, 93
'Sledging' 154, 166, 168
Smith, A. C. 197
Smith, E. J. 79
Smith, M. J. K. 60, 62-5, 68, 79, 81, 83, 85, 94, 98-9, 142, 148, 173, 190, 196-7
  as captain 81
  'sweeping' the slow left-hander 98-9
Smith, W. A. 128
Snow, J. A. 61-4, 67, 100, 112, 174, 205, 208
Sobers, Sir Gary 72, 97-116, 174, 228
  leads by example 105-6
  partnership with Pollock at the Oval 72
Solkar, E. D. 198
Solomon, J. S. 35
Stackpole, K. R. 151, 157-8
Statham, J. B. 18, 32
Steele, D. S. 203, 210-11, 220, 226
Stevenson, G. B. 240
Stollmeyer, J. B. 98
Swanton, E. W. 'Jim' 51, 172
Surridge, W. S. 201

Sydney Daily Telegraph 168
Sydney Morning Herald 37, 168

Tallon, D. 36, 229
Taylor, Clive 198
Taylor, K. 40, 44, 55
Telegraph see Daily Telegraph
Thomson, J. R. 13-14, 178-9, 182, 190-91, 193, 200-2, 206, 220, 226
Times, The 41, 207
Titmus, F. J. 41-6, 48, 52-5, 64-8, 78, 85, 92, 94, 100, 108, 110, 117, 128-9, 131, 133, 136-7, 179-82
  rated best off-spinner by Burge 44
  successes against Pollock 64
  umpiring decisions go against in Australia 180
Tresidder, Phil 37
Tribe, G. E. 77
Trueman, F. S. 15, 41-2, 44, 46-9, 52-6, 169
  front-foot law, trouble with 42
  reaches 300 wickets in Tests 56
Tucker, Dr. Bill 123
Turner, G. M. 141-171
  adopts new methods 147
  1000 runs in May 144
  comparisons with Len Hutton 161-2
Tyson, F. H. 18, 32

Underwood, D. L. 122, 128-9, 131, 133, 136, 172, 182, 208, 214, 216, 227-8, 247
  as night-watchman 214, 227

Van der Merwe, P. L. 61, 67-9, 72
Venkataraghavan, S. 198-9
Veivers, T. R. 44-5

Wadsworth, K. J. 146, 154-6, 157, 163, 167-8

Walker, M. H. N. 151-4, 161-3, 166-7, 179-80, 202, 227, 232-4, 236, 242-3, 245

Walters, K. D. 83, 86, 89, 151-3, 160-61, 170, 172-89, 201, 228, 243
100 in a Test session twice 187

Wardle, J. H. 31

Warner, Sir Pelham 13

Washbrook, C. 88

Wasim Bari 126

Wazir Mohammad 120

Wellings, E. M. 84, 87, 95

Whitbread Scholarships 239

Whitehouse, J. 196-7

Willey, P. 211-3, 220

Willis, R. G. D. 177-87, 188, 208, 227-8, 231, 247

Wisden 15, 37, 39, 72, 76, 82, 121, 123, 135, 147, 154, 176-7, 194, 196-8, 200-2, 213, 223

Wood, B. 198

Woodcock, John 71, 99, 207, 215

Woolley, F. E. 63, 68

Woolmer, R. A. 209, 211, 220, 225-7, 232

Worrell, Sir Frank 37, 97, 100

Yarnold, H. 135